# THE ENGLISH FOLLOWERS OF ELIJAH

Fr. Richard Copsey, O.Carm. M.A. (Oxon.), S.T.L., Ph.D. was born in London and joined the Carmelite Order after some years as a teacher. He studied for the priesthood in Ireland and also qualified as a psychologist there. He has held a number of roles in the Order, as a lecturer, headmaster of St Edward's School, Cheltenham, prior provincial and a member of the Carmelite Institute in Rome and editor of its journal *Carmelus*. In recent years, he has written widely on Carmelite history and spirituality. In 2020, his *Biographical Register of Carmelites in England and Wales 1240-1540* was published which has become a standard reference work for the Order.

# THE ENGLISH FOLLOWERS OF ELIJAH

Portraits of some of the Carmelite friars
in the English Province 1242-1540

**Richard Copsey O.Carm.**

EXPLORING CARMELITE HISTORY 1.

St. Albert's Press
Faversham, Kent

Prepared for publication with the help of New City publishing house.

First published 2024

Saint Albert's Press, Carmelite Friars, P.O. Box 289,
Faversham, Kent ME13 3BZ
https://stjudeshrine.co.uk/
email: shrineoffice@stjudeshrine.org.uk

ISBN-10: 0-904849-62-7
ISBN-13: 978-0-904849-62-2
EAN: 9780904849622

Front Cover: The arrival of the Carmelites in England,
painting by Adam Kossowski, in Aylesford Priory, Kent.
Other illustrations are acknowledged at the end.

Printed by Books Factory

# Dedication

In Memory of

Fr Kevin Alban, O.Carm.

Provincial of the British Province of Carmelites

who suggested that I should write this book

and

was intending to write the preface

but who sadly died on 4th May 2021.

# Contents

# Introduction

The first Carmelites arrived in England in 1242, brought from the Holy Land by returning English crusaders. They were from a community of hermits, who had formed in a narrow valley on Mount Carmel, not far from the crusader port of Acre. The hermits had begun to gather soon after Acre was recaptured by the armies of the Third Crusade, led by King Richard the Lionheart of England and King Philip II of France. It was sometime around 1212-1213, when the hermits petitioned Albert, the papal legate and patriarch of Jerusalem, for formal recognition as an approved religious community. In response, Albert composed a series of instructions, or "Way of Life" for them, outlining what they must do to be formally approved, laying down some spiritual guidelines. Sadly Albert died in 1214, and so was unable to continue guiding the hermit community.

In the 1230s, the narrow strip of land held by the crusaders, which extended from Acre in the north, down the coast to Jaffa, came under increasing pressure from the surrounding Arab forces. The constant threat of attack led the hermits, most of whom would have been of European descent, to seek safer places to live. In 1235, the first group left Mount Carmel and headed for Cyprus, where they made a foundation at Fortamia (now called Karmi/Karaman), on the north coast of Cyprus, five miles inland from the port of Kyrenia, and on the slopes of a mountain range, at the peak of which stands the castle of St Hilarion. A second group of hermits left around 1238, and settled at Messina in Sicily. The third group, which contained some English hermits, came to England. They were brought back by a group of returning English crusaders, arriving late in 1241. These hermits made two foundations, the first was at Hulne Priory, just outside Alnwick in Northumberland, on land given by Sir William de Vescy and the second, a few weeks later, at Aylesford in Kent, granted by Sir Richard de Grey.

However, being members of an Order unknown in Europe, the hermits initially met with some opposition. Moreover, their reception was not helped by the strange cloaks which they wore, which had wide brown and white stripes.

In some places, they were called the “pied” or the striped friars. In England, it took five years before the bishop of Rochester would formally recognise the community in Aylesford, and allow them to have a public church with a bell and a cemetery. Once given, this formal recognition meant that the community could welcome lay people to attend mass in the chapel, who could also ask to be buried in the cemetery. In spite of this episcopal reluctance, a third foundation was quickly made at Lossenham, near Newenden in Kent invited by Sir Thomas Aucher, and then a fourth foundation was made at Bradmer in Norfolk (this community was later transferred to higher ground in Burnham Norton which was a few miles away). The rapidly growing number of foundations throughout Europe, led to the Carmelite hermits meeting for a first general chapter held outside the Holy Land, at Aylesford in the summer of 1247. At the chapter, a new prior general, Gerald, was elected and, after some discussions at the chapter, two English friars were sent to the Pope in Avignon to petition for some changes in their, “Way of Life”, and for formal approval of it, as an approved religious Rule. This was granted, and the Carmelites took their place as one of the new mendicant orders of friars.

In the years that followed, the Carmelites enjoyed a period of rapid expansion, especially under their prior general, Saint Simon Stock, who held office from around 1258 to 1265. By 1300, there were 30 houses in England, and this increased to 39 houses by 1360. The province stayed at this level, until the dissolution of the Order in England in 1538, during the reign of King Henry VIII. The number of friars in the province grew steadily and reached its peak of just under 1,000 friars towards the end of the 14th century.

However, there was one important international event which interrupted this steady growth, and that was the Second General Council of Lyons which met in 1274. The primary purpose of the Council was to seek the re-unification of the Roman and the Orthodox branches of the Church. A secondary reason was that many of the bishops were uneasy about the proliferation of new religious orders in the Church, and were concerned about the behaviour of many of their members, and the lack of any effective control over them so, when Pope Gregory X summoned the Council to meet, he asked for some reports, on the situation regarding the new orders, and what should be done to remedy it.

At the Council, the negotiations with the Orthodox delegates took precedence, and a plan for re-unification was agreed. Sadly, when the delegates returned home, this plan was overwhelmingly rejected by the Orthodox faithful.

As for the foundation of new Religious Orders, the Fourth Lateran Council which had convened in Rome in 1215, had decreed that no new Orders were to be created. However, this decree had been widely ignored, and there had been a proliferation of new religious groups. Consequently, the Council Fathers meeting in Lyons, decided to take a very strict line and to suppress all the Orders, which were founded after the decree of the Lateran Council. By now, the Dominican and Franciscan Orders were well established, with a large number of communities throughout Europe and the Holy Land. Their friars were well trained, and the more talented had gained doctorates in theology and other ecclesiastical disciplines. Some of these talented friars had been promoted to high offices in the Church as bishops or cardinals. So, the Council Fathers decided that these two Orders were to be exempted from this decree. Nevertheless, the Carmelites and Augustinians put up an energetic defence against their suppression, arguing that they had been founded before the decree of the Lateran Council. The Augustinians claimed that they could trace their foundation back to St Augustine of Hippo (†430), and the Carmelites went one better and claimed descent from the prophet Elijah and his followers, the sons of the prophets, who had dwelt on Mount Carmel before the time of Jesus. These claims needed a carefully argued response, but, by this time, the Council Fathers were eager to return home, so the final decree on the suppression of new Orders reads as follows:

> "… Of course, we do not allow the present constitution to apply to the orders of Preachers and Minors; their approval bears witness to their evident advantage to the universal church. Furthermore, we grant that the order of Carmelites and that of the Hermits of Saint Augustine, the institution of which preceded the said general council, may remain as they are, until other regulations are made for them. …"

Pope Gregory X died soon after the Council ended, in January 1276, and his successors proved to be more relaxed about this decree. Gradually, both the Augustinians and the Carmelites were formally recognised by the Church until in the early 1300's, they were given the same recognition and privileges as the Franciscans and the Dominicans.

However, in the immediate aftermath of the Council of Lyons, the threat of suppression did lead to a major reform of the Order, and to a search for support from various influential persons, both lay and ecclesiastical. Letters of support were obtained from King Edward I of England and from various bishops, both in Europe and the Holy Land. Even the Grand Masters of the

Knights Templars and the Hospitallers in the Holy Land, sent a letter in support of the Carmelites, in which they mentioned how the Order raised funds in Europe for the defence of the Holy Land. Within the Order itself, the system of formation was improved and *studia generalia* (international houses of studies) were set up in Paris, London, etc. where students from the whole Order could pursue higher level studies in philosophy and theology leading to university doctorates. Steps were taken, to change the striped cloak worn by the hermits on Mount Carmel to a simple white one which looked more impressive, and this change of cloak was approved by the Pope in 1287. The white cloak was seen to be more appropriate for an Order, which was now known as "the brothers of the blessed Mary of Mount Carmel". This new title had been adopted in the early 1250's and reflected the increasing devotion to Our Lady of the Order which was a significant change from their original title of, "the hermit brothers of Mount Carmel".

Out of the large number of Carmelite friars who were members of the Order in the English Province, from 1242 to 1538, there is information in the records of just under 5,000 of them. Many of them are known solely from their occurrence in the lists of ordinations, found in the surviving registers of the diocesan bishops, but, fortunately, there are a number of other important sources. Among the most important of these are the notebooks compiled by a young Carmelite called John Bale. He was a member of the Province from 1507 until he left the Order in 1536 (when he left having adopted the new Protestant beliefs). Fortunately, during his time in the Order, Bale had a great interest in its history, and in the significant Carmelite writers and superiors. Nearly all of Bale's notebooks still survive, and comprise over 3,000 pages of notes he wrote during his travels in England, overseas in France, in the Low Countries and Italy. These notes made during his journeys form an invaluable source for studying the history of the Order. The names of various English Carmelites also appear in the papal registers, and in the many English state papers and court records. The information which was gathered from all these sources has recently been published in my book entitled, *A Biographical Register of Carmelites in England and Wales 1240-1540* (Faversham: St Albert's Press, 2020). This Biographical Register contains just under 5,000 entries, and lists all the known details on those members of the province who can be traced, and includes as well the prominent Carmelites who visited the province, the students from other provinces who studied in England, and the female anchorites who lived in the cells attached to a number of Carmelite houses, and who, although not formally members of the Order, were under the pastoral care of the Carmelites.

In the following chapters, a number of notable figures from the medieval province are described. They were not all saints or praiseworthy characters; in fact, some were notably less than perfect, but they give a glimpse of the different types of those who joined the Order. Inevitably, part of the reason they have been chosen, is because there was enough information on them to give an informative account of their lives. Wherever possible, contemporary accounts from persons, who knew or had met them are included, as well as extracts from what they themselves wrote.

The Carmelites portrayed in the following chapters differ from the more formal, scholarly entries in the *Biographical Register*, in so far as they are more descriptive, and where it would be helpful, they are linked to current events.

Various features of the life in an Order are explained, where they may be helpful, for readers who have little knowledge of religious orders. It is therefore hoped that these portraits will prove interesting, especially to those for whom Latin (which was the common means of communication in the medieval period), is a significant obstacle, and who find religious life in the medieval period, a little mystifying.

The portraits follow a chronological order with one notable exception. As the Carmelite John Bale, is such a significant source of information, on the medieval province and its members, and is often quoted, his portrait is therefore given first. Moreover, this avoids continually having to refer to who he was, and the historical notes he made. More scholarly entries on the friars who feature in the following chapters can be found in my *Biographical Register*, where the individual entries contain all the known biographical details on each friar, a list of any works he wrote, all surviving manuscripts along with a comprehensive bibliography of relevant books and articles. As a principle, in this book, all the individual portraits, quotations and sources for further reading are in English (or are accompanied by a translation). For those seeking sources in other languages, then please consult my book, *Biographical Register*.

Following this Introduction, there is a short list of books on the general history of the Carmelite Order, and a list of any abbreviations used. After each individual portrait, there is a reference to its entry in my *Biographical Register*, and also in *Additions and Corrections* to the *Register*, which can be found on the Carmelite website. (A revised edition of the Register is currently in preparation). If there is an entry in the *Oxford Dictionary of National Biography*, for a Carmelite, this is noted as well as any helpful books or articles in English. Where a Carmelite is cited in this book, his name is given in bold type if there is a portrait on him, in one of the chapters.

A note for the future: a series of, *Early Carmelite Documents in English*, is in preparation, and will hopefully provide English translations of some of the significant Carmelite texts, for anyone studying the history of the Order. Volume I will contain documents from 1200 up to 1380.

My grateful thanks are due to the many people who have helped me in preparing this book, especially to my provincial, Fr. Brendan Grady, O.Carm., who has continually encouraged and supported me in my studies, to Matt Betts who has overseen the revival of St Albert's Press, and to the members of New City publishing house (Focolare Movement) in Welwyn Garden City, who have seen this work through to press, and especially to Ms. Maria Dalgarno and Mrs Susan Scullino who have prepared my text for publication.

Richard Copsey, O.Carm.
raccopsey@googlemail.com

# Selected Bibliography

**General Reading on the Carmelite Order:**

The standard history on the Carmelite Order is:

Joachim Smet, O.Carm., *The Carmelites*, (Darien, Illinois, 1975-1985) 4 vols. (vol. 1 covers the period from 1200 to the Council of Trent).

Joachim Smet, O.Carm., *The Mirror of Carmel. A brief history of the Carmelite Order*, ed. William J. Harry, O.Carm., (Darien, Illinois: Carmelite Media, 2011). This a one volume abbreviation which was being prepared by Fr Joachim before he died. The published edition sadly omits all the footnotes and other references.

**For the Carmelites in England and Wales:**

See the *Carmel in Britain* series which contain collections of articles on the Province:

*Carmel in Britain. Essays on the Medieval English Carmelite Province*, Volume 1: People and Places, ed. Patrick Fitzgerald-Lombard, O.Carm., (Rome: Institutum Carmelitanum, 1992).

*Carmel in Britain. Essays on the Medieval English Carmelite Province*, Volume 2: Theology and Writing, ed. Patrick Fitzgerald-Lombard, O.Carm., (Rome: Institutum Carmelitanum, 1992).

*Carmel in Britain. Studies on the Early History of the Carmelite Order*, Volume 3: The Hermits from Mount Carmel, Richard Copsey, O.Carm., (Rome: Institutum Carmelitanum, 2004).

*Carmel in Britain. Studies on the Early History of the Carmelite Order*, Volume 4: Thomas Netter of Walden. Carmelite, Diplomat and Theologian (c1372-1430), eds. Johan Bergström-Allen & Richard Copsey, O.Carm., (Faversham: St Albert's Press, 2009).

# Abbreviations

*BRCEW* Richard Copsey, O.Carm., *Biographical Register in Carmelites in England and Wales 1240-1540*

*ODNB* *Oxford Dictionary of National Biography*, (Oxford Univ. Press, 2004). [The ODNB is also available online]. These entries are marked ODNB followed by volume and page numbers.

*Early Carmelite Documents*
Richard Copsey, *Early Carmelite Documents in English*. Vol. 1: 1200-1380 (in preparation)

# 1

# JOHN BALE

## (1495–1563)

John Bale, bishop of Ossory, canon of Canterbury Cathedral

The little village of Covehithe lies on the Suffolk coast, 5 miles north of Southwold, and 28 miles south-east of Norwich, the county town of Norfolk, and John Bale was born there on November 21st, 1495, to Henry and Margaret Bale. It appears that John was the eldest of nine children. At that time, Covehithe was a small town that was beginning to decline due to coastal erosion, and its population had dropped to around 300 inhabitants. However, it maintained its own quayside, where local fishermen landed their catches of herring and other fish. The town was also home to a small linen industry, weaving the locally grown flax, and hosting an annual fair on St Andrew's Feast Day (30th November), which attracted people from the surrounding villages and farms.

Sadly, a present-day visitor will find little trace of the town which Bale knew. Approaching the village along the narrow Mill Lane, then Beach Road, the visitor reaches the parish church of St. Andrew's, but, apart from the church and a few houses, nothing else of Covehithe remains. Beach Road continues past the church for a few hundred yards, and then ends abruptly when the road finishes at the edge of a low cliff, with the beach a steep drop below. The Covehithe which Bale knew, lies half a mile further on, buried under the waves of the sea, which is steadily eating away at the shoreline.

Soon after his birth, the newly born John Bale was baptised in the parish church. At that time, St Andrew's was a large gothic church built during the 14th and 15th centuries, and Bale was baptised in its 15th century octagonal font. Sadly, nowadays, only the lower parts of the walls of the old church remain. Due to the encroaches of the sea, and the consequent decline of Covehithe in the 17th century, the large church fell into disrepair and, with the numbers of parishioners diminishing, the roof was removed and, in 1672, permission was given to build a smaller thatched church inside the walls of the old church. The font in which Bale was baptised did survive, and continued in use.

Little is known about the circumstances of Bale's family, except that they were very poor. Bale did record one experience which he had during his early years when, in 1506, he was taken to Norwich by his father and there they witnessed the burning of a young boy for heresy:

> I have read in the chronicles of that city, that it has been diversely often plagued by the slaughter of innocents. And in the year of Our Lord 1506, I beheld it in action, a most wonderful event, being then but a lad of eleven years of age. When their blind bishop and clergy, with their full consent, had burned a young man there, after the most tyrannous manner (I think) that ever was seen, only for having the Lord's prayer in English, and for not allowing that prayer to be said idolatrously in Latin to their dead saints, neither followed in them nor in their clergy any repentance for that cruel slaughter….

Within a few years, it became clear to Bale's parents that they had a son who was very talented, however they did not have the resources to provide a suitable education for him. The one option for their son to get a good education and develop his potential, would be if he were to join a religious order. So, in

1507 when he was 12 years of age, they took him to Norwich, where he joined the Carmelite community there.

At that time, the medieval English Province of Carmelites was divided into four distinctions or regions, and Norwich was the senior house in the Norwich distinction. (The other houses in the distinction were Blakeney, Burnham Norton, King's Lynn and Yarmouth). Norwich was not only the largest community in the distinction with a community numbering around 40-50 friars but, as the senior house, it provided a *studium provinciale* (regional study centre) offering advanced courses in theology for talented friars from the other houses in the distinction, leading to a licence in sacred theology (S.T.L.), an internal award given by the Order.

It is likely that John Bale would have received some basic education in Covehithe before his entry in the Carmelites, as it is known that his parish priest ran a small school. So, it is likely that he could read and write English. Once in the Carmelite priory, he would have received a good general education, with an emphasis on reading and writing in Latin. Latin was the *lingua franca* of the Order and the mass, divine office and studies in theology were all undertaken in Latin. Once he had a basic proficiency in Latin, Bale would have entered the novitiate which lasted for one year. Then he would have begun his studies for the priesthood, beginning with two years of philosophy, and then four years of theology. Bale's intellectual ability soon became apparent to his teachers and so, in 1514, his superiors decided that he should transfer to Cambridge, and continue his studies at the university there. Among the other Carmelite students in Cambridge, at this time, was John Barret, a contemporary of Bale's from Norwich, who, after the dissolution of the Order in 1538, would become a canon in Norwich cathedral. Another contemporary of Bale was Robert Barnes, the Augustinian friar. The two became good friends but some years later, Barnes became a follower of Luther. His life ended in 1540, when he was burnt for heresy. One of Bale's teachers at Cambridge was Geoffrey Downes, who would later become chancellor of the diocese of York (1554-1561).

As a friar, Bale would have lived in the Carmelite house in Cambridge, and undertaken his studies, under the direction of the Carmelite *magister regens* (senior doctor of theology). Some historians have claimed that Bale was a student in Jesus College, but there is no evidence for this and, as a friar, Bale had no need to be a member of a college.

Bale's earlier studies in Norwich, meant that soon after arriving in Cambridge, he was eligible to be promoted to holy orders, and so was ordained a sub deacon on December 22nd, 1515, in Lyddington church, then a deacon on October 20th, 1516, in Barnwell priory church, and a priest on March 7th, 1517, also in Lyddington church. Soon after his ordination as a priest, Bale was appointed *"iuvenum informator"*, or a tutor to the young friars.

Even before his ordination, there is evidence of Bale's growing interest in the history of his Order. Cambridge University Library preserves what is probably his earliest surviving notebook, (C.U.L. Ms. Ff 6.28) where, on the first page, he wrote (in Latin):

> *"John Bale, Carmelite from Norwich*: This book is the lawful possession of John Bale, a student in the University of Cambridge, and a member of the Order of Carmelites from the convent in the distinguished town of Norwich, written in his own hand, by the grace of God. Amen."

This dates the notebook to soon after Bale's arrival in Cambridge, and before he was ordained a priest, that is between 1514-1517. The book contains the liturgical offices, for the Solemn Commemoration of Our Lady of Mount Carmel along with some Carmelite saints, i.e. Cyril of Constantinople, Berthold, a prior general, Albert of Trapani, Angelus of Sicily, and lastly for the prophet Elijah. Bale would have found these texts in the Carmelite library in Cambridge, and copied them for his own use.

A second early notebook is held in the Bodleian Library, Oxford, (Ms. Selden supra 72). This notebook appears to be a series of copying exercises, which Bale gave to his students, after he had been appointed *iuvenum informator*. It contains short works by various Carmelite authors. In places, Bale has given the title of a work, and then left the rest of the text to be copied by a student. On folio 41, he signs himself as "John Bale teacher of the young", which dates this notebook to sometime after 1517. The notebook contains a short chronicle by Robert Bale (†1503), prior of Burnham Norton, (no relation to John Bale), a list of priors general by John Bale himself, a work *In praise of the Carmelite Order* by John Baconthorpe, and two short historical pieces by William of Coventry. The notebook was compiled some time before 1523.

From 1517 onwards, Bale applied himself seriously to collecting information on the history of the Carmelite Order, and its outstanding members. His historical studies were quickly recognised and, around 1523, his Carmelite superiors gave him permission to travel abroad, to the Low Countries, to further his research. We have no exact dates for this, his first visit to the Continent, but the notes that Bale made during his travels, can be found in two of his notebooks preserved in the Bodleian Library, Oxford (Ms Bodley 73 & Ms Selden supra 41). A few misplaced pages from this trip are found in a later notebook, now in the British Library (Ms. Harley 1819).

One notebook, Bodley 73, gives the best clues as to the places Bale visited during his travels in France and the Low Countries, but, as Bale's notes are bound together in a rather haphazard order, interspersed with other notes which he made whilst travelling around England, it is very difficult to compile a chronological sequence of his movements.

On his outward journey, Bale appears to have stopped in London before making his way south, probably via the Carmelite houses at Aylesford and Sandwich, and then across the channel to the Carmelite house in Calais. Whilst in Calais, probably recovering from the rigours of his cross-channel passage, Bale copied an old chronicle which he found in the Carmelite house there. Then, after Calais, he made his way northwards through Ypres, Enghien and on to Ghent, where he stayed for some months. Among the other places, which Bale visited during his stay and where he made notes are, Bruges, Mechelen, Antwerp, Brussels, Valenciennes, and the Carmelite sisters at Vilvoorde. From Bale's own biographical details which he gives in his later history of the English Province, *Anglorum Heliades* (written in 1536), he claims to have spent some time studying at Louvain University.

Bale reserved his second notebook (Ms Selden supra 41), for the longer pieces, which he copied whilst in the Low Countries. Many of these seem to have been manuscripts which he encountered, whilst he was in the Carmelite house in Ghent. Among them, there are a number of compositions by blessed Baptist of Mantua (†1516), the Carmelite prior general, which had been brought back from Italy by the prior of Ghent, Adrian van den Echout (†1499). Also Bale copied some works by the humanist scholar, Arnold Bostius (†1499), who had spent nearly all his life in the Carmelite community in Ghent. Among the works of Bostius which Bale preserves, there is one of the only two surviving manuscripts of *De Patronatu et Patrocinio Beate Virginis Marie*, written in 1479, a long composition, describing how the Virgin Mary is the patron of the Carmelite Order, how she protects it and has worked miracles on its behalf.

Finally, there are two other works which Bale copied in the Low Countries, but which were bound in a later notebook, British Library Ms Harley 1819. One of these is an anonymous life of St Anne, the Mother of the Virgin Mary. This life, containing 53 chapters written in Latin, is clearly by a Carmelite, and possibly written originally in Flemish. The second work is a series of 'elegant' letters written by the Carmelite Mathias Emich, which he composed whilst he was a student in Cologne.

It is difficult to know exactly how long Bale was away in the Low Countries. Certainly, he seems to have left in 1523 or possibly early 1524, and he was away for about two years. He records visiting the Carmelite sisters in Vilvoorde in 1526, a visit which must have taken place early in the year, as Bale was back in Cambridge in the middle of that year. Then, in early August, he left Cambridge in order to attend the provincial chapter being held at Hitchin, which would have been celebrated around the Feast of the Assumption, which is held on August 15th. Whilst at the chapter, Bale composed a poem to celebrate the event.

At the conclusion of the provincial chapter in Hitchin, Bale made plans for a second trip abroad, this time aiming to travel all the way to Rome. Once again, he may have used the argument with his superiors, about the value of continuing his theology studies at the Order's *studium generale* in Rome. In preparation for this journey, Bale started a new notebook, which is now in the British Library (Ms Harley 1819). Luckily, this book is better organised than Bale's earlier notebooks, and it is reasonably easy to follow his journey through France and Northern Italy. Bale had, by now, adopted the general practice, of inserting a heading at the beginning of each set of notes, which indicated where these notes were made. Occasionally these headings are missing, possibly forgotten or omitted when Bale stops in a Carmelite house, where he hasn't found anything worth recording. Fortunately, Bale also recorded a list of the places he visited, opposite the chapter headings of the life of St Anne, which he had copied in the Low Countries. This second list helps us compile a more complete to Bale's route through France. Having retraced Bale's journey myself, it is clear that there are a few other unmentioned Carmelite houses, where it is likely Bale stayed overnight during his travels, but found nothing worth recording.

Bale started this second journey from Hitchin at the end of the provincial chapter, probably on Monday August 20th, 1526, and made his way down to London, in the company of other delegates from the chapter, who were returning to their communities. From London, Bale continued down to Aylesford in Kent, and then on to Sandwich, where he stayed in the Carmelite house there until a suitable passage to France became available. From Calais, he set out for Paris, passing through the Carmelite houses in Montreuil and Rouen on the way. Rouen would have been a place of particular interest to Bale as his great Carmelite hero, Thomas Netter* of Walden was buried in the chapel there.

After a short break in Paris, Bale continued his way south, passing through Orléans, Bourges, Saint-Amand, Moulins, Clermont-Ferrand, Lyons and Vienne. This journey during the winter of 1526-27 must have been quite a trial, but Bale makes no comments on the weather, or his experiences during his travels. From Vienne, he turns east and heads up into the mountains, visiting the Carmelite houses at Pinet, Pont-de-Beauvoisin and La Rochette (the last two are not mentioned in his notebook). At this point, Bale was faced with the long trek of over 110 miles across the Alps, and down to Turin. There were no Carmelite houses on this route, and Bale does not give any indication of where he stayed or rested on his journey. Approaching Turin in April 1527, Bale elected to stay at the Carmelite house in Rivoli, which is 9 miles short of the city. There was a reason for not continuing into the city, as it had been under threat of attack by the Imperial troops, and the Carmelite house there, founded only a few years previously in 1524, had been sited just outside the walls, but it had been demolished to leave the ramparts clear for the defence of the city. The small Carmelite community had found sanctuary within the walls in the parish church of San Benigno. Advised by the Carmelites in Rivoli, Bale abandoned any hope of lodging in the city, and instead chose to visit two other small Carmelite houses on the south side of Turin, at Moncalieri and Vinovo. Then, learning that the Imperial Army was marching south to besiege Rome, Bale prudently revised his original plan of visiting the Holy City, and retraced his steps back into France.

A gap occurs in Bale's notes at this point, but it is likely that he took a southerly route across the Alps, through Briançon and Gap, arriving in Avignon around the end of June 1527, where his historical notes begin again. After Avignon, Bale continues his journey westwards, stopping at Nîmes, Lunel, Montpellier, Béziers, Narbonne, Carcassonne, Montréal, Castelnaudry, and finally Toulouse. In Toulouse, Bale encountered William Gregory, a Scotsman, who had joined the Carmelite Order whilst a student in Paris. Gregory had become a member of the reformed community in Albi, and rose to high office in the developing reformed Congregation of Albi. As prior of Toulouse, Gregory offered Bale a warm welcome, and invited him to stay for a while in his community. In fact, he encour-

* An asterisk indicates that the person has a separate chapter elsewhere in this book.

aged Bale to continue his studies at Toulouse University, and assured him that he could guarantee that Bale would be awarded a doctorate if he remained for a year. As Bale himself later notes, he stayed for some weeks in Toulouse, using it as a base from which to visit the neighbouring Carmelite houses, particularly Albi, and it is likely that he attended a few lectures in Toulouse university, which he would use as evidence of his continuing his studies whilst abroad when, on his return to Cambridge, he sought to be awarded his baccalaureate.

In the autumn, leaving Toulouse, Bale continued his progress westwards following the Gironde River, passing through Castelsarrasin, Agen, Aiguillon, Langon, until he reached Bordeaux, probably in late September 1527. Whilst in Bordeaux, Bale was able to copy a life of the English Carmelite, Saint Simon Stock*, written in 1500 by a former prior, Menaud de Rosiers (†1508). Then, Bale headed northwards through Jonzac (where the Carmelite convent still remains beautifully preserved), Poitiers, Tours, Orléans and Paris. Finally, Bale reached Montreuil and Calais again, and so made his way across the Channel to London, where he rested for a while. However, he was not idle in London, and took the opportunity to copy Nicholas Cantelupe's short work, *In Praise of the Carmelites,* which was the poem on Richard II's reconciliation with the city of London, being composed by the Carmelite Richard of Maidstone*, and the lengthy *Liber festivalis* (Book of Feasts), by the Augustinian Alexander of Ashby.

Bound into Bale's earlier notebook (Ms Selden supra 41), is an unfinished work, entitled *A Chronicle or Collection of the History of the Carmelite Order.* This is an early attempt by Bale himself, to compose a history of the Carmelite Order. The text is not a discursive account but, like Bale's later compositions on the Order, it is a collection of short biographical entries, on the important figures in Carmelite history. This work is still only an unfinished outline and, in it, Bale divides the history of the Order, according to the years during which each prior general held office. The name of the prior general is placed in a circular frame, along with a short account of his life, and the remainder of the pages are divided into two columns, which Bale filled up as he acquired more information. The early sections suffer from a lack of content, especially the legendary period from Elijah down to Berthold, and there are many other empty spaces. However, as Bale approaches his own century, the pages are filled with entries on significant Carmelites, whom Bale has learnt about during his travels.

This composition was probably never intended for any formal publication, but rather served as a chronological framework, and an aide-mémoire for Bale, as he organised the information he had gathered. Evidently, he was adding further details up until 1539.

Once back in Cambridge, early in 1528, Bale petitioned for his baccalaureate, citing studies abroad (i.e. at Louvain and Toulouse) and the university grace book records:

> "… It is granted to brother Ball (sic) of the Carmelite Order that, after he has studied theology for ten years in the theology faculty in this university and in places overseas…"

The final requirements for the bachelor's degree, including preaching a sermon at St Paul's Cross, London, were to be completed by St Martin's Day (July 4th) 1529. Bale continued his studies for the doctorate, but there is no record of when he had completed the requirements, and there is no entry in the surviving university registers of him having incepted as a doctor. However, by 1534, he was being addressed as 'doctor'.

Sometime in 1530, Bale was appointed prior of the Carmelite house in Maldon, and he received a licence to preach in the London diocese, from bishop John Stokesley, on February 16th, 1531. Later, after he had adopted Protestant beliefs, Bale claimed that he had been suspended from preaching by bishop Stokesley in 1531, because he would not "leave the Gospel" (i.e. his Protestant belief in the Bible), and swear to publicize an anti-Lutheran tract by bishop William Barlow. But it has been pointed out that, "reminiscences after the fact are tricky", and there is no record of Bale being suspended from preaching, so Bale may have reinterpreted past events in the light of his newly adopted Protestant beliefs.

Bale remained in Maldon until 1533, when he was transferred to become prior in Ipswich, the only Carmelite house in his home county of Suffolk. It was whilst he was there that Bale came under the influence of Thomas, Lord Wentworth, who lived at Nettlestead, a village only six miles northeast of Ipswich. Wentworth was the leading nobleman in Suffolk, a convinced Protestant and a patron of young intellectual reformers. It was probably due to his superiors noticing Wentworth's influence on Bale that, after only a year in Ipswich, he was moved north and appointed prior in the Carmelite house in Doncaster.

However, once established in the diocese of York, Bale's newly acquired reforming ideas quickly led him into trouble. On July 24th, 1534, he was licensed by archbishop Lee to preach in the diocese of York. 1534 was a significant year for the church authorities as Thomas Cromwell, at the behest of his master, king Henry VIII, was attempting to steer the Act of Supremacy through Parliament. This Act declared the king to be the supreme head of the Church in England, in place of the pope, and was finally passed in November. It is likely that, in giving Bale licence to preach, archbishop Lee was hoping that Bale, with his doctorate from Cambridge, would help promote the king's policies. Bale himself records having preached in Ripon, where his views ran into some fierce opposition;

> "… where myself was once baited of [the Anti-Christ's] Bashan bulls, for maintaining the King's prerogative against their Pope.."

In fact, only a week after receiving permission to preach, Bale was involved in an unseemly quarrel in Doncaster, when he and Thomas Kirkby, the warden of the Franciscan convent, attacked each other's views in sermons preached in their respective churches. On August 1st, the archbishop appointed four senior clergy to look into the affair, and to report back to him, but the result of this enquiry is not recorded.

Just over a year later, Bale was involved in another dispute in Doncaster. This time his quarrel was with the vicar of the local parish church. On January 24th, 1536, Archbishop Lee wrote to Thomas Cromwell, describing the efforts he was making to ensure that the clergy should not preach on the subjects, which were forbidden by the king, e.g. purgatory, veneration of saints, etc. He mentions an episode in Doncaster where a "light fryer" (almost certainly Bale – a white friar) was involved:

> "… one other contention between the vicar of Doncaster and a light friar there, whereupon I charged the said vicar, that he in no wise should preach on any article mentioned in the order taken by the King's Highness, and because I was credibly informed that the said friar preached some of the said articles, and that after such sort that the people were much offended, I commanded the vicar, that he should not suffer him to preach, and for as much as the said vicar and others had certain articles against the said friar, which he had preached, I sent for him first by a gentle letter, but he would not come, but answered me plainly, he would ask counsel, and so went to London. Afterwards at his return I caused him to be cited, but he would not appear, and now I have given commission down to examine the articles, and for because he has preached much slanderously, to the offence of the people, I shall discharge him from preaching."

In one of his later books, Bale recalls that archbishop Lee examined him; "… upon the article of honouring and praying to the saints, divided into xvii articles…"

This would seem to relate to the Doncaster episode. Baler mentions that his Cambridge mentor, Geoffrey Downes, was present and smiled as Bale answered questions which were put to him by an old priest.

With his licence to preach revoked, Bale left Doncaster and made his way south to London, and to the royal court at Greenwich, probably seeking some form of patronage. However, his efforts appear to have brought little return, and it was the antiquary John Leland, who proposed to Bale that he should use his historical notes on his Order to write a history of the Carmelites in England. So Bale went back to the Carmelite house in Ipswich, where he had been prior, and, during the summer of 1536, he composed his *Anglorum Heliades* (The English followers of Elijah), complete with a dedicatory introductory letter addressed to Leland. Bale had a fair copy of this work made, but he continued to add some marginal corrections and additions until 1539. The work is divided into two books. The first book contains an account of the development of the Carmelite Order in England in 54 chapters, whilst the second book is composed of a series of biographical entries, of the significant Carmelite authors, together with a list of their works. For most of this work, Bale writes appreciatively and sympathetically on the coming of the Carmelites to England, and the development of the Order over the centuries. The reader would never suspect that this was written by anyone other than a devout Carmelite. It is only when Bale arrives at the last few chapters that he becomes more critical, and begins to express his own personal views. In chapters 51 and 52, he writes of people and events which happened during his own time in the Order. He reflects on superiors whom he knew personally, which makes him an invaluable witness, even though he cannot resist being severely critical about most of them. In the final chapter, Bale gives full vent to his own views and opinions, and reveals his deeply felt reforming attitude:

> Thus I shall end this account with a brief conclusion. The sons of Elias were poor hermits, of small repute among men, humble, retiring, unknown, and even despised. They owned no lands, and lived hidden in valleys, in woods, and in mountainside caves. Indeed, they were not at all unlike those of whom Paul says: "…they wandered about dressed in sheepskins and goatskins, amidst want and distress, and ill-usage; men whom the world was unworthy to contain, living a hunted life in deserts and on mountainsides, in rock fastnesses, and caverns underground. One and all gave proof of their faith…" Then their chief business was religion, the perfection of their life. Remaining in the flesh, but not living according to the flesh, they fiercely shunned vice and evil desire. In those days they were endowed with the Holy Spirit, of fervent devotion, occupied in contemplation of God, and shining with a multitude of divine virtues. This time having passed, they devoted themselves to scholarship, and gave themselves to the study of the various sciences. So from among them came many who were wise and learned men.

> Then they came to the notice of princes, put on airs and graces and having obtained employment, were finely dressed, rewarded with honours and titles, enriched with gifts. From that time forward they relaxed, and the religious spirit, the ardent devotion, and the innocent simplicity of life of the early fathers dried up and dwindled away. True holiness and fervour gave way to a pre-occupation with ceremonies, in a search for a reputation among people. Hence, they began to be ambitious, proud, acquisitive, and to erect fine buildings for themselves. Luxurious and effeminate, they now lapsed from concern with ceremonials into mere superstition and hypocrisy. So that, in the end, being thoroughly lukewarm, lazy, and idle, they became the dregs, prey to the basest of vices. Now nothing can be expected of them in the future, but forgetfulness of God and great impiety, utter wretchedness and decline, total abjection, and contempt, unless God in his mercy should interpose his hand. Which, with repeated tears, I beg of him who is blessed throughout the ages.

During 1536-1539, Bale appended two further works in his own hand to his *Anglorum Heliades*, and the three compositions were bound together in British Library, Ms Harley 3838. The first of these works is entitled, *A Short Catalogue of a Few of the Carmelite Writers from Elijah the Thesbite to Berthold their First Master General.* This work contains a series of biographical entries on all the "Carmelite", authors from the founding of the Order by Elijah, up to Berthold, who was the last superior before the Rule was given to the Order, by the Latin Patriarch of Jerusalem, Albert of Vercelli. The entries are all derived from various medieval histories, and Bale's composition is valuable in the way it describes the legendary history of the Order. The second work is a continuation of the first, with the title: *A Catalogue of the Outstanding Writers and Theologians of the Carmelite Order.* This work contains biographical entries for all the Carmelite authors, from the first prior general Brocard (c1200) up to Bale's time. It is a synthesis of all Bale's notes and jottings, many of them made during his travels on the continent, and these have a unique historical value.

In the autumn of 1536, Bale made his formal break with the Carmelite Order and took up a post as parish priest in Thorndon, Essex. From this point onwards, his interests change, and Carmelite history is mostly left behind as he becomes progressively more involved in promoting Protestant ideas. Bale writes numerous polemical books and pamphlets, and composed a number of plays, which could be performed in the houses of wealthy supporters of the Reform. His historical interests now broadened to extend beyond the Carmelite Order, to cover all the British authors and their works, which he could trace.

After three months in Thorndon, Bale was reported to the authorities for spreading heretical views and, on January 25th, 1537, he found himself in prison in Greenwich, under investigation by the Privy Council. His release was engineered by Thomas Cromwell, who then employed him in arranging performances of his plays to spread Protestant views. During this period, Bale married Dorothy, a widow. However when Thomas Cromwell was executed in 1540, he was forced to leave his wife and son, and go into exile. In 1548, following the succession of king Edward VI, Bale returned to England and, in 1552, he was appointed bishop of Ossory in Ireland. This was not a very inviting appointment as most of the Irish remained firmly Catholic and anti-English. Bale was consecrated as bishop in Dublin on February 2nd, 1553, but his stay in his diocese lasted only for six months until August, when the news arrived of the accession of the Catholic Queen Mary to the throne. Bale was forced to flee overseas again, and this time he took refuge in Frankfurt. On the accession of Queen Elizabeth in 1558, Bale was able to return, and was appointed a canon of Canterbury Cathedral, where he spent his remaining years. He died on November 15th, 1563, and was buried in nave of the cathedral. His wife, Dorothy, was granted a pension.

The Carmelite Order in England is extremely fortunate to have had John Bale as one its friars, during the early years of the sixteenth century. His interest, energy and dedication rescued so much of the Province's history from oblivion, in the upheaval caused by the Reformation, and the suppression of the Order in 1538. His surviving notebooks contain nearly 3,000 pages of closely written information on the Order, and the list of persons, mentioned in them, runs to over 3,600 names. Moreover, thanks to his travels in the Low Countries, France and Italy, our knowledge of Carmelite history in these countries is also increased. As will be seen from the following portraits of some of our medieval English Carmelites, much of the knowledge that we have of them is due to the painstaking notes made by Bale.

A sad aspect of Bale's life, from a Carmelite point of view, is his departure from the Order in 1536, and his adherence to the Protestant Reformation. But Bale was, above all else, a man who lived by his principles come what may. He did not suffer fools gladly, and when he argued, he put real vigour into expressing his view. Not for nothing was he known as "bilious Bale". His criticisms of the Carmelite Order in his own day were, in many aspects, well deserved. The Order had lost some of its fervour, laxity had crept in, and abuses were growing. The real problem, though, was that the Order was failing to attract persons of real commitment and ability, who would have the strength and leadership skills needed to introduce, and carry through the necessary reforms.

Inevitably Bale's own reforming tendencies, like many converts to new beliefs, were carried to extremes. His rejection of the celibate life, helped him to justify his leaving the Order, and his marriage, but it left no room for those wishing to devote their lives wholly to serving God. It would be unfair to accuse Bale of hypocrisy or deviousness, but his initial view of a Church in England, directed by the king, ran into trouble when he himself had to flee the country as king Henry VIII's views on religion became more traditional, after the fall of Thomas Cromwell. This happened again when Bale had to seek refuge abroad on the accession of Queen Mary to the throne, and her re-introduction of Catholic practices. Yet, for all his inconsistencies, Bale is a fascinating character. He must have been infuriating at times, especially when he held fast to unpopular views, but he was a person who demanded attention. His views, sincerely held, needed to be answered, and his enthusiasm and commitment were impressive. He was a first class historian, the equal to all his contemporaries, a playwright of no mean talent, a prolific writer of serious and more popular religious works, and, as he himself would want stressed, he spent his life trying to do what he felt God wanted him to do.

The following sonnet to Bale was written by the young poet, Barnabus Googe, in 1561 when Bale was 66 years of age.

***To Doctor Bale***

Good aged Bale, that with thy hoary hairs
Dost yet persist to turn the painful book,
O happy man, that hast obtained such years,
And leav'st not yet on papers pale to look,
Give over now to beat thy wearied brain,
And rest thy pen that hath long labored sore;
For aged men unfit sure is such pain,
And thou beseems to labor now no more.
But thou, I think, Don Plato's part will play,
With book in hand to have thy dying day.

**References:**

*BRCEW* 93-108: *ODNB* 3, 482-486.

Richard Copsey, O.Carm., "John Bale: preserver of Carmel's past", in *Historiography and Identity: Responses to Medieval Carmelite Culture*, ed. Jens Röhrkasten & Coralie Zermatten, (Zurich: LIT Verlag, 2017) ,145-167.

Leslie Fairfield, *John Bale: Mythmaker for the English Reformation*, (West Lafayette, Indiana: Purdue Univ. Press, 1976).

# 2

# SAINT SIMON STOCK

**(†1265)**

Simon Stock and the Scapular Vision

Any account of notable English Carmelites would be expected to start with Saint Simon Stock, who is the best known member of the medieval English Province, and its only saint. However, this immediately faces us with a problem because we know so little about his life with any historical certainty. The major reason for our ignorance is that all the internal records, covering the early years of the Order, have been lost. As the Order expanded from being a small eremitical community on Mount Carmel, into an international Order with houses throughout Europe, there was initially no specific house where the prior general resided. For historical reasons, Mount Carmel still remained as the Mother House, but its distance from Europe, and its increasing perilous situation due to the Muslim attacks, led to Mount Carmel, and the other houses in the Holy Land at Acre and Sidon, being increasingly isolated.

During the early years, as the hermits established themselves in Europe, and following the first general chapter, which was held in Aylesford in 1247, whoever was elected prior general, travelled around from house to house, visiting the various provinces, accompanied by a friar who served as his secretary. They carried, in their luggage, the register recording the general's actions, the minutes of the general chapters and other official documents. This system appears to have worked well for a number of years until disaster struck in 1271. The prior general, at that time, was Nicholas the Frenchman, and it was while he was in the East, visiting the houses in the Holy Land Province; that is, the communities in the Holy Land, on Mount Carmel and in Acre and Sidon, but also including the communities on Cyprus at Fortamia, founded near Kyrenia, on the north coast c1235, and Nicosia in the 1260's. During his visitation, Nicholas stayed for a while in Cyprus, at the house in Fortamia, whilst there, he wrote a letter addressed to all the members of the Order. This letter, called *The Flaming Arrow*, exhorted all the Carmelites to return to a more eremitical style of life, devote themselves to prayer, and avoid too much contact with the world outside their priories. Nicholas finished writing his letter in February 1271. Early Carmelite historians have assumed that, after finishing this letter, Nicholas resigned his office and retired to live as a hermit, but there is no evidence for this. In fact, it would have been strange for Nicholas to resign before seeing what the reaction to his letter was. A better explanation is that Nicholas was preparing to distribute the letter when he fell ill and died on April 29th, 1271. So, the letter remained unread in Cyprus. This explains the fact that no early copies of the letter survive, and that knowledge of its existence only reached Europe in the early 1400's, when a copy arrived from Cyprus.

The death of Nicholas not only prevented members of the Order from reading *The Flaming Arrow*, but his demise in Cyprus also led to the loss of the early registers of the prior general, and other official documents belonging to the Order. Whether this was due to the documents remaining in Cyprus, and being destroyed at some later date, such as during the Turkish conquest of the island in 1571, or whether the documents were dispatched to Europe, and lost in a shipwreck, or some other catastrophe on their travels, is open to conjecture.

Early Carmelites writing on the history of the Order, such as Sibert de Beka, Jean Trisse and others, have no knowledge of the early priors general of the Order, and all start with the Englishman, Ralph Fryston* of Alnwick in Northumberland. He was elected prior general on September 8th, 1271.

It was not until a later prior general, Jean Grossi, who was a keen historian, searched through some of the old liturgical books of the Order, that he found references to prayers being said for some previously unknown priors general, including a "Nicholas", an "Alan" and a "Simon". In his list of priors general, composed in 1390, Grossi could only record the dates of their memorials but, in recent years, Carmelite historians have now pieced together a tentative list of the early priors general. At the first general chapter held in Aylesford in 1247, a "Godfrey" was elected prior general (and not Simon Stock as previously thought). Godfrey's name occurs on a document in 1249, about the founding of a Carmelite house in Pisa. He is probably also the "G. prior of Carmel" who is mentioned in a will relating to the Carmelite house in Sidon on June 1st, 1254. However, he seems to have died soon after, as a chapter was held later in 1254, in London, when it seems likely that Alan was elected as the new prior general. His name was found by Jean Grossi in an old ordinal in Cologne. We have no records of Alan's period in office but, it is likely that he held office only for a short time, probably from c1256-c1258, when he was replaced by Simon Stock. Emanuele Boaga, President of the Carmelite Institute in Rome, suggested that Alan died on November 12th, 1256, but there is no record of a general chapter soon after that date. Simon's name was discovered by Fr Grossi in an old ordinal, in the Carmelite house in Orange in France, where he found the entry:

> "Brother Simon Stock of the English province, who was buried at Bordeaux and worked many miracles; he died on the 16th day of May."

This ordinal must have been composed sometime after the foundation of the house in Orange, in 1307, but the entry probably made use of earlier records. Another reference to Simon occurs in the necrology of the Carmelite convent in Florence, composed by Giovanni Bartoli c1374. For the earliest entries, Bartoli made use of older sources. His entry for Simon Stock reads:

> "May 16th, Brother Simon Stock of the English province was prior general and a holy man and worked many miracles: he is buried at Bordeaux in the province of Gascony."

So, having these tentative dates for Simon Stock as prior general, what else can we know about him? The answer is very little! There is, however, a very early story preserved by the Dominicans, which mentions a Simon who was a prior. This is found in a collection of miracle stories, which the Dominican friar, Gerard de Frachet, composed between 1256-1259, at the request of the Order's general chapter. The story that Gerard de Frachet collected was as follows:

> "A certain brother in the Carmelite Order was tempted to leave the Order when he heard that brother Jordan had drowned. He became more and more disturbed saying to himself: "All men who serve God are wasting their time; either this man was not a good man and thus he perished, or God does not reward well those who serve him." Having thus decided to leave [the Order] very soon, that very night a beautiful figure, surrounded by an immense light, appeared to him. Trembling with fear, he prayed, saying: "Lord Jesus Christ help me and show me what this is." And at once, the figure replied: "Do not be upset, dearest brother, for I am brother Jordan, about whom you are disturbed; and thus will everyone be saved who serves Our Lord Jesus Christ until the end." And he disappeared, leaving him consoled about all these things. This brother and the prior of the same Order, Symon, a religious and trustworthy man, narrated these happenings to our brethren."

The Carmelite historian, Fr Joachim Smet, has argued that the prior Symon, mentioned in this story, was probably the prior of Mount Carmel, as blessed Jordan drowned soon after setting sail from Acre, and so it was probably Simon Stock. This is quite plausible, but Blessed Jordan died in February 1237, and his fate would have been well known even in Europe, and so the location of this story could have been any Carmelite house. More plausibly, the Carmelite brother, who was tempted to leave the Order, was probably a young hermit and so likely to have been studying for the priesthood. In the Holy Land, young hermits from Mount Carmel probably followed the courses in philosophy and theology, at the Dominican house of studies in Acre. This Dominican house had a good reputation and, with the numbers of hermits on Mount Carmel increasing, there would have been a need for priests to serve the community, to celebrate mass and hear the confessions of the hermits, as well as any visiting pilgrims. Also, it is known that the Carmelite hermits went to hear the confessions of the Knights Templar, in the nearby fortress of Atlit, on the coast below Mount Carmel. So the brother who had this vision could very likely have been staying in Acre, whilst pursuing his studies at the Dominican house. It seems there was a small Carmelite community in Acre in the 1250's, although its formal recognition by the Church, and the opening of its chapel to the public did not happen until 1261. If the brother in Frachet's story was studying in Acre, then the memory of blessed Jordan's death would be very fresh in the Dominican community, and prior Symon could have been the prior of the small Carmelite community in Acre. Whether this was Simon Stock is open to conjecture.

Simon Stock's period as prior general lasted from 1258 to 1265 but it is frustratingly undocumented. It is likely that Simon Stock, as prior general, commissioned another English Carmelite, Henry de Anna*, to act as his vicar in the founding of new houses in northern France. The records show that there were numerous new foundations made during this period, as the Order spread throughout Europe and, as prior general, Simon Stock must have played an important role in encouraging and supporting these new ventures. There were around twenty-five communities in the Order when Simon Stock was elected as prior general, and there were fifty-one houses by the time that he died in 1265. In effect, the number of Carmelite houses in the Order doubled under Simon Stock's leadership. Also, it is likely that Simon Stock would have attended the general chapter which was held in Aylesford in 1261.

An interesting foundation was made towards the end of Simon Stock's period in office. This was the Carmelite house established in Bordeaux. At that time, Gascony was under the rule of the English King Henry III, and there were many English merchants and royal officials living in the city. There is a distinct possibility that Simon Stock, was the son of an English family who lived in Bordeaux. This would help explain why Simon's name does not occur in any of the contemporary English records. Also, if he was born in Bordeaux, then it is quite understandable that in 1264, he would have encouraged the establishment of a Carmelite community in his home town. Similarly, if his family were from Bordeaux, this would help explain why Simon visited the new community there, the following year, in 1265. But sadly Simon fell ill, during his visit, and died on May 16th, 1265.

There is no doubt that Simon Stock was not only a most effective prior general, but also a man of great faith, who lived a very holy life. Soon after his death, his tomb became a place of pilgrimage, and miracles were reported from those seeking his intercession. If Simon was born in Bordeaux, then this would help explain the quick emergence of devotion to a local saint.

As happens with many of the saints, legends began to emerge concerning the life of Simon Stock.

Menaud des Rosiers, the prior of Bordeaux, wrote on a life of Simon in 1500, and, in it, he gives a description of the events, which surrounded Simon's burial and his tomb.

> "After some days, the most merciful God wishing to praise and magnify his beloved Simon Stock, a vivid light shone forth at night from his tomb, so that it seemed to be full day. His frightened brothers turned to the archbishop of the city. The archbishop amazed at this new miracle, called together the clergy and people, for the light had already frightened the brothers for fifteen days. The archbishop arrived in a procession, with a great company of religious, and ordered the gravestone to be removed; a great perfume came forth and the bones shone like gold. The pious archbishop placed the bones in an urn, and ordered that such a treasure should be preserved with great care. And many miracles were worked at that time which, I will omit, because they would be tedious reading.
>
> This was related to me by two of the venerable fathers of our convent in Bordeaux, of whom one was a hundred years or more of age, brother Peter Comitis, and the other ninety years or so, brother John Fortis. This very year (which is 1500) brother Augerius de Vineis, doctor of sacred theology, has built a chapel and shrine for Simon Stock, in the same convent of Bordeaux."

The evidence of the two old brothers in Bordeaux, must refer to the miracles worked at the tomb, which took place in later years, and their witness would date the existence of a local cult to Simon Stock back to the early 1400's. The focus of the devotion, though, is clearly on the relics of Simon Stock and their miraculous powers. Some years later, in 1604, the prior general, Henry Silvio visited the Carmelite house in Bordeaux, and he records that:

> The body of St Simon Stock is contained intact in a painted casket, set in an elevated position in a special chapel. This saint is held in the greatest veneration in the city, and his office is said in our convent on May 16th. It is true that because of wars and devastation by heretics of the convent, which was built 500 years ago, first outside the city, then transferred to its present location inside the city, as can be most clearly shown, there are no writings or documents concerning this saint who was our general, and the relics are venerated only by tradition. There are still in this province, religious of 85 and 90 years of age, who testify that the afore-mentioned relics were always venerated, and held to be those of St. Simon Stock. A duplex office was composed in his honour, as can be proved by the very ancient choral books which contain the proper office of St Simon, all in chant.

A later witness is Martinien Pannetier, one-time prior of Bordeaux, who perished on the guillotine, during the French Revolution in 1794. Pannetier wrote two short works, *The Life of St. Simon Stock*, and *Instructions for the Confraternity of Our Lady of Mount Carmel*, intended for the lay members of the Carmelite Third Order. Pannetier records some of the miracles worked at the tomb, one of which concerns a former prior:

> …the Rev. Father Pierre Ratigui, prior of the convent of the Carmelites of Bordeaux, was at death's door due to a deadly illness, abandoned by the doctors, and without hope of recovery. He was moved to place himself under the protection of St Simon Stock, and he asked to be carried into the saint's chapel where he assisted at mass, which was celebrated in honour of the saint. During the mass, he held in his hand a lighted candle, entrusting himself with confidence to the intercession of his protector. When the mass ended, his prayers were completely fulfilled: he was immediately cured and restored to his former good health.

Raymond de Ratigny is known to have been prior in 1614, so the miracle mentioned by Pannetier must have taken place around this date. It is significant that the prior, wishing to be cured, does not turn to the scapular, but to the relics of Simon Stock: He is carried into the chapel in order to be near the tomb. Although fairly late, the story would seem to preserve the original focus of the cult which was based on miracles occurring at the tomb.

## The Scapular Vision

Sometime late in the 14th century, a catalogue of Carmelite saints emerges. The original version was possibly composed by the German Carmelite, John of Hildesheim (†1375). However, as this catalogue was copied and distributed, extra details and new entries were added. Around 1390-1400, a new entry was added concerning a "brother Simon" which read:

> Saint Simon, an Englishman of great holiness and devotion, who always begged the Virgin in his prayers that she would bestow some special privilege on his Order. To him, the Virgin appeared carrying a scapular in her hands and said: 'Let this be a pledge to you and to your brethren: whoever dies wearing it shall be saved'.

At the same time, or soon after, three other new entries were added, clearly linked to this account of brother Simon and his vision. These were:

> Saint Louis, king of France, who, when he had captured the Holy Land, brought the brothers of the Order from Mount Carmel back to the West with him, and established them, some in Paris and some in other places. Thus the Order had its beginnings in the West, and afterwards Louis died clothed in the habit of the Order.

> Saint Edward, king of England, who on account of his great devotion always turned to the glorious Virgin. Hearing that the brothers of the Blessed Virgin Mary of Mount Carmel had been brought across the seas, he sought diligently to have a foundation, and gave them his own palace in Oxford as a convent. Finally, at his own wish, he was clothed in the habit of their Order when he died.
>
> Saint Henry, first duke of Lancaster, a man of outstanding holiness, when he learnt of the miracle and privilege shown by the glorious Virgin to saint Simon, namely that whoever died wearing the scapular would be saved, always himself wore the scapular of the Order. Whence he showed his great devotion to the Blessed Virgin. At length, he died and was clothed in the complete holy habit."

This *Catalogue of Saints* is the earliest account of the vision of the Virgin Mary, and the scapular promise in any Carmelite text, and occurs over 100 years after the event described. However, there are several inconsistencies in this account. Firstly, the "brother Simon" who has the vision, is not described as a prior general, which is a strange omission. Then, in the three supporting entries, there are further anomalies. Saint Louis is described as the person who brought a group of Carmelites with him, on his return to Europe and established the Order in the West which is doubly inaccurate. There is no record of any Carmelites accompanying Saint Louis as he returned to France in 1254, and the Carmelite foundation in Paris was not made until four years after St Louis returned. Nor was Saint Louis the first to bring the Carmelites to Europe as, by the time of his return in 1254, there were four houses in Sicily, seven in England, and one each in Italy and Germany, and moreover even one in France at Les Aygalades near Marseilles (c1244).

As for the other entries, there is no record of any lay person wearing the Carmelite scapular out of devotion at this early date. It is true that, in the 13th century, there were lay devotees attached to the Carmelite church in Florence, who joined the friars on formal occasions and in the processions, but they wore a smaller version of the Carmelite white cloak (as they still do to this day). Similarly, King Edward II did make a promise to the Virgin Mary, as he sought to escape from the Battle of Bannockburn, but he fulfilled this promise by giving Beaumont Palace, his residence in Oxford, to the Carmelites. As for Henry, Duke of Lancaster, there is no evidence he had any special links with the Carmelites and on his death in 1361, his major bequest was to the hospital in Leicester, which his father had founded, and where he himself asked to be buried, in the hospital chapel.

The emergence of the scapular vision, at this date, may be due, partly, to the emergence of similar miracle stories, about religious habits, in other Orders. The Benedictines had a story about a monk who was in the monastery infirmary where, due to the heat, he was persuaded to take off his cowl. Sadly, he died not long afterwards. Then, during the night, whilst the monks were praying before his coffin, the dead monk stood up, and went to kneel before the sub prior, explaining that he had been sent back from heaven by Saint Benedict, because he was not properly dressed. The sub prior replaced his cowl, and the monk lay down again, and passed away peacefully. A closer analogy to the scapular vision, can be found among the Dominicans who were, at this time, propagating a belief that Reginald of Bologna had been shown the white habit of the Dominicans by the Virgin Mary who told him, "This is the habit of your Order" and so he joined the Order. This gave rise to the conviction that their habit had been given to them by the Virgin Mary. Then, a later legend arose that the Virgin Mary had given the Rosary to Saint Dominic. Around the same time, the Franciscans were preaching that Saint Francis descended into Purgatory once a year, and released all those who had died wearing the Franciscan habit. This led to lay devotees being dressed in the Franciscan habit just before they died.

For the Carmelites, the identification of "brother Simon" with the prior general Simon Stock, did not occur until the early fifteenth century. This was due to the fact that, as mentioned above, the existence of Simon Stock as an early prior general was only re-discovered by Jean Grossi in 1390. The identification of "brother Simon", as Simon the prior general, seems to have happened sometime after 1400. It first appears in the Carmelite Jean Grossi's *Viridarium* (lit. *Pleasure Garden*: i.e. a short history of the Order) written c1415. From this point onwards, the legend of the scapular vision grew rapidly.

In 1423, the prior of the Carmelite house in Ghent, John Hazeiaghere, travelled to Bordeaux to ask for some relics of Simon Stock, to add to the community's burgeoning collection of relics. He was given an arm, two ribs and a bone from Simon's throat, accompanied by a letter of authentication, signed by the provincial and vicar-general of Gascony, John de Burgh, and the prior of Bordeaux, William Costall (who had studied in the Carmelite house in London for some years). Most of the text of the letter of authentication still survives and it describes Simon Stock as having lived a saintly life:

> "… And after he was taken from our midst, his life was approved clearly through the wonders and many miracles which took place…

> … therefore brother John Hazeiaghere, the bearer of these letters, of the same Order and from the French Province, a religious man and of proven character, as we know from other experienced persons, and devoted to this saint, has humbly asked us if we would consider him worthy to receive some of the relics of St Simon that he might carry them to his Province to the glory of God and the praise of St Simon. We therefore moved by paternal piety, wishing with all zeal to serve the Province of France and being willing to be moved by his request, we give to the said brother John Hazeiaghere the arm of this saint, two ribs and a part of his throat. And possessing these holy relics, we ask that they shall be received with devotion and in good faith, and put in an honoured place, so that in this, God may be praised in everything for ever and ever. In witness to all this, the official seal of the Vicar and Prior, here present, have been attached … from our convent of Bordeaux, the 4th November 1423 AD."

Curiously, there is no mention of the scapular vision. Until then, the devotion in Bordeaux to Simon Stock, was clearly based on pilgrimages to the tomb of the saint, and the prayers offered for his intercession. It appears to have been the prior of Ghent himself who brought the story of the scapular vision as, soon after his visit, a liturgy was composed in Bordeaux for the feast day of Simon Stock (16th May), which included the scapular vision. Belief in the scapular vision took root very quickly and, by 1500, Menaud de Rosiers, the prior of Bordeaux, is writing a long life of Simon Stock, which includes many extra details about the life of Simon Stock and the miracles he worked, which Menaud has found in other late writings or, more likely, invented. In his text, we are told about Simon having been born in Kent, the younger son of a farmer who died when he was seven years old. It is claimed that Simon was brought up by his elder brother, and devoted his life to prayer and contemplation, living as a hermit in the trunk of a tree. When the Carmelites arrived in Aylesford, Simon was inspired to join them. Other writers around the same time added further details such as the fact that the scapular vision took place on July 16th, 1251 and Simon had lived to be 100 years old, etc.

In 1642, in response to a critical attack on the Carmelite accounts of the scapular vision, and the Sabbatine privilege – by Jean Launoy, a professor of theology in Paris – the then prior of Bordeaux, Jean Chéron wrote a long defence of the Order in a work entitled, *The Scapular Privilege and the Vision of Simon Stock Justified.* After quoting all the Carmelite authors, he could find, Chéron produced at the end of his book, the text of two manuscript fragments which he said were in his possession. Chéron claimed that these fragments were written by Peter Swanyngton, the secretary of Simon Stock, and contained an account of how Simon Stock had told Peter Swanyngton, about the vision he had witnessed. Sadly Chéron never produced the manuscript fragments which he claimed to have. It was only in 1911, that a French historian, Père Louis Saltet, published a carefully researched article, which demonstrated all the historical inaccuracies in Chéron's text, and demonstrated that the Swanyngton fragments must have been invented by Chéron himself.

However, all these later legends should not obscure the fact that Simon Stock, the prior general was a significant figure in the development of the Order. He led the Carmelites from c1258 to 1265, and it was his leadership which guided and inspired the Order during a period of rapid expansion. Moreover, he was not only a good leader and administrator, but his life and religious devotion, led to him being regarded as a very holy person. Soon after his death, his tomb became a place of pilgrimage. Moreover, there are reputable reports of cures being achieved through his intercession. As the Order faces many challenges in the 21st century, perhaps it would be appropriate to ask for his guidance, and for his intercession, that those who follow in his footsteps may be able, in their turn, to serve the God whom he loved so much.

**References:**

*BRCEW* 369-274: *ODNB* 50, 651.

Saggi, Ludovico, O.Carm., "Saint Simon Stock", in *idem, Saints of Carmel*, (Aylesford, England: Carmelite Fathers, 1975), 261-265.

Copsey, Richard, O.Carm., "Simon Stock and the Scapular Vision", *Journal of Ecclesiastical History*, 50:4 (Oct 1999) 652-683. A later version of this article can be found in *Carmel in Britain*, vol 3: *The Hermits from Mount Carmel* (Faversham, 2004) 75-112.

# 3

# RALPH FRYSTON

Ralph Fryston of Alnwick, prior general

Ralph Fryston of Alnwick was a significant figure in the early history of the English Province although, once again, little is known of his life with any degree of certainty. Even his name has come down to us in many different forms, e.g. Ralph Fresburn, Ralph the German, etc.

Ralph was one of the party of hermits from Mount Carmel who came to England at the end of 1241. According to legend, Ralph, accompanied by Yvo Berch, led a group of Carmelites to Hulne, just outside Alnwick in Northumberland in 1242, where they founded the first Carmelite house in England, on land provided by William de Vescy, lord of Alnwick. This foundation was followed a few weeks later, by a second foundation at Aylesford in Kent.

Our first historical reference to Ralph is found in an early list of general chapters, where it is recorded, that he was elected prior general at the chapter held in Paris, on September 8th, 1271, in place of Nicholas the Frenchman, who had died in Cyprus earlier that year. There is a second piece of evidence supporting his election, which was written by the Carmelite Pieter Wasteels, in 1643, with quotes from a letter written by Ralph which began:

> "To all the Christian faithful who shall read these words, brother Ralph, humble prior general of the brothers of the Order of the Blessed Mary of Mount Carmel, sends greetings in the Lord …."

The letter ends:

> "… dated at Paris in our house, in the year of Our Lord 1271, on the octave of the Nativity of Our Lady [15 Sept]."

Sadly, Wasteels did not record the contents of this letter, and the original has since been lost. As it is very likely that Ralph would have held a senior position in England, before being elected prior general, it is reasonable to suppose that he was the prior provincial in the years before his election. If this is so, then he would have met the previous prior general, Nicholas, who visited the province in 1266. That Ralph was provincial, before being elected general fits in with a note made by John Bale*, who claims that, in the year following his election, Ralph made a visitation of England, and was present at the provincial chapter held in London in 1272, when Roger Crostweyt was elected provincial, presumably in place of Ralph himself.

Unfortunately, soon after his death, one of the scribes recording the acts of the general chapters, misread Ralph's name. In Latin, Ralph's name becomes "Radulphus Alnevicus" (Ralph of Alnwick) but the scribe, unfamiliar with English towns, misread this as "Radulphus Alemanus" (Ralph the German). This mistake was perpetuated by later historians.

It was during Ralph's time as prior general, that the Church began to plan for a General Council to be held in Lyons in France (see Introduction). In order to prepare themselves for this Council, the Carmelites brought forward their next General Chapter, and met in Bordeaux in January 1274. It would seem that Ralph anticipated the problems which the Order would face at the forthcoming Council and, as he was growing older, he decided to resign as prior general, and hand the responsibility over to a younger and more capable friar. When the Carmelite Chapter met, they elected Pierre Millau as prior general to succeed Ralph. Ralph himself retired to Hulne Priory, his filial house where he had joined the Order, and once again he took up the life of a simple friar, giving himself to prayer and contemplation.

However, after two years, Ralph's life was disturbed again. A General Chapter was convened to meet in Montpellier in May 1277, and Ralf was summoned to be present. On August 2nd, 1276, King Edward I issued a letter asking for safe-conduct:

> "Safe-conduct, for one year, for Ralph de Fryston, prior-general of the Carmelites, going beyond seas to his general chapter."

It appears from the one year safe-conduct that the elderly Ralph intended to take his journey fairly gently, probably wanting to visit some of the French Carmelite houses on his way. However, there is no record of him being present at the Chapter, and so it would seem that he was unable to go. Most likely, he fell ill before he could set out and died shortly afterwards.

Although we know so little about Ralph, he must have been a well-respected member of the province. His fellow Carmelites in the province, saw him as a suitable provincial to lead the province and then, his fame extended farther afield, and he was elected by the whole Order to be its prior general. Bale, in his history of the province written in 1536, claims that Ralph came from a distinguished Northumbrian family, and that he fought under Richard I in the Holy Land. Unfortunately, for this to be true, Ralph would have been over 100 years old when he died. Bale did, though, preserve a short poem commemorating Ralph, and his role in the foundation of Hulne Priory, which reads:

> "Leaving their ancestral home, Ralph with Ivo
> Led the Carmelites to establish here their home.
> Tired from their journey, he settled them round a spring,
> The spring of Hulne which gushed out from amidst the dry ground.
> Then, in old age, death overtook him. After a holy funeral
> Divine grace caused bright lights to shine around his grave."

**References:**

*BRCEW* 288-289.

# 4

# GILBERT OF NORWICH

## (†1287)

Gilbert of Norwich, bishop of Hamar

The cartulary, (a collection of deeds and other legal documents), for the Carmelite house in King's Lynn, still survives, and in it there are a couple of references to a "Gilbert of Norwich", who was the bishop of Hamar in Norway. The first records that, on October 24th, 1273, whilst he was staying at Middleton, three miles from King's Lynn, the bishop granted an indulgence of 40 days for all the faithful who visited the Carmelite chapel in King's Lynn, devoutly recited an *Our Father* and *Hail Mary*, and gave an offering towards the building of the chapel.

The bishop was back again, and in the Carmelite house on August 2nd, 1276, when he granted a second indulgence of 40 days for all the faithful who having been to confession, were truly contrite and, for the salvation of their souls, came to hear the preaching of the Carmelite brothers, wherever and whenever, they proclaimed the Word of God.

It is not surprising that a bishop from another diocese should be acting in a large diocese like Norwich, especially as the Bishop of Norwich was often away on royal business. John Bale*, our Carmelite historian, was a member of the community in Norwich in the early 1500s and, in one of his notebooks, he compiled a list of 42 illustrious Carmelites who were buried in the chapel there. The first entry on his list is:

> "Brother Gilbert of Norwich, bishop of Hamar, who died in the year of Our Lord 1287, on 30th October."

Clearly, by using the title "brother", Bale believed that Bishop Gilbert was a member of the Order, and he refers to him as such in other later entries in his notebooks.

Apart from an entry in the papal archives that a "Gilbert" was consecrated the Bishop of Hamar on March 4th, 1263, the rest of his life remained tantalisingly unknown. Then, totally unexpectedly, an email arrived for me, from Dr Brian Ayers, of the University of East Anglia, with a request for information on Bishop Gilbert as, he wrote, he was exploring his life but from a completely different starting point. He was working on the history of the parish churches in Norwich, and had noticed that, in an account of the now vanished St Crowche's parish church (Holy Cross), by the 19th century historian Francis Blomefield, there is the following passage:

> "In this churchyard, Adam and Botild, father and mother of Bishop Gilbert, were interred, whose graves many pilgrims and other devout people used to visit, there being an *indulgence* to all that came thither and prayed for them, of 300 days of pardon."

So, it seems that bishop Gilbert was English, and born in the parish of St Crowche, probably around 1230.

By the time of the next reference to Gilbert, he has been ordained to the priesthood, and was serving as the archdeacon of Shetland from 1260. At this period, Shetland was part of the kingdom of Norway. Evidently, Gilbert's ability came to the attention of king Haakon IV who appoints him as the "king's priest" (or confessor). As the bishop of Hamar in Norway died later the same year, the king decided to put forward Gilbert as his replacement. However, Einar, the archbishop of Trondheim, objected and proposed another candidate. In order to settle the matter, Gilbert was sent off to Rome in 1262, to bring the two proposals for the Pope to decide upon. Faced with the choice, Pope Urban IV chose Gilbert, and so, after his return early in 1263, Gilbert was consecrated bishop, in the cathedral church in Bergen, on 4th March.

Very quickly, Gilbert began to be used by the king on important diplomatic missions. In September 1263, he was one of four envoys sent to negotiate a peace treaty with the king of Scotland, Alexander IV. The envoys met King Alexander in Ayr, and put forward King Haakon's demand for the recognition of his rule over the Western Isles, and the Isle of Man. The envoys returned to Norway with the king of Scotland's terms, but no agreement was reached. So the king of Norway decided to settle matters by force, and led a large fleet to enforce his rule over the Western Isles. Apart from one brief skirmish, the king failed to engage the Scots into any decisive encounter and, as winter was approaching, he retired to the Isle of Orkney. During the winter, the king fell ill and died in the bishop's palace in Kirkwall at midnight on December 15th. Gilbert was one of those present at his deathbed and then returned to his diocese afterwards.

In 1265, King Haakon's son, King Magus VI, re-opened the peace talks with the Scots and, after Easter that year, Gilbert was one of two envoys sent to re-open negotiations for a peace treaty. The two of them travelled by ship down to King's Lynn where they stopped briefly, probably hoping to learn of the attitude of the English King Edward III. However, king Edward was engaged in a conflict with his own rebellious barons, which was only resolved by the Battle of Evesham on August 4th. By this time, the two envoys had moved northwards to York, and from there up to Perth in Scotland, where they met with the Scottish king. Then they returned to Norway, with the terms of a possible peace treaty, for king Magnus. By these terms, Norway recognised Scotland's sovereignty over the Western Isles, in return for a lump sum of 4,000 marks and an annuity of 100 marks. This agreement, signed on July 2nd, 1266, became known as the Treaty of Perth.

The next time, Gilbert appears in the records is when he visits King's Lynn on October 24th, 1273, and gives an indulgence (as recorded above). From this time forward, Gilbert appears to have remained in the diocese of Norwich, acting as an assistant to bishop Roger Skerning, and then to his successor in 1278, bishop William Middleton. At some time, after he became a bishop, probably on one of his visits to Norwich, Gilbert appears to have granted the indulgence, to all who came and prayed over the grave of his parents.

Around 1275, Gilbert seems to have formally resigned from his See, and, from that time on, he spent the rest of his life in the Norwich diocese. On January 13th, 1280, he dedicated the site of the newly founded Carmelite house in Yarmouth. Also, John Bale* records that Gilbert sponsored the Carmelite student, Peter Swanyngton, in his studies for the doctorate which he completed in the late 1290's. Sadly, Gilbert died before Peter Swanyngton had completed his studies.

Although there is no specific evidence of Gilbert joining the Carmelite Order, Bale seems quite clear that he was regarded as a *frater* or brother. It would seem highly likely, therefore, that Gilbert took up residence, in the Carmelite house in Norwich, and was regarded as a member of the community. Whether he formally applied to join the Order is not known. This could have happened, or alternatively, he could have been granted a letter of confraternity, which declared him an honorary member of the Carmelite family. Whichever is true, certainly when he died, Gilbert was buried with an appropriate ceremony in the Carmelite church, and the community were proud to have had him present among them. Gilbert was a man of great talents, a dependable and trustworthy servant of kings, and one who spent his life in serving and helping others.

**References:**

*BRCEW* 48-49 (see also *Additions & Corrections*).

Brian Ayers, "Bishop Gilbert of Hamar: A Norwich Cleric, Envoy and Administrator in Thirteenth Century Norway", *Collegium Medievale*, 34 (2021), 203-227.

# 5

# HENRY DE ANNA

## (†1300)

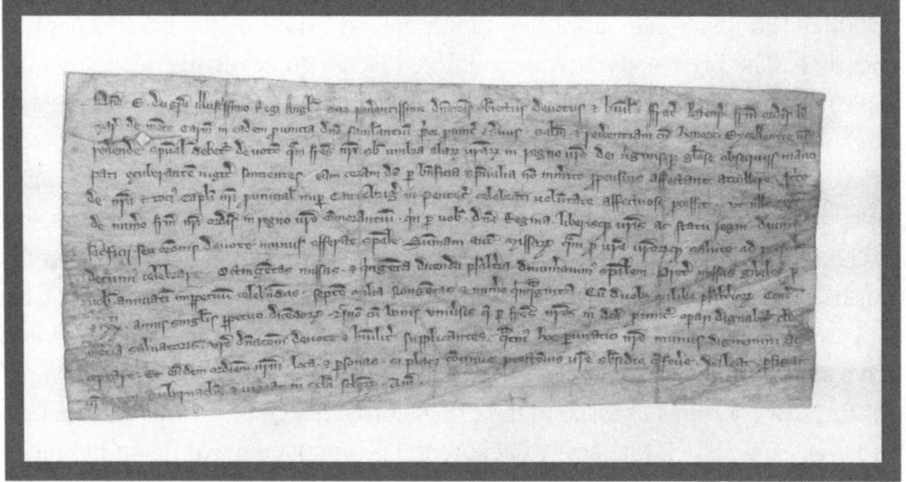

Letter from Henry de Anna to King Edward I, c1283

Throughout the second half of the 13th century, the English province was fortunate in having a very active and active leader, Henry de Anna. (He is usually called "Henry de Hanna" by historians, but examples of his signature still survive where he signs himself as "de Anna"). Our lack of documents from the 13th century means that we know very little about Henry's early life; moreover, the notes made by our major source for this period, John Bale*, are frequently confusing. From his surname, it is likely that Henry's family originally came to Norfolk from France, or the Low Countries. Henry joined the newly founded Carmelite community in Bradmer, near the coast in Norfolk, during the 1240's. (Due to the marshy land at Bradmer, this community moved to Burnham Norton, further inland, in 1253).

Nothing is known of Henry's early years as a Carmelite, but he must have been a student of great ability. John Bale* claims that he was the first prior of the house in Oxford, when it was founded in 1253. However, this is an error as the surviving documents record that the first superior of this new foundation, was John of Rochester. It is quite possible, though, that Henry de Anna became the prior there some years later. Bale states that he was elected prior provincial in 1254, but again he must be wrong, as there are contemporary documents which indicate that the provincial's name at that date began with a "W." If Henry was elected provincial, then it could not have happened until around 1260. Henry now becomes a senior figure in the province, and Bale notes that Henry was appointed to undertake various commissions on behalf of the prior general at this time. The prior general who appointed Henry to act as his deputy, would have been his fellow Englishman, Saint Simon Stock* (†1265) or his successor, Nicholas the Frenchman, who was elected in June 1266. Interestingly shortly after his election Nicholas visited Oxford and wrote some letters from there. According to Bale, Henry was sent by the prior general to go to France, to assist in the founding of new houses there. In 1260, Paris was the only house in the north of France, and so since Henry had his family origins in France or the Low Countries, it would help explain why Henry was chosen for this role. It would have been quite understandable for Simon Stock, as prior general, to use one of his English confreres to assist in the expansion of the Order in the region, north of Paris, especially if his family background meant that he was fluent in French and/or Flemish. It is likely that Henry assisted in establishing communities in Valenciennes (before 1259), Metz (before 1262), Liège (before 1265), Bruges (1264) or Ypres (1265). (Note: In the 17th century, Valenciennes put forward documents to "prove" it was founded in 1238, but there is no contemporary evidence to support this claim). Bale adds, without giving any details, that Henry also undertook similar commissions in Germany, Scotland and Ireland.

Henry came out of office in 1272, when Roger Crostweyt was elected provincial. However, once again, Bale claims that Henry was appointed as vicar general, but this time for the English prior general, Ralph Fryston* (who held office until 1274), and after this for his successor, the Frenchman Pierre Millau. One of Henry's roles would have been to preside at provincial chapters, when the prior general was not present, both in his own province as well as for neighbouring provinces. Henry himself was elected provincial for a second time, around 1281, and his appointment was confirmed at the general chapter which took place in London at Pentecost in the same year. As an experienced delegate at the chapter, it is to be expected that Henry would have played a significant part in the drawing up of a new edition of Constitutions for the Order. (This set of Constitutions is the earliest edition to have survived). Also, Henry probably played a part in designing the strategy to avoid the possible suppression of the Order, following the decree of the Council of Lyons in 1274.

After the General Chapter, Henry returned to England to oversee the future development of the province. There were already communities in Oxford and Cambridge, so these cities offered opportunities for further studies in theology, at their universities, to the more talented students of the province. The Carmelites, like the other three mendicant orders, gained permission to present one candidate a year, in each university, to incept as a Doctor of Theology. As the average time taken to complete the doctorate programme, was around 10-12 years after priestly ordination, sending students for a doctorate was an expensive investment. However, it was under Henry that the first candidates to study for the doctorate were chosen. The first English Carmelite to gain a doctorate in theology was Humphrey Necton, who incepted soon after 1292, in Cambridge. Fortunately, Humphrey's studies were financed by the bishop of Ely. He was followed a few years later at Oxford University, by Peter Swanyngton, and again his studies were financed by a generous bishop, the Carmelite Gilbert of Norwich*, bishop of Hamar in Norway, who lived in retirement in the Carmelite house in Norwich.

In spite of the academic prowess of the two universities at Oxford and Cambridge, it was probably due to Henry de Anna, that neither of the two Carmelite houses there was ever designated as a *studium generale* (international student house). Such a designation would have allowed the other European provinces to send students to these houses, and so occupy some of the two precious places a year, which were allotted to the Order for students to incept as doctors. Instead, it was the Carmelite house in London which was designated as a *studium generale* for philosophy and, over the subsequent years, it hosted a significant number of foreign students, especially from Germany. At this period the Irish and Scottish houses were still part of the English province, and so they could send students to Oxford and Cambridge. This privilege seems to have been continued even after the Carmelite provinces of Ireland and Scotland, gained their independence at the end of the 13th and beginning of the 14th centuries.

Soon after his election, Henry wrote a diplomatic letter to King Edward I, assuring him of the prayers of the Carmelites for himself and his family, and asking for his protection of the Order. This letter begins:

> "To Lord Edward, by the grace of God, the most illustrious King of England which is subject to your most reverend sovereignty, your devoted and humble brother of the Order of the Blessed Mary of Mount Carmel, prior

> provincial of the servants of God in the same province, sends greetings and honourable reverence. …"

The letter goes on to promise that the Carmelites in the English Province will say a great number of masses, prayers, etc. for the well-being of the king and the repose of the souls of his ancestors, etc. This is the first of nine letters written by Henry, which still survive. Most of them are addressed to the king and his officials, asking them to arrest and return errant friars, who have left their communities without permission, and were travelling around dressed in lay clothes. One of these letters, written in 1293, whilst Henry was in Aylesford, reads as follows:

> "To the most excellent prince, Lord Edward – by the grace of God – illustrious king of England, Lord of Ireland and duke of Aquitaine, brother Henry, prior provincial, and servant of the brothers of the Order of the blessed Mary of Mount Carmel in England, sends greetings in him, through whom kings reign and princes rule.
>
> As John Berkynge and Philip Beckeles formerly professed brothers in this Order have cast off the habit of the Order, and travel from place to place dressed in secular clothes, with evil intent, and wander in danger of their souls, and giving scandal to our Order, we humbly beseech your excellent majesty and ask that ,as far as you can, you will give orders, through letters to your servants, and the faithful, that the said John and Philip may be placed under arrest without any delay and released into our custody so that they may be appropriately punished according to the discipline and rule of our Order for the salvation of their souls. May your excellent reign which has lasted long and will continue for much longer. Given at Aylesford on the 10th kalends of December 1293 A.D."

Bale also records that he found an entry in an old register in Burnham Norton that Henry de Anna had made a visitation of the house on February, 19th, 1283. Visitations, at this time, were serious affairs. The provincial with his secretary, another friar, would arrive at the house to be visited. For the prior general or his vicar, who were probably unknown to the community, they would be asked to produce a document identifying themselves and authorising them to conduct a formal visitation. The visitators, and the community, would then process to the chapel where the visitator would introduce himself, and outline the procedure for the visitation. Every friar would be interviewed about his religious life and the religious life of the community, such as: what was the daily timetable; were friars observant in their attendance? Was the office said reverently?, etc. The financial records of the house would also be inspected and questions like: Was money owing to the house? Was the income being used wisely, etc., had to be answered.

Henry de Anna remained in office for a long period, and he played a significant role in the overall direction of the Order. It is known that he attended the general chapter held in Montpellier in 1287, as his signature occurs on a decree of 26th July, which approved the adoption of the white cloak (instead of the striped cloak worn on Mount Carmel). Later that year, he presided at a provincial chapter, which was held in Lincoln on September 14th, when the change of cloak was introduced in England. As far as we know, Henry de Anna presided at the provincial chapters held in Oxford (1289), Lynn (1291), Oxford (1296) and Ipswich (1300). There were probably other provincial chapters held during this period, as provincial chapters normally took place each year in the week in which the Feast of the Assumption fell (15th August) but unfortunately no records of them survive. One other letter which survives, was written by the Archbishop of York, on April 27th, 1289, asking Henry de Anna to receive an Augustinian canon, John Manlovel, into the Order.

From all this information and from other details given in his surviving letters, it is possible to trace many of Henry de Anna's movements during the 1290's. In 1291 he was probably away at the general chapter, which was held in Trier, Germany, around Pentecost (10th June). Then, on his return, he convened the provincial chapter, which was held in Lynn around August 15th. Our next trace of him is on December 1st, 1293, when he signs a letter to the king, whilst he was in Aylesford. By December 9th, he was back in London, when he signed another letter seeking the return of an errant friar. The following year, he was presumably present at the general chapter, held this time in Bordeaux at Pentecost (6th June) 1294. Henry was back in London by August 9th, when he signed another letter to the king. Then he would have hurried to attend the provincial chapter, held later that month in Oxford. The following year, we have more indications of Henry de Anna's movements. He signed another letter to the king from London, on May 27th, 1297, which left him very little time to reach Bruges, where the general chapter was due to begin at Pentecost (June 2nd). However, he had returned to London by August 16th, when he signed another letter. As this date was when the provincial chapter normally met, presumably Henry signed it whilst attending the chapter, which was meeting in London that year. Our next letter signed by Henry de Anna, is dated February 2nd, 1299, whilst he was once again in London. Henry must have been away during March, as a letter seeking the return of the Carmelite Thomas Bavent was signed by Humphrey Necton, who was vicar general. Henry was in Northampton when he signed his last surviving letter on September 9th.

Henry attended his final provincial chapter, in Norwich in August 1300. After the chapter, Henry appears to have visited the Carmelite houses in Norfolk, Burnham Norton, and King's Lynn. From there he made his way to Stamford where he became ill. He died on November 28th, and was buried in the chapel at Stamford. (In his printed books, Bale gives the year of Henry's death as 1299, however this is a misreading of his earlier notes).

Sadly we know little about the personality and other qualities of Henry de Anna, but he is worth remembering for his skilful and successful leadership of the province, during what would have been a difficult period. For 12 years and then 19 years, as provincial, he held the province together. He encouraged scholastic achievement, and watched over the steady growth in numbers of friars and new foundations, not only in England but also in Scotland and Ireland. A later prior general, blessed Baptist of Mantua (†1516), who only knew Henry de Anna by repute, wrote an epitaph to him which ably sums up his qualities (even if it repeats some historical inaccuracies):

> "Here lies Henry de Anna from Burnham, his full name
> A learned man who lived a holy life
> Noted for his virtues, this brother gained the highest office.
> Second leader of the British province
> He received the new cloister besides the banks of the Isis:
> Then, sent to the French, he founded many houses there.
> Returning to his own English, he remained as leader
> Until, in old years, he passed peacefully away."

**References:**

*BRCEW* 55-56:

6

# JOHN BACONTHORPE

(†1349+)

John Baconthorpe, provincial

In his history of the English Province written in 1536, the Carmelite John Bale* wrote that, at its peak:

> "… many of [the Carmelites] were men of great learning … at this time there such a number of learned doctors and other erudite men that you would not have thought there could be so many or their equal in the whole kingdom."

Bale, at this time, was embracing Protestant views and, on the point of leaving the Order, during which he had some harsh criticisms to make about the Carmelites of his day, so such complimentary words were real praise indeed.

Perhaps the greatest of these "learned doctors" was John Baconthorpe (or 'Bacon') who was born in the village of Baconsthorpe in Norfolk c.1292, and possibly related to the Bacon family who lived in Baconsthorpe Castle. Bale and others claim that Baconthorpe joined the Carmelites in nearby Blakeney but as this house was only founded sometime between 1304-1316, it is more likely that Baconthorpe joined the Order in Burnham Norton, and that when Blakeney was founded, he was among those sent to form the new community. Once in the Order, Baconthorpe quickly gave evidence of his intellectual ability and, after his initial studies, probably undertaken in Norwich, he was sent to do advanced studies in the University at Oxford. If he was related to the Bacon family, then it is likely that they helped to finance the costs of these further studies.

At Oxford, Baconthorpe studied under another Carmelite Robert Walsingham (†1312), and it was possibly Walsingham who recognised the exceptional talents of the young Baconthorpe, for he was soon transferred from Oxford to study for his doctorate in theology at Paris. Baconthorpe is known to have been there, lecturing as a bachelor in theology on the Bible and on the standard theology textbook, Peter Lombard's *Four Books on the Sentences*, sometime before 1318. He incepted as a doctor of theology, probably in 1322, and, the following year, as was the custom, he presided as regent master in the Carmelite *studium generale* (international house of studies) there. He is recorded as being in this position by the general chapter, which met in 1324 in Barcelona, where the delegates voted for a grant to cover his expenses. Whilst at Paris, Baconthorpe started writing his own commentary on *The Sentences*, and John Bale records that:

> "*Magister* John of Bacon, a town in England, doctor in both law and theology, completed [his commentary on] the first book of *The Sentences* in Paris on the Wednesday before the Feast of St. Mark, 1325 A.D. [24th April]"

It was probably during his time in Paris that Baconthorpe wrote four short works on the Order, defending the Carmelites against criticisms from the other religious orders, and from the parochial clergy. These works would have served also as useful guides for the younger Carmelites in formation. The following extract comes from the beginning of one of his earliest compositions entitled *A Collection of the Historical Sources and Laws for Defending the Foundation and Confirmation of the Order of the Blessed Mary of Mount Carmel:*

> "The Order of Carmel is noted for its great antiquity, such that there is no record of it in the law. For in the decree of the Council of Lyons which begins: 'The diversity of religious orders', makes mention of the Lateran Council, and then adds afterwards: 'The foundation of the Carmelite Order precedes the said general council', nor does it place any precise time on how much it preceded the council. From this it is clear that it preceded the council by such a great period, that no record of its antiquity can be found in the law. Moreover, in the first Constitutions of this Order, written in antiquity, there is found: 'that from the time of the prophets Elijah and Elisha, who lived on Mount Carmel', some contemplative men succeeded them on the same mountain, and they were called 'the brothers of Carmel'; and after Christ's Incarnation, they built a chapel in honour of the blessed Mary and assumed her name in their title.

Around 1326, Baconthorpe returned to England where he began lecturing in the Carmelite house in Cambridge. Then, the following year, the prior provincial Richard Blyton resigned due to his royal duties, and Baconthorpe was elected provincial in his place. Almost immediately, he became involved in politics, and was probably one of the two Carmelites who were in the group of delegates sent by Parliament to accept the abdication of King Edward II, on January 20th, 1327. Later that year, Baconthorpe was away at Albi in France, attending the general chapter being held there, where his appointment as provincial was confirmed. It was probably whilst he was in France, that Baconthorpe was one of three Carmelites who were summoned to Avignon by Pope John XXII, to defend the Church against the attacks on papal supremacy.

Baconthorpe presided at provincial chapters held in Nottingham in 1328, and London in 1329. However, in 1330, politics came back to trouble him again. In March 1330, at a session of Parliament held in Salisbury, Baconthorpe, together with his predecessor Richard Blyton, were accused of being involved in the Earl of Kent's plot. The Earl of Kent, believing that King Edward II was still alive, hatched a conspiracy to set him free, but his plan was quickly discovered. The Earl of Kent was executed, and Baconthorpe and Blyton, for their part in the conspiracy, were banished from the country. Galfrid le Baker's contemporary account of this episode is:

> "The same year, that is the third year of the king's reign, at the instigation of those who hated his father, the king held a parliament

> in Winchester where, at the prompting of his mother and her husband Roger Mortimer, the said Earl of Kent, the king's uncle, and many other nobles and religious friars, namely the provincials of the Dominican Order and of the Carmelites of the blessed Mary, and brother Richard Bliton, were accused by him of having conspired, as was said, to free the king – his father – from prison and to restore him to power. But all this was false and sheer phantasy. Yet the earl, because of some confessions that he made and certain letters that were found on him, was beheaded – although such confessions and letters, even if they were true, should not to have been sufficient to bring this punishment on such a worthy man. The others, though, that is the provincials of the Dominicans and the Carmelites of the blessed Mary, were exiled; but the bishop of London was set free; the cleric Robert of Taunton and some friars from the Carmelite and Dominican Orders were committed to prison."

Baconthorpe spent his period in exile at Paris, where he took up his teaching role again. In a way, later generations should be grateful for Baconthorpe's six years in exile. Freed from the duties of being a provincial, and the administration of a large province, he was able to devote himself to theology, in the stimulating environment of the university in Paris which was the most prestigious university in Europe at that time. He was in the company of some of the leading theologians in the Church, and his ideas benefitted greatly from their scholarly competition. Baconthorpe's own reputation as an original thinker grew, and he became a prolific author. He produced a large number of compositions. Sadly, apart from his commentary on *The Sentences,* the postil on St Matthew's gospel, and his four short works on the Carmelite Order, most of Baconthorpe's works have been lost. However the sheer volume of his output is impressive. In the list of his known works, there were commentaries on most of the books in the Bible, treatises on many of Aristotle's works, as well as discourses on the writings of St Augustine and St Anselm, and an impressive collection of sermons, addresses, etc.

Around 1336, Baconthorpe was permitted to return to England where he became a lecturer at Oxford. Whilst there, he continued with his commentary on *The Sentences* and he finished this work sometime around 1345. One of his other compositions at this time was a commentary of St Matthew's gospel. This work probably started as a course of lectures given c1336-1340. The following excerpt is taken from the introduction to this commentary:

> "The methodology in this work will be according to the teaching of Augustine in book 2 of his *On Christian Doctrine*, chapter 15, where he teaches that, if the doctors of philosophy and human laws say anything true, then they ought to make use of it in preaching the gospel. However,

> the fables of the poets are not to be accepted, except where they are used in explaining morality when preaching. In the *Decretals* distinction 86, chapter 'Since many', Gregory states that, having heard the writings of the bishop Desiderius, so much joy flooded into his heart that he was unable to contradict that which he argued. But then he heard that the bishop had expounded on secular literature, that he had recited the fables of Jupiter and explained their morality in his preaching. This Gregory found so offensive, and he was so vehemently repelled that the good things which the bishop had said in his words, were changed into anguish and sadness; and he added that the reason was because the praises of Christ should not be uttered by the same mouth as the praises of Jupiter. Another reason was that for him a fable represented something false, just as a parable was a representative example of truth; but falsehood is to be destroyed everywhere, not expounded and this was why the Philosopher, both in speculative science and in morals, first refuted the legendary and false ideas and then afterwards put forward true arguments and examples, as appears in the first book of his *Physics*, the first book of the *Metaphysics*, the first of the *Ethics*, as this example will show. Now just as the People of Israel when leaving Egypt, begged for gold and silver jewelry and clothing for a better use, not on their own authority but at the command of God. Therefore, led by God, I aim in this commentary on the gospel, that they may find a better and more extensive understanding in each of the readings, and discover in the contents some worthwhile philosophical truths, morals and canon law, together with theology, briefly explained and extensively gathered together."

Sometime in the 1340's, Baconthorpe appears to have moved down to London, as a Latin bible which belonged to the Carmelite house in London, contains the inscription:

> "Memorial of the reverend doctor of theology, brother John of Bacon, which he left to the convent of brothers of the Order of the Blessed Mary of Mount Carmel, London, 1248 A.D."

Aside from the scribal error in the date which should have been 1348, this book appears to have been a gift from Baconthorpe in his old age, (he was approaching sixty years), when he was disposing of some of his beloved books. Baconthorpe was still alive in 1348 as his commentary on Aristotle's *Ethics* was addressed to John Thoresby as chancellor, a position which Thoresby did not occupy until June 16th, 1349. Three years later, Thoresby was promoted to become archbishop of York on August 16th, 1352, so it would appear that Baconthorpe died sometime between these two dates. He was buried in the Carmelite church in London.

Around 1490, Laurent Bureau, a Carmelite from Dijon, composed a long Latin poem on the life of Baconthorpe, and the following two passages give the flavour of it. (The "Francisco" mentioned in the second excerpt was the Carmelite Francis de Medicis, who edited Baconthorpe's commentary, on Book I of *The Sentences* printed in Paris in 1485):

> "England gave birth to me, everyone called me John
> And I was honoured with the name of Bacon.
> When I desired to drink holy draughts from the fountainhead
> I went to Paris, where they flow most freely,
> And there, of all that study, toil and care could achieve,
> I wanted nothing to be neglected by my wit.
> For the holy writ was not my only care,
> The canons of the pontiffs pleased me too.
> . . . . .
> At last, after my death, I went to rest in my native land.
> It is sweeter to have the soil of one's home to cover one's bones.
> Then I lay buried for many ages:
> Thus time renews all things and puts them to flight.
> Francisco, a physician and a member of the order,
> Granted it to me and my writings to live again,
> Making them take shape in many volumes.
> He was the cause of my being read by learned men.
> I owe much to this man and much to my readers,
> And so do you, whoever you are, who purchase knowledge."

The Italian Carmelite, Blessed Baptist of Mantua, also composed a poem on Baconthorpe's commentary on the *Sentences* which describes the great esteem in which Baconthorpe was held by his fellow Carmelites.

> "What is this book which has lately come from darkness into light?
> It is Bacon's, the great pride of Mount Carmel.
> No one has better fathomed the mind of Averroes:
> If you follow him, you will become a second Aristotle.
> He it is who rejects the path of shadowy Scotus
> And walks in new ways through the Sacred Scriptures.
> All who love wisdom should keep close to him;
> All wisdom abounds in that work's sacred fountains."

**References:**

*BRCEW* 85-93: *ODNB* 3, 183-185

The expert on Baconthorpe's writings was the late Fr Bartolomé Xiberta, O.Carm., who wrote mostly in Latin or Catalan. However, there are useful entries on Baconthorpe in many Encyclopaedias, etc.

# 7

# JOHN OF WELWYK

## (c1347)

Medieval drawing of Monte Cassino Abbey

One of the sad realities of researching the friars, in the medieval Carmelite province, is that, for the large number who can be traced, all we have is a name or a reference in a legal or church document. It is frustrating that we know nothing about their lives, what they did, or what experiences they had whilst living in a religious community. However, occasionally, in a few cases, we can get glimpses of the course of an individual's life and of various events in which they featured. Such a reference occurs in a petition to the papal curia by the Carmelite William of Welwyk dated 2nd May, 1347. A summary of the petition in the papal archives has been printed:

> "John de Welwyk, a Carmelite, bachelor of theology, of the diocese of York. Signification that on completing for his purgation and enjoined penance, and in fear for his life unless he publicly acknowledged that he was justly punished, he left his habit, and was deputed reader by Raymund, then bishop of Cassino, among the monks of that church, where he remained for nine years. He, having been absolved for excommunication and irregularity, prays for licence to pass to the order of St. Benedict, so that he may be received in the monastery of Subiaco, or in some other monastery of that Order in the lands of the realm of Sicily. Granted. Avignon, 6 Nones May."

From these brief details and using a fair amount of imagination, it is possible to create an outline for his life. From his surname, John of Welwyk's family probably came from the small village of Welwick, 18 miles southeast of Kingston-Upon-Hull in Yorkshire. The village is not far from Patrington, a village associated with another Carmelite who features later in this book, the better known Stephen Patryngton*. From some of the later details of Welwick's life, John appears to have been born c1295-1298 and hence would probably have entered the Carmelite community in Hull when he had reached 14 years or more. Hull was only founded c1290-1292, so it was still a small community when Welwyk joined. He would have spent his early years there, learning to read and write in Latin; how to take part in and understand the liturgy of the mass, and the daily round of saying the divine office.

After a formal year in the novitiate in Hull, Welwyk would have commenced his studies for the priesthood. As the community in Hull was still small, he would probably have been sent to the regional house of studies in York, to study philosophy and then theology. At York, if a student was particularly talented, then he might continue his studies by following the two year advanced course leading to a licentiate in sacred theology (S.T.L.). This was an internal award of the Order. On the other hand, if the student showed exceptional talent, he might be among the few chosen to proceed to advanced studies at a university. Unfortunately the ordination register for the archbishop of York, during this period, has been lost, so it is not possible to discover when John was ordained but, as he is described in the papal document as being a bachelor in theology, he appears to have studied for around 5-6 years at university, by which time he would have been 30 years of age or so. Which university he attended, is not recorded, but the fact that Welwyk was sent to university, indicates that probably he had some financial support from his family, or from a patron to finance his studies. Studying at a university was expensive and having financial support was important.

It was probably soon after having gained his bachelor's degree, that Welwyk became involved in some misadventure. Whatever it was, it must have been a serious matter as the papal petition records that, even after John had gone to confession, been absolved and fulfilled a suitable penance, he still felt that he was in mortal danger. This leads to the implication that the fault he committed was a serious criminal act, or a sexual one. If it was criminal, then it could have been that John was involved in a fight or conflict of some kind. If his antagonist died as a result of the fray, then it is quite conceivable that John remained in danger of a reprisal from the family or relatives of the person who died. In the medieval period, most people carried a knife with them, mainly for use at mealtimes, as cutlery was not normally provided. This meant that a quarrel could rapidly escalate and, with knives drawn, serious wounds be inflicted. There are several cases in the records of a Carmelite killing a fellow Carmelite during a fight. An alternative explanation of John's predicament could be that he was involved in a relationship with someone's wife or an unmarried young woman. This could lead to an aggrieved husband or furious parents or relatives wanting to take revenge on the friar who had violated their loved one, especially if the affair had resulted in an unwanted pregnancy. As an ordained friar, Welwyk would have had 'privilege of clergy' so the secular courts would have referred him to his own superiors for punishment, but outsiders tended to see this as a way for the clergy to avoid due punishment for their crimes.

Whatever fault Welwyk had committed, it is clear that he went about in fear for his life, and this fear was such that he saw the only solution to the problem was for him to flee the country. So he took off his religious habit, disguised himself in lay clothes and boarded a ship for the continent. If, as has been supposed, Welwyk had joined the Carmelites in Hull, then it is possible that he had friends among the ship owners or sailors who were engaged in trading with France and the Low Countries, from the port of Hull. So, he could have begged or paid for his passage, especially if his parents or friends were able to provide some funds or were involved in shipping themselves.

Once on the continent, Welwyk appears to have made his way along one of the pilgrim routes leading to Rome. Possibly he saw himself as a pilgrim expiating his sins by completing such a penance. Whatever, once in Rome, fortune appears to have favoured Welwyk who needed some way of earning his living.

Sometime around 1328, he met the bishop of Monte Cassino. The bishop at the time was also the abbot of Monte Cassino, named Raymond de Gramat, a Cluniac Benedictine from Autun in France. Bishop Raymond was a learned man with a doctorate in canon law. On July 13th, 1326, he had been sent with the bishop of Anagnina to the marches of Ancona near Naples. On his arrival, he was appointed to the position of Abbot of Monte Cassino and Bishop of the Monte Cassino diocese.

Bishop Raymond had been in office for a year or two, before he met John of Welwyk who, with a degree in theology would have seemed like an answer to his prayers. The monastery of Monte Cassino was going through a difficult period. The abbey was in decline, and the numbers in the community decreasing. Bishop Raymond had been appointed to provide some fresh energy, and to revive the religious life of the community. Evidently, the bishop saw in John of Welwyk, a talented individual who could teach theology to the monks. The wording of the petition above states that he was appointed "reader" by the bishop, which is a slight misreading of the Latin '*Lector*'. In Latin 'Lector' does mean 'a reader' but, in this context, the correct English word is 'lecturer', as John's role was to give classes to the monks. When the bishop offered this post to Welwyk, it is easy to see why he jumped at the chance. It seems unlikely, though, that Welwyk explained his true ecclesiastical situation to the bishop. As Welwyk was formally excommunicated, for having left the Carmelites without a dispensation, the bishop would not have been able to offer him the position. So Welwyk probably kept silent about the reasons for his departure from England.

It would appear that, after teaching at Monte Cassino for nine years, Welwyk felt confident enough to reveal his true situation to the bishop. The petition mentions that John had been absolved from his excommunication and his clerical irregularity, which would imply that John had revealed all to the bishop and been formally absolved. One can only imagine the conversation between Welwyk and the bishop, but it seems that the bishop had a high regard for Welwyk, and wanted to resolve his situation in the best possible way.

As the abbot of Monte Cassino, the bishop would have had sufficient experience to make a judgement on whether John's future lay in the religious life, and the past nine years would had given him some good evidence of John's suitability. Hence, the petition to the pope, which clearly comes with the bishop's support, for John to be allowed to transfer to the Benedictine Order. The choice of abbey was left open, so probably Welwyk was still making up his mind as to where to go. He may have thought that it was time to leave Monte Cassino and make a fresh start elsewhere. Subiaco, the Benedictine monastery east of Rome, is mentioned as a possibility, or a Benedictine monastery in the Kingdom of Sicily. At that point of time, the Kingdom of Sicily included not only the island of Sicily, but also the lower parts of Italy, including Naples and the regions to the south, such as Puglia, Calabria, etc. Bishop Raymond's own career was rising, and, on December 1st, 1339, he was appointed coadjutor to John, Bishop of Anagnina, who had just been named as vicar general for Rome. It seems that Bishop Raymond was destined to be the next bishop of Anagnina. Sadly, he died the following year, so was unable to see whether John of Welwyk made a success of his new vocation.

To take a slight diversion, there is an interesting link between Bishop Raymond and England. The bishop possessed a fine illuminated Latin Bible which had been copied in Naples around 1330, during his time as abbot, and it was in his possessions when he died. However, the Bible was seized by Pope Benedict XII, and taken to Avignon. The Bible, now called the Clement Bible after a later pope, currently resides in the British Library, and can be viewed on the internet in all its splendour.

The entry in the papal register gives permission to John of Welwyk, to spend the rest of his life in a Benedictine monastery, in the southern regions of Italy. It would be nice to know which abbey he joined, and if he spent the rest of his life, faithful to his monastic vows. After all his experiences, John had earned the restoral of his clerical state, and a chance to live out his vocation. It is to be hoped that, in his prayers, he remembered his friends and family back in England.

**References:**

*BRCEW* 235:

# 8

# WILLIAM OF COVENTRY

## (†1360+)

Remains of the Cloister Garth of the Carmelite Priory, Coventry

Some years ago, a request came in from someone wishing to know more about the Carmelite friar – William of Coventry, – as they were compiling a family tree, and were sure that he was one of their ancestors. My protestations that, as a member of a Religious Order with a vow of chastity, this claim was unlikely, led to the riposte that: "… you know what things they got up to in those days!" The fact that William had a reputation for being a holy man was brushed aside, and the identification of him as one of their ancestors was confirmed, so they thought, by having the same surname as their family. However, claiming him as an ancestor because of his surname, betrays a misunderstanding of the origins and use of surnames, in the medieval period. The one constant feature about an individual, at that time, was his first or Christian name. Normally, in a Christian family, a baby was given the name of a saint. However, there were a limited number of popular saints, so many babies received the same first name. In a survey of first names among 4,500 Carmelites in England, before the Reformation, the most popular was John, and nearly one third of all Carmelites had this as their first name. Hence, in order to distinguish between all the "Johns", etc., surnames were added, either to give more information such as the individual's family lineage, i.e. John son of William (hence Williamson) or their craft or trade, i.e. John the Smith or John the Butcher. Once given, of course, a surname would carry down to the son and so on. Place names were normally only given when the person involved, or their family, came from outside the locality, i.e. they were "comers in" as they say in Yorkshire. So, John of Coventry might have acquired the surname Coventry. If he or his family had moved at some time to live elsewhere, such as in Lichfield or Northampton, he would then become known as John from Coventry. In a religious community, this would be a simple way of distinguishing the various friars called John. Conversely, a person would rarely acquire the surname "Coventry" if he was actually living in the town of Coventry, as this would not distinguish him from all the other John's living in the town.

In the case of the Carmelite, William of Coventry, there is another possibility. The "of Coventry", may have been attached not because the person himself has moved, but rather something belonging to him. This applies to our subject, the Carmelite William of Coventry. It is possible that he acquired the surname "Coventry" because of the three short works that he wrote on the history of the Order. Copies of his works were acquired by other Carmelite houses in England, and thus the addition of "of Coventry" would have helped the other houses to identify which "John" had written them, that is, this book was written by Brother William from the community in Coventry, i.e. William of Coventry.

Very little is known about William of Coventry and his life. It is reported that he was a cripple, probably through an accident, or an innate problem with his hip. He appears to have joined the new community in Coventry, as a servant, shortly after 1342, when the house was founded. He was a religious person and so, after a while, he joined the Order. However, because of his disability, he could not be ordained, so he became a lay brother. Later, he became known as *Claudus Conversus* (the crippled lay brother). No contemporary references have so far been traced which refer to William, and even our usually reliable Carmelite historian John Bale, has difficulties in giving his dates. In his earlier notes, Bale claimed that William lived c1340, but in his later printed works Bale gives the date when he lived as c1360.

Although he remained a lay brother, William did not lack intellectual ability, and he deserves to be remembered as being one of the first English Carmelites, to write an account of the history of the Order. His history is divided into three short compositions. The first, *A brief chronicle of the origin and wonderful development of the Carmelites*, gives a general overview of the legendary history of the Order, from the time of the prophet Elijah down to 1298, i.e. the date at which the Order was formally approved by pope Boniface VIII, as one of the four mendicant Orders. William's second work, *The double flight of the brothers from Carmel*, recounts the history of the Order in the East, describing its expansion into Cyprus, Sicily and the other islands in the eastern Mediterranean, and their expulsion from the Holy Land after the Battle of Hattin in 1187. Then William describes the return of the Carmelites to Mount Carmel after the recapture of Acre, by King Richard the Lionheart, and the second flight from Mount Carmel, when the Muslims tightened their grip around Acre in 1238. The third work, *The coming of the Carmelites to England*, describes the miracle of the spring of Elijah, which provided water during the siege of Acre, and then the journey of a group of the hermits to England, brought by two English crusaders, Richard de Grey and John Vescy (this latter name is an error by William of Coventry. It was William Vescy who brought the Carmelites). In the following passage at the end of this work, William of Coventry describes the coming of the Carmelites to England:

> "Among [the crusaders] were two noble English knights, namely Sir Richard de Grey and Sir John Vescy. These took two brothers with them back to England where they gave them two sites, one in the forest near the Scottish border, which is called Hulne, near Alnwick. This place is in a remote forest two miles from the nearest other existing habitation. To the other was given a place in Kent, very decayed by the passage of years, which is called Aylesford. This happened in the year 1240 AD. As it is recorded in verse:
>
> In the year twelve hundred and forty
> The Carmelites occupied Hulne at that time.
>
> There they live, continuously engaged in devout prayers to God and the glorious Virgin, increasing and multiplying, and also in other places founded by pious persons, resolved to work unceasingly, all for the salvation of souls. Indeed in the wisdom of our Almighty Father, which reaches firmly from one extremity to the other, arranging everything

> harmoniously, Jesus Christ wanted to distribute the Carmelites, the brothers of his Mother, prepared and with their feet shod to spread the gospel of peace conscientiously throughout the various parts of the world, in order to bring knowledge of salvation to his people, who, with the Father and the Holy Spirit lives and reigns for ever and ever. Amen."

William of Coventry's three short works are a remarkable achievement for a lay brother, in the mid-14$^{th}$ century, amidst all the terrible ravages of the Black Death (1348) and other afflictions. It is the more surprising considering that William had very few historical sources available to him. From the details included in his compositions, William of Coventry had access to two earlier Carmelite works, Jean de Cheminot's *Mirror of the Brothers of the Order of Blessed Mary of Mount Carmel,* which was written in 1337, and also an anonymous list of *Houses in the Holy Land,* which dates from the same period. For his account of the crusade of Richard the Lionheart, William takes his details from Roger of Howden's chronicle of the reigns of Henry II and Richard I, which contains an account of the recapture of Acre in 1191, at which Roger was present.

In the composition of his third work, it seems likely that William modelled his account on a similar work by the Franciscan, Thomas of Eccleston, who wrote *A tract on the coming of the Franciscans to England,* around 1258-1259. In a brief passage of this work, Eccleston mentions the coming of the Carmelites to England brought by Richard de Grey.

Apart from these sources, it is difficult to know what other accounts William of Coventry had available. It is likely that he had some other Carmelite notes or references, which have now been lost. From these sources, William does preserve some miracle stories, one of these refers to the spring of Elijah, which stopped flowing when the Carmelites were forced to flee from Mount Carmel:

> "Therefore, in the year of Our Lord 1238, the seventh year of pope Gregory IX, the twenty-third year of the most illustrious king of England Henry III, many Christians came to the Holy Land, to Ptolomaida, which is called by another name Acre, to defend it from the pagans and, if God had willed it, to have expelled the Turks from the land. At that time, the pagans were making many cavalry raids on the lands close to Acre. Now it is known that on Mount Carmel, that is four miles distant from Acre, water flowed from the fountain of Elijah, which is on that mountain close to the cells and oratory that the brothers had constructed in honour of the Virgin Mary, which did not produce water unless the brothers were living there. Knowing moreover that that fountain, of which there was not another similar to it in the world, could be of great assistance to the Christians who were nearby and almost under siege, the pagans would not allow the brothers to stay on the mountain but forced them to take flight. Therefore the brothers came to

Ptolomaida or Acre, and lived among the Christians there serving as priests for the pilgrims.

"Afterwards, during the summertime, the Saracens, wanting to harm the Christians in Acre as much as they could, threw the carcasses of animals and the bodies of the Christians that they had slain into the river of Acre, which is called Belum. These, then, because of the heat of the sun and the fierce currents in the waters, began to rot, giving off a deadly stench and poisoning the waters. The Christians who had fled there because there was no drinkable water in the springs, all of them having been poisoned by the Turks, now began to fall ill, especially because the fiery nature of the Cretan and Cypriot wines, which they used to slake their thirst began, because of their potency, to drive them frantic.

"The Christians then making enquiries if there was any well left unpoisoned, asked the brothers of Carmel whether the Saracens had poisoned their spring which is called – the fountain of Elijah – for they knew that it did not give any water when the brothers were absent; and therefore it was thought sufficient, by the Turks, that the spring should be left abandoned by the brothers of that place. Then a body of armed men was sent to Carmel in order to learn the truth who, on their return, announced that they had found the mountain safe, the cells dug up and left as rubble, and the spring dried up.

"The nobles, therefore, summoned the brothers and asked them if the fountain had produced water while they were living on Carmel. They replied that this was so. Surprised by this, the nobles, accompanied by an armed force, took the brothers with them on to Carmel. Once there, the brothers wept sorely to see such a holy place and the home of their fathers, the prophets, dedicated to the Mother of God, deserted and this provoked the bystanders also to weep. At length, one of them, seeking to comfort the brothers, said kindly: "Men and brothers, this desolation was prophesied long ago but also mercy was promised through Jeremiah saying: 'I looked and behold, Carmel was deserted and all its towns destroyed before the face of the Lord and the face of his anger.' And also: 'I shall bring Israel back home and he shall graze on Carmel.'

"Thus comforted the brothers went up to the summit, that is to that place where Elijah the prophet, the father of our Order, brought down rain by his prayers after three years and six months of drought. There, on their knees, they praised God and the Lady of the place, the Mother of Jesus Christ, and their holy predecessors, asking that the water of the fountain should flow again, as it used to for God's servants. Then, before they were able to rise from their prayers, the waters began gushing out abundantly from the fountain. Many Christians from different nations witnessed this and, because of the miracle that Christ was pleased to do in response to the prayers of the brothers of his Mother, they took some of the brothers with them to the various parts of the world, founding houses for them in honour of their advocate, the Virgin Mary."

When William writes on the coming of the Carmelites to England, there are a number of errors in his account, such as naming John de Vescy as the bringer of the Carmelites to Hulne, as noted above. However, in this instance, William of Coventry may have been misled by one of his sources; for example, the same mistake regarding William de Vescy occurs in an anonymous world chronicle, composed by a Carmelite in Sandwich around 1310.

The exact date when William composed his three works is not known but the Carmelite house in Coventry was not founded until 1342, and the composition of Jean de Cheminot's work, which William quotes, is dated 1337. Hence William could not have written his works before the late 1340's. How far and how quickly his works circulated is also not known. Certainly, John Hornby, in his defence of the Order at Cambridge University in February 1375, quotes historical details which he must have taken from William of Coventry. Similarly, the Catalan Carmelite Felip Ribot in his "Chronicle of William of Sandwich" which forms one of his *Ten Books on the Way of Life and the Great Deeds of the Carmelites*, written c1385, gives details which must have come from William of Coventry's third work, on the coming of the Carmelites to England. Our best guess for the date of the composition of William's works would seem to be sometime in the 1350s.

William of Coventry is remembered primarily for his three works, which have survived over the centuries. However, they are more than just a source for early Carmelite history as they represent the efforts of a devoted brother who was, through no fault of his own, prevented from being ordained, and from the academic education which would have come with it. But his works speak for him, giving witness to someone who contributed to the Order in the best way that he could, enriching our historical resources, and surely, behind his writing, there lies the evidence of a devoted, careful, talented brother who gave praise to God throughout his life.

**References:**

*BRCEW* 470-471: *ODNB* 13, 737

Andrew Jotischy, "Crusading and Crusaders in Medieval Carmelite Texts: William of Coventry and the Holy Land", in *Historiography and Identity. Responses to Medieval Carmelite Culture,* Jens Röhrkasten & Coralie Zermatten, ed., (Zurich: Lit Verlag, 2017), 79-90.

An English translation of William's three short historical works is being prepared for publication in *Early Carmelite Documents.*

# 9

# JOHN PASCHAL

## (†1361)

Llandaff Cathedral nave, looking eastwards.
John Paschal was buried in the Lady Chapel at the east end.

John Paschal was born in Suffolk and became a Carmelite in Ipswich. He was quickly marked out because of his intellectual ability, and sent to do further studies in Cambridge University, where he incepted as a Doctor of Theology around 1340.

Once Paschal had completed his year as *magister regens* (senior lecturer) at the university, he came to the attention of a fellow graduate of Cambridge University, William Bateman, who was serving as an auditor in the papal curia in Avignon, and acting as the royal proctor for King Edward III. Paschal soon began to undertake a number of errands for Bateman, travelling to and from Avignon on his behalf.

As a doctor of theology, Paschal was permitted to have another friar as his secretary and a personal servant. It was probably at this time that Paschal engaged a Dutchman, Arnold de Zutphen, as his servant. Arnold's name is preserved in a collection of 70 sermons which he copied, probably in Avignon, for Paschal. Unfortunately, Zutphen thought that these sermons were written by Paschal himself, and it was only recently that Patrick Nold at Oxford University identified them as being written by the Franciscan cardinal Bertrand de la Tour.

Paschal was in Avignon or on his way there in December 1343, when the news came of the death of Antony Bek, the bishop of Norwich. Bateman was provided to the See on January 23rd, 1344 and quickly foresaw that, due to his commitments in Avignon, he would need a suffragan bishop to carry out his episcopal duties in the diocese of Norwich during his absences. Paschal was in Avignon at this time and Bateman proposed his name to the pope as a suitable candidate. Pope Clement VI quickly agreed and, on February 16th, 1344, he appointed Paschal to the See of Llandaff (which was not vacant at that time). Paschal was consecrated in Avignon a few days later and then, on February 28th, he was granted a number of privileges by the pope. Among these privileges was permission to found a Carmelite house in his diocese (which never materialised). Another permission was for John Grey, Lord of Codnor and Alice, his wife, and other relatives, for their confessors to give them plenary absolution at their hour of death.

The Codnor family, were influential donors to the Carmelites, and had given the sites for the priories in Aylesford (1242) and London (1247). A third papal permission gave a benefice for Arnold, Paschal's servant, which was in the gift of the dean and chapter of Maastricht. Other privileges granted benefices for some named individuals, and permission for Paschal to appoint three notaries public, and promote three unnamed clergy to benefices.

After this, Paschal set out to return to England and travelled in the company of another Carmelite, the Irishman Ralph O'Ceallaigh, who had just been consecrated bishop of Leighlin. They made their way through France and then found a ship to carry them across the Channel to Sandwich in Kent. Unfortunately, the two of them arrived just as the town was involved in the preparations for King Edward's proposed invasion of Flanders. The two Carmelites were immediately arrested by the town bailiffs, on suspicion of bringing papal bulls and letters prejudicial to the king. News of the arrest of the two Carmelites was sent to London and, on 5 April, the king replied to the mayor as follows:

"As it has been communicated to us that you have arrested two brothers of the Order of Carmel, newly consecrated bishops by the Supreme Pontiff and bearing bulls and letters prejudicial to us into the port of Sandwich, we want you to know that it is not nor was it ever our intention that any order of ours should instruct you to place under arrest anyone who has been consecrated bishop. And therefore we order you that you should immediately release these bishops together with their servants who are under arrest and grant them liberty to leave freely. However, any letters prejudicial to us which you find that these bishops or their servants may be carrying, you are to transmit whole and intact to our council in London. Given by the king at Marlborough on 5 April 1344."

Paschal made his way to Norwich where, later in the year, he performed one of his first episcopal actions by consecrating a new cemetery in the Carmelite house there. Being a bishop, did not sever Paschal's links with the Order, and, on August 9th 1345, he was addressed by the pope in a bull as "the bishop of Llandaff and vicar-provincial of the said Order in England". The bull gave protection to the friars, over offerings received in the side chapels of their churches, which were being claimed by the rectors of the parish churches. From his title, Paschal would appear to have been acting a vicar for John Folsham, the provincial of England, who was away attending the general chapter which was held in May that year.

Paschal's services as a bishop were also in demand in other dioceses, and he is recorded as carrying out ordinations in the diocese of York in September and December in 1345, and in March, April and June 1346. On January 2nd, 1347, John Eaglescliffe, the current bishop of Llandaff, died and the canons of the cathedral, seemingly unaware of Paschal's right of succession, elected John of Coventry, the archdeacon of Llandaff, as his successor. Paschal appears to have been in Avignon at the time, and this election was quickly set aside by Pope Clement VI, who reserved the appointment to himself. On February 19th, 1347, he provided Paschal to the bishopric and Paschal set off hurriedly for England where, on 3rd June in Canterbury cathedral, he was admitted to the See of Llandaff by the archbishop of Canterbury. Then, on the following day, he made his profession before the high altar in the cathedral, in the prescribed form as follows:

"In the name of God, Amen. I, John Paschal, consecrated bishop of the church in Llandaff at the Roman Curia, promise openly before everyone due and canonical obedience, reverence and submission to my reverend father Lord John, archbishop of Canterbury, primate of all England and legate of the Apostolic See and to his successors in the church of Canterbury canonically appointed and the holy metropolitan church of Canterbury. And I promise that I will be a faithful supporter in defending, preserving and maintaining the decrees of the Roman pontiff, his delegates and his successors, and the laws of the aforesaid holy church of Canterbury. So I place my trust in God's help and God's holy gospels. And all the above, I confirm by signing here with my own hand."

The temporalities of the See, were then ordered by the Black Prince to be delivered to him on July 2nd 1347. Soon afterwards, Paschal was travelling again and, on September 13th, 1348, he dedicated the cemetery and the site for the new extended church in the Carmelite house at Aylesford. Whilst in Kent, he acted as suffragan, for the elderly bishop of Rochester until his death. Then, on October 5th, he was given a commission to consecrate churches and altars in the diocese of Canterbury following the death of archbishop John de Stratford. Paschal was back in his diocese in December when he visited Lady Elizabeth de Clare in Usk and again in March 1349

In 1352, a dispute came to a head between Paschal and his archdeacon in Llandaff, John of Coventry. John had been the candidate elected by the cathedral chapter after the death of the previous bishop. Evidently, John did not take kindly to his failure to be consecrated bishop, so he appealed to the pope in Avignon and cited Paschal to appear before the curial court there. Unfortunately, John of Coventry and his supporters forgot about King Edward's *Statute of Provisors*, issued in 1351, which forbade dispossessed clerics from appealing to the pope against decisions made in the royal courts. On June 29, 1352, the king appointed a commission, led by the sheriff of Gloucester, to enquire why Paschal was being cited over matters which should be decided by the king.

Little of Paschal's writings survive, but there is the text of one mandate which he issued at a convocation of the clergy. Evidently, there were a number of abuses, being committed against the clergy and against the church, over the titles to the possession to church lands, and the terms of leases concerning the rent being charged or the terms of some of the leases. On April 20th, 1354, at a synod of the clergy held in the cathedral, Paschal issued an ordinance threatening excommunication against anyone committing these abuses. The mandate reads:

"In the name of God. Amen. I, Friar John, by divine permission Bishop of Llandaff, with the council and consent of all our clergy, constitute and ordain that all and singular persons who, of their own authority, invade or occupy houses, lands, meadows, feedings, or other temporalities or spiritualities whatsoever belonging to our Church of Llandaff or any other church whatsoever; or if they have taken leases thereof for any certain term

> from the same churches or their representatives, or have them received them to farm or by way of security, or rashly presume to hold them beyond the term assigned by the representatives of those churches in such contracts, beyond or against the will of the said representatives, or to occupy them, or to conceal the form of the said contract, and also to usurp, embezzle, divert, or otherwise to inflict injuries or harm to those churches in this respect; and any who give aid, counsel, or favour to such rashly presumptuous persons in this respect, and those who knowingly buy or receive goods furtively taken away from any whatsoever ecclesiastical locality of our diocese, are exposed *ipso facto* by authority of this present Synod to a sentence of greater excommunication, and we especially reserve to ourselves the absolution of such persons."

Between December 1357 and August 1359, Edward, the Black Prince, famous for his victory over the French at the Battle of Poitiers, visited Lady Elizabeth de Clare frequently and Paschal was introduced to him by Lady Elizabeth.

Paschal died in his palace at Becton, on October 11th, 1361, and was buried under a marble stone in the Lady chapel in Llandaff cathedral. Sadly there are no traces left of his tomb but his memorial lies in the service that he gave to his diocese and his king.

**References:**

*BRCEW* 197-199: *ODNB* 42, 963

Patrick Nold, "British Library Royal 7.B.1 Reconsidered: A Franciscan Sermon Cycle". *Carmelus* 45:1 (1998), 155-162.

# 10

# OSBERT BEAUFEU OF PICKENHAM

## (†1360-1370)

Osbert Beaufeu of Pickenham: illumination from a manuscript copy of his *Determinationes*.

As mentioned earlier in the entry on William of Coventry* (Chapter 8), during the medieval period, a person was known primarily by their first name. Surnames were added mainly to distinguish between people who shared the same first name. The surname could be a family name, indicating the individual's parentage, or a place name indicating where they or their parents were born or their nationality, if they were abroad. Added to all this, there would be variations in the spelling of names or place, which created even more complexity. For one Carmelite called Osbert, it is possible to trace nineteen variations for his surname, which is surprising considering he is the only English Carmelite so far traced with this first name. Osbert's family surname was probably Beaufeu, but he was more commonly known by the village where he, or his family, came from, that is Pickenham, a small village near

Swaffham in Norfolk. So, in the surviving records, he is sometimes known as Osbert Beaufeu, using his family name, or more commonly Osbert of Pickenham, which indicates where he was born or when he is referred to outside of England, is called Osbert Anglicus (the Englishman).

The main reason for Osbert being known by all these different variations, is a result of his fame as a theologian, and the books which he wrote. Osbert was born soon after 1300, and joined the Carmelite community in King's Lynn (known at that time as Bishop's Lynn), which is about 20 miles from Pickenham. Lynn served as a house of studies for its own friars studying for the priesthood and also for young Carmelites belonging to the smaller communities at Burnham Norton and Blakeney. Osbert quickly gave evidence of his intellectual ability and so, after his initial studies in philosophy, he was probably transferred to the senior house in the distinction (region) at Norwich, for his theology studies. From there, he was sent to study at Oxford University. He was well advanced in his studies there and had been ordained when on February 11th, 1336, he was admitted to hear confessions in the diocese of Lincoln.

Osbert completed his doctorate sometime in the late 1340's, and then would have served his year as *magister regens*, lecturing in the Carmelite house. Exactly where Osbert spent the next few years is not clear. Possibly he stayed in Oxford, but the Carmelite historian John Bale, and some other early writers, claim that he was in Paris for a period, lecturing at the university and in the Carmelite *studium generale* there. Then, Osbert returned to England sometime in the 1350's and was appointed the prior in the Carmelite house in London, where he lectured in the *studium generale* and gained a great reputation for his teaching. Bale writes about him:

> "He was prior for a time of the London house, an office he filled receiving great praise and admiration; and a large number of scholars came to hear his lectures. As a teacher he combined a clear delivery with great skill in preparing the content of his lectures."

Of Osbert's theological works, only a series of *Questions* survive. In the medieval period, lecturers in theology would hold regular sessions, answering questions on theology, which had been brought to them, or to which the lecturer felt that he had something to contribute. Afterwards, these *Questions* would be written out in full, so that they could be copied and distributed. Osbert's *Questions* were obviously very highly regarded, and copies have been found in many different places, such as Bruges, Reims, Florence, Ferrara, Bologna, Erfurt, Madrid, Prague, etc. Usually Osbert's *Questions* are found in a collection of 20 such compositions. The first eight of these *Questions* are Osbert's lectures on Book One of Peter Lombard's, *The Sentences* (the accepted textbook on theology). *Question 9* was thought to be Osbert's introductory lecture to the course on the Bible, but recently it has been identified as an introductory lecture to *The Sentences*, which studied the fundamental biblical texts. *Question 18* has also been attributed to Osbert.

Osbert died in London sometime during the 1360's, and was buried "in a majestic tomb with a French inscription". Laurent Bureau wrote an epitaph for him:

> "He whom England engendered is a child of Carmel,
> Called holiest by his own right,
> This is Osbert, called by the epithet of Angle,
> Whereas rather he was surely an angel.
> So much virtue in his soul, so much knowledge of the truth
> That, to the country of his fathers, he made a worthy contribution.
> If you consult the works that he left, laced with keen shrewdness.
> Nothing could be more pleasing to the ears."

*References:*

*BRCEW* 270-272: *ODNB* 44, 203-204

Leonard Kennedy, C.S.B., "Osbert of Pickenham", *Carmelus*, 35 (Rome, 1988), 178-225.

# 11

# JOHN REPPES

## (†1373+)

Remains of the Papal Buildings in Avignon which John Reppes visited often.

Among the Carmelites in the medieval period, there were some friars who were noted for their great spirituality and devotion, who inspired others by their way of life. Some were great preachers who could stir the hearts of the faithful, and some who gave quiet service, carrying out tasks and commissions diligently and competently. John of Reppes was one of the latter. He was clearly very talented and reliable and he spent a large proportion of his life serving the king and other nobles.

Reppes was probably ordained around 1318, and undertook his studies in the Carmelite *studium generale* (international study centre) in London. He was appointed as prior in a number of houses, before returning to London to be prior there when, in 1335, he was named as an executor in the will of Henry Bydyk, and appointed to supervise the use of a bequest of 48 marks (£32) which had been left towards building work on the Carmelite church in London.

As prior of the important Carmelite community in London, Reppes soon became a significant figure in the capital city, and he was appointed as confessor to Henry Grosmont, the Earl of Derby and some other noble families. In 1343 the Earl sent him on a mission to the papal curia in Avignon. Whilst there, on October 23rd, and on the recommendation of the Earl, Pope Clement VI, made Reppes, a papal chaplain which gave him a degree of freedom from his vow of obedience to his religious superiors. On the same day, he was given special faculties for hearing confessions in a papal decree which read:

> "John de Reppes, Carmelite, prior of London. Signification that he has held the office of prior in many convents, is confessor of the earl of Derby and other earls, barons and ladies in divers dioceses, that divers prelates bring to him their cases, and licence him to hear confessions, because he is not in their dioceses; wherefore he prays for faculties like those of bishops to hear confessions and enjoin penances throughout the realm. Granted for perpetuity and for exempts and non-exempts.
>
> Avignon 10 Kalends November."

It was not clearly stated what Reppe's mission in Avignon was but it is likely that he was involved in the negotiations for extending the peace treaty, between England and France which had been agreed in the Truce of Malesdroit earlier in the year. Reppes was still in Avignon on November 20, when the Pope gave him a letter of recommendation, to the Benedictine abbot and convent of Westminster, and Reppes made his way back to London.

Reppes was back in Avignon the following year, bearing some letters from Henry, the Earl of Derby, and others from Queen Isabella, from Mary of St Paul, the Countess of Pembroke and from Blanche, the Lady of Wake. On April 15th, 1344, Reppes received answers to these letters from the pope and was given a letter of safe-conduct for his journey back to England.

Once again, Reppes did not remain long in England, and was soon on his way to Avignon. This time, he was bearing letters from the Earl of Derby and John Stratford, the Archbishop of Canterbury, for the pope, and also other confidential letters from the Earl and King Edward III to John Otford, who was one of the king's envoys, in the peace negotiations. On October 8th, 1344, the pope issued a letter to the Archbishop of Canterbury, which reads:

"To John, archbishop of Canterbury. The pope has received his letters by John de Reppes and commends him for his labours touching the reformation of peace, about which the pope has conferred with the said envoy, and with John de Offord, to whom the king's, and his, and the earl of Derby's letters have been presented. The archbishop's envoy will bring a verbal report of what was then agreed upon, and the inexpediency of the pope's coming to the place suggested by the earl, until he hears more of the intention of the parties, between whom the pope urges him to continue his labours for peace."

On October 12th, Reppes was given two further letters, one for Thomas Hatfield, keeper of the secret seal, and the other for John Gynewell, the future bishop of Lincoln. In the meantime, Reppes had petitioned the pope for some special permissions for himself. On October 17th, the pope gave him a series of personal privileges in reward for his services. One of these was permission to preach, without needing to obtain a licence from the local bishop. Another granted him the same privileges as a Doctor of Theology; that is, to live in whichever house of his Order that he chose, to have a *socius* (secretary or assistant) and a servant (to prepare his meals, etc.). A third privilege gave him the right to retain the chamber, which had been assigned to him by the prior general in the London house, for life. Other privileges gave him the right to have a portable altar for the use of himself and his *socius*, to possess funds for his funeral, and for the wages of those who served him, his relations and other pious uses, and a final privilege, to be exempt from the jurisdiction of his superiors in the Order, and to be under the direct protection of the Holy See. In effect, these privileges gave Reppes the same independence and control over his own affairs that he would have gained if he had been consecrated as a bishop.

Reppes remained in Avignon for a few weeks longer as he was present at the negotiations between the English delegates and the papal officials which started on October 22nd, then, he left for home and his arrival in England on November 3rd, is recorded by Adam Murimuth in his *Chronicle*:

"… on the 3rd day of November, a certain Carmelite brother arrived in England from the Roman Curia, who was called John of Reppes, a man of a very worldly way of life, … who first visited the archbishop and afterwards met with the king."

Reppes was back in Avignon on December 12th, 1344, bearing letters from Henry Grosmont. He is mentioned in the replies which Pope Clement IV wrote to Grosmont, and to the archbishop of Canterbury. He is referred to, as well, in a long letter written by the pope to King Edward II, on the possibility of a truce.

Once Reppes had delivered these letters, he was soon on the road again back to Avignon. He was in the papal city in April 1345, and it was probably during this visit that he was appointed as a papal penitentiary, which gave him further independence from his Carmelite superiors.

Reppes' next mission to Avignon took place in 1346, when he was sent by Henry, Earl of Lancaster, to report on the negotiations for peace between England and France, which were being conducted by Aymar de Poitiers, the pope's nephew. At this time, the Earl himself was campaigning in Gascony, and so Reppes was given a letter of safe-conduct in order to report to the Earl there. The peace negotiations continued slowly and Reppes was back in Avignon on April 6th, 1347, when the pope gave him a letter for King Edward, who was then involved in the siege of Calais. The pope urged the king to call a truce and end the siege, but Edward was determined to capture Calais before agreeing to any truce. Reppes was also given letters for the archbishop of Canterbury, and the Earl of Lancaster, as well as a letter of safe-conduct for himself, as he journeyed across France.

Calais surrendered to the English forces on August 3rd, 1347, and a peace treaty between England and France, was signed on September 28th. At this time, the king sent Reppes to Avignon, as one of his envoys, and there are records of two substantial payments by the king to cover Reppes' expenses in Avignon. Reppes' presence in Avignon is mentioned by the pope in a letter to Philip, the king of France, dated January 24th, 1348. Reppes remained in Avignon for some months, as his presence there is recorded in letters dated February 17th, 1348, and May 30th, 1348.

After his return from Avignon, Reppes' work as an envoy, appears to cease. He was now over 50 years of age, and so probably found the constant travelling difficult. In 1367, he was appointed as prior of the Carmelite house in Cambridge, a position he held for two years. It appears that he died c1373.

Reppes is an enigmatic character. He was a competent and trustworthy servant of the Earl of Lancaster and King Edward III, and appears to have established a good relationship with Pope Clement IV. It was not only that he could be trusted to convey confidential letters and state papers between England and Avignon, but, as he gained experience, he seems also to have acted as a formal envoy between the English crown and the Roman Curia, actively engaged in the search for a peace treaty between England and France. However, this diplomatic activity inevitably led to a certain tension between Reppes, and his religious obligations as a Carmelite friar. It could not have been easy to observe a vow of obedience when the king or the pope were making heavy demands on his time and activities. It is easy to understand Reppes asking the pope for special privileges which granted him some exemption from his duty of obedience to his religious superiors, and left him free to perform his diplomatic duties. However, there is a thin line between the privileges which facilitated Reppes' duties, and those which enabled a more indulgent lifestyle. Reppes gained the privileges normally reserved for Doctor of Theology, e.g. having a Carmelite brother as his *socius* or secretary and a servant, as well as a cell where he could entertain visitors, and also the privileges normally reserved to bishops, such as the liberty to preach and to hear confessions in any diocese, and the right to have his own funds for paying servants, etc. Clearly Reppes needed to be able to fulfil his work alongside members of the nobility and senior clerics in the royal and papal courts, but there is also probably an element of truth in Adam Murimuth's comment that he lived a "very worldly way of life". Sadly, it is only Reppes' diplomatic activities which can be traced in the surviving documents, and there is no record of his spiritual life. However, he deserves to be remembered for his efforts to serve the king, and other important figures in England, and for his long tiring journeys and dedication trying to facilitate a peace treaty, between England and France, which were his way of serving Christ.

**References:**

*BRCEW* 205-207:

For Reppes' diplomatic activities, see:

Karsten Plöger, *England and the Avignon Popes. The Practice of Diplomacy in Late Medieval Europe*, (London, Legenda, 2005):

Barbara Bombi, *Anglo-Papal Relations in the Early Fourteenth Century* (O.U.P., 2019).

# 12

# WALTER KELLAW

## (†1367)

Excavations on the Carmelite House, Northallerton, in 2007

Walter Kellaw was born in Northallerton in Yorkshire, around 1312, and joined the Carmelite community in York. He would have completed his initial formation in York, and was probably ordained there but, sadly, the ordination register for archbishop William Melton (1317-1340) has been lost.

Kellaw was evidently a talented student and he was chosen to continue his studies in theology at Oxford. He had incepted as a Doctor of Theology by February 19th, 1348, as he was described as *"sacre pagine professore"*, when he was given a licence to hear confessions in the York diocese for one year. As this was the time of the Black Death, there was an urgent need for confessors to replace those who had died. Kellaw's licence was renewed on August 7th, 1351, and again for a third time on February 16th, 1353.

Around this time, Kellaw served as confessor to Ralph, the fourth Lord Neville (d. 1367) and his wife Alice (d. 1374) who was the daughter of Hugh, Lord Audley. Then, at the general chapter held in Metz on June 8th, 1348, Kellaw was appointed provincial of the English province. As provincial, Kellaw would have presided at the provincial chapter, which was held in Nottingham in August that year. On December 3rd, 1348, Kellaw presented the Carmelite John of Berkhamstede to hear confessions in the Lincoln diocese.

Early in 1350, Kellaw would have been involved in the establishment of two new foundations, one in Ludlow and the other in Doncaster. The Ludlow foundation was the result of the generosity of Sir Laurence of Ludlow. An inquisition was held on January 10th, and permission was given to accept the property in February. The Doncaster foundation followed soon after. Inquisitions were held on August 23rd, and again on November 6th. Permission was given on November 30th, but there was a delay until May 7th, 1351, when the Archbishop of York was forced to write and ask the Abbot and Convent of St Mary's Abbey, York, to show any reason why the new site for the Carmelites should not be consecrated. It appears that the community took up residence there soon afterwards.

On May 23rd, 1350, Kellaw's signature and seal as provincial were appended to an agreement between the Carmelites in York, and the parish priest of St Crux's in York, the parish in which the Carmelite house was situated. This agreement was signed at the archbishop's palace in Cawood near Selby. The following year, Kellaw's signature and seal are attached to a document, which granted a perpetual mass of the Blessed Virgin Mary and other spiritual benefits to brother Hugh of Dowdale for his generosity towards the Norwich house.

Dowdale was a knight who had joined the Order, and used his wealth to help the various Carmelite houses in Norfolk. In the case of Norwich, Dowdale gave £100 towards the cost of a new dormitory, £22 for a new set of vestments, £7 for a censer, two phials and a basin of silver, and 10 marks towards a stone gate worth 10 marks. Also, he had begun and completed the south aisle of the church in Norwich at his own cost.

Then, on August 8th, 1352, Kellaw was summoned before the king's council:

> "To the provincial prior of the Carmelites in England to be before the council on Thursday after the octaves of the Assumption next."

Two other clerics were also ordered to appear before the royal council. These were brother Ranulph from Chester Abbey, and the Dominican provincial prior. The subject of this consultation was not stated. It may have been linked with the peace negotiations which were taking place with France, as the Carmelite John Reppes*, had been one of the king's envoys for some years. Alternatively, the royal council might have been discussing the development of the English occupation of Calais, which had been captured on August 4th, 1347. After the expulsion of the French inhabitants, an English community had been quickly sent to take over the Carmelite priory in Calais, and on September 10th, 1347, they were granted an extension to their property, taking over buildings left empty by their French owners. Then, on January 8th, 1352, an annual royal subsidy of 20 marks (£13 6s. 8d.) was awarded to the community.

The following year, Kellaw unexpectedly resigned his office as prior provincial at the provincial chapter, held in Norwich in August 1353. The reason for his resignation was unclear. Other provincials resigned due to age or ill-health, but this was clearly not the case for Kellaw. His resignation may have been because the king wished to use his services, as happened when Richard Blyton resigned as provincial in 1326. However, Kellaw's time out of office did not last long. His successor. William Lubbenham, fell ill soon after taking office and could not continue, so at the following provincial chapter held in Maldon in August 1356, Kellaw was re-elected as provincial and held office for the next three years.

One of Kellaw's first achievements during his second period in office, must have brought him great personal satisfaction. His own home town of Northallerton did not have any house of friars, and somehow Kellaw managed to persuade King Edward III to sponsor a Carmelite foundation there. In the *Calendar of Patent Rolls* on November 8th, 1356, there appeared the following royal grant:

> "Grant in frank almoin to the prior provincial and Carmelite Friars in England of a croft called Tentour Croft in Northallerton, in the county of York, with a meadow adjoining containing 3 acres, 1 rood of land, which the king had of the gift and feoffment of John Yole of Northallerton, to found a house of the Order to the praise and honour of God and his mother the glorious Virgin Mary, to pray for the souls of the king's progenitors, kings of England, and for him and his heirs, as founders and patrons of the house."

Other permissions came, as might be expected for a royal foundation, from the Benedictine prior and convent in Durham, who held the advowson for the parish, and from the bishop of Durham, who agreed to the transfer of the title to the land. Quite how Kellaw managed to obtain this royal support is not clear, but as the confessor to Ralph, fourth Lord Neville, and his family, Kellaw would have had a powerful supporter at court. Similarly, his appearance before the royal council in 1352, would have brought him to the king's notice. Soon, further land was gifted to the new foundation, bringing its plot up to six acres. Also, the community benefited from other gifts, from their close relationship with the Neville family over the years. In fact, Margaret, the daughter of Lord Neville and wife of Lord Percy of Northumberland, chose to be buried in the Carmelite church when she died in 1372.

Kellaw retired as provincial for the second time in 1358, and his successor, John Cowton, was confirmed at the general chapter held in Bordeaux on September 8th that year. Cowton had probably not yet returned from the general chapter by October 18th, as Kellaw was still acting as provincial, when he presented four Carmelites from Ludlow, to the bishop of Hereford for licences to hear confessions. After this, Kellaw appears to have retired to Northallerton, where he spent his remaining years. It is claimed that he was the prior there, which would be quite understandable for a retired prior provincial. He died in August 1367 and was buried in the chapel there.

Interestingly Kellaw's name appears in a copy of Raymund of Peñafort's *Summa de casibus poenitentiae* which was in the Carmelite library in Hulne Priory, probably a gift he had made at some time when he was provincial. John Bale* claims that Kellaw wrote three works, *Determinaciones quasdam theologicas* (Responses to some Theological Theses), *Quodlibeta* (Theological Disputes) and *Sermones aliquot* (Collection of Sermons). But these are very common titles and, as Bale does not give any incipits (opening sentences), this usually indicates that he has not seen the works himself. However, Kellaw's legacy was in a life that was lived by placing his talents and energy at the service of God, his Order and his country.

**References:**

*BRCEW* 453.

# 13

# THOMAS BROME

## (†1379+)

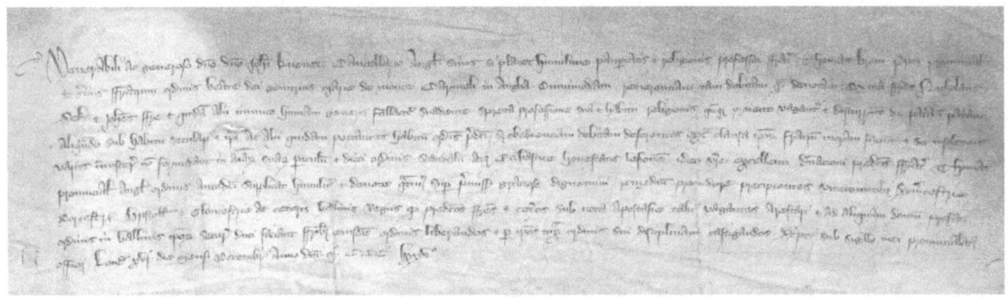

Letter from Thomas Brome to the Chancellor of England seeking the return of two Carmelite friars

Thomas Brome is one of the Carmelites who lived during the fourteenth century, but whose contribution to the development of the English Province is not usually fully appreciated. Brome joined the Order in Maldon, Essex, and was sent from there to study in Cambridge where he was ordained a priest around 1340. He continued to study theology in the university and, in 1353, he is recorded as being granted the privilege of choosing his own confessor, who could give him a plenary indulgence at the moment of his death. Finally, in 1358, he incepted for his doctorate. The granting of the plenary indulgence, and the fact that Brome was able to study for the doctorate, indicates that he came, probably, from a wealthy family or had an influential patron.

After Brome had completed his year as regent master, lecturing in Cambridge, he appears to have moved to the London house, where he was appointed prior. Then, in June 1362, he was appointed prior provincial at the general chapter, which was held in Trier, Germany. On his return, Brome would have attended the English provincial chapter, held that year in Cambridge, and which met during the week, as was customary, containing the feast of Our Lady of the Assumption on August 15th.

Once in office, Brome would have spent significant periods of his time travelling around the province, visiting the individual communities, presiding at the annual provincial chapters, and travelling abroad to attend the general chapters, which took place in one of the Carmelite houses in Europe every three years, usually at Pentecost. On one such occasion, after he had attended the general chapter held in Le Puy-en-Velay, in June 1375, Brome made a detour to the papal curia in Avignon, accompanied by another English Carmelite, Thomas Maldon, in order to procure notarised copies of some important papal bulls, relating to "the antiquity, title and confirmation of the Carmelite Order". The two of them were in Avignon on October 10th, to receive these bulls, and so were rather delayed on their return to England. It is not recorded whether the convening of the provincial chapter was delayed until after their arrival.

Brome's signature occurs on a number of legal documents, etc. which were completed during his period as provincial. In the Aylesford cartulary, he signed two agreements concerning the establishment of a community chest, a copy of which fortunately still survives. The first agreement was made with a learned ecclesiastic, Simon of Brendon, a Doctor of Theology, who gave ten marks (£6 13s 4d) on July 7th, 1365. Community chests were intended to provide loans for those in need, etc. However, the sum deposited had to be carefully preserved and each year at the provincial chapter, a delegate from the community had to confirm that it was still intact: that is, all the loans had been repaid or accounted for. If the community failed to maintain the money deposited in the chest, then the agreement with Simon of Brendon ordered that the remains of the sum should be given to the Carmelite house in Sandwich.

Three weeks after this gift, on August 1st, a couple, John Skynner and his wife, from Aylesford made a further deposit, this time giving a sum of five marks (£3 6s. 8d) under the same conditions. Brome's signature occurs on another agreement, which he signed, whilst at the provincial chapter, being held in Winchester on August 15th, 1367. This agreement ratified a generous donation, from Thomas Stathom and his wife, to the prior and community in Chester of 100 marks (£66 13s 4d) which was to enable the completion of the priory buildings.

In 1368, Brome's signature occurs on a letter of confraternity which was given to John Browne and his wife Ymggota. Then, on December 16th, 1375, Brome wrote to John Knyvet, the Chancellor of England, asking for his help concerning two friars, Nicholas Sek and John Fre, who had left their community, and were wandering around in secular clothes in the south-west of England. The Chancellor was requested to order his sheriffs to locate these two runaways, arrest them, and return them to their Order.

However, Brome's main claim to fame does not rest on the few times where his name features in the records, but rather in the firm direction and guidance that he gave to the province, during the seventeen years that he remained in office. The Carmelite historian John Bale*, basing himself on some lost provincial records, writes about Brome:

> "He revived many forgotten customs and restored religious observance to its pristine purity. He was a great lover of chastity, and for that reason had a great devotion to John the Evangelist and the holy King Edward. He had statues of them placed in almost all the houses of the Province. Often when he visited the Order's houses, his first concern would be to inspect the church, and to ensure its maintenance, or even improvement of its standard of public worship. He was looked on by all as an exemplary contemplative and observant religious, whose example was to be followed. A visit from him brought healing to the sick and pleasure to the healthy."

Bale also records that Brome donated some stained-glass windows to the Carmelite house in London, with representations of Mary, the Mother of Christ, and of St. John, chosen because of their chastity.

Brome's long period in office, and his care for regular religious observance, did provide later historians with the means to solve one long-standing puzzle about the administration of the province. Due to the number of houses (39 in total), the English province was divided into four distinctions or regions. However, no record of which houses were in each distinction, survives and all previous attempts to discern the names of the houses in each distinction have had to depend on inspired guesswork. However, Brome's long period in office and his care for the regulation that the annual provincial chapter should be held in each distinction in turn, finally provided the means of unravelling this problem. The houses in each distinction can now be listed as follows:

| *London Distinction* | *Oxford Distinction* | *Norwich Distinction* | *York Distinction* |
|---|---|---|---|
| Aylesford | Bristol | Burnham Norton | Hulne |
| Lossenham | Northampton | King's Lynn | Lincoln |
| Cambridge | Gloucester | Yarmouth | Berwick? |
| Sandwich | Stamford | Blakeney | Newcastle |
| Ipswich | Winchester | | Nottingham |
| Maldon | Chester? | | Appleby? |
| Shoreham | Sutton (Plymouth) | | Kingston-on-Hull |
| Hitchin | Marlborough | | Boston |
| Calais? | Coventry | | Scarborough |
| | Denbigh? | | Doncaster |
| | Ludlow | | Northallerton |
| (10 houses) | (12 houses) | (5 houses) | (12 houses) |

There is still some uncertainty as to which distinction a few of the houses belonged, as no chapter was held in them during Brome's period in office, so they have been allocated to a distinction from their geographical location. One interesting finding, which explains some of the difficulty encountered by previous attempts to list the distinctions, is that the Norwich Distinction had only five houses in it. This was a disadvantage for the Norwich distinction as it meant that the individual houses had to host provincial chapters more frequently. Hosting a provincial chapter was expensive, as the chapter lasted for one week, and there would be around 100 friars attending. But there was an important advantage for the Norwich houses, as the Carmelite Order was only allowed to present one candidate to study for the doctorate in theology in Oxford, and in Cambridge each year. Suitable candidates were chosen from each distinction in turn. Hence, with only five houses, there was a greater chance of friars, from the Norwich distinction, being sent to study for a doctorate than for the friars in the other larger distinctions.

**References:**

*BRCEW* 390-391: *ODNB* 7, 816.

Richard Copsey, O.Carm., "The Formation of the Medieval English Friar: From Dominican Model to Carmelite Practice", in *Omnia disce* – Medieval Studies in Memory of Leonard Boyle, O.P., ed. Anne J. Duggan, Joan Greatrex & Brenda Bolton, (Aldershot: Ashgate, 2005), 245-262

# 14

# JOHN MEPSALE

## (†1390+)

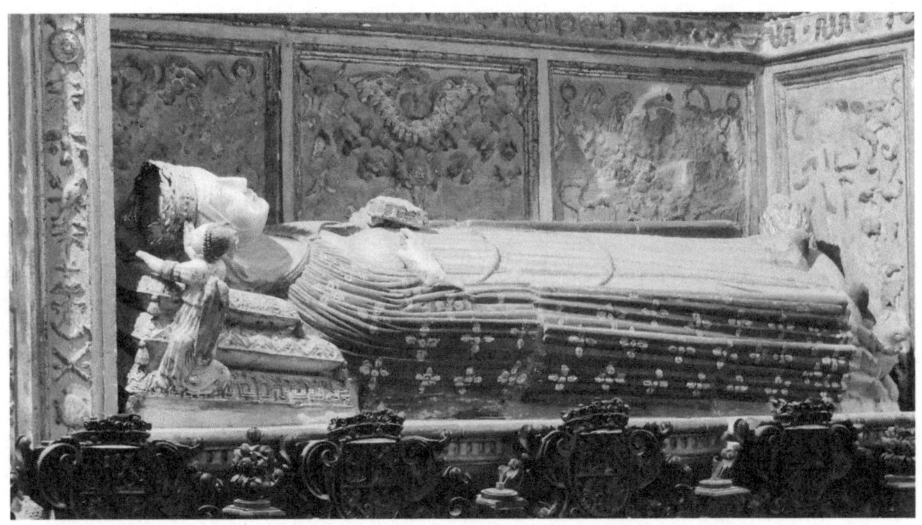

The Tomb of Queen Catalina of Castile, daughter of John of Gaunt

Many readers might think that anyone who joins a religious order, will spend most of their life enclosed in a monastery or a convent. Especially for the Carmelites who were founded as a community of hermits on Mount Carmel, this ought, perhaps, to be true. However, following their forced migration from the Holy Land, the Carmelites were compelled to adapt to a different type of role in Europe. Following the example of the Franciscans, Dominicans and other mendicant orders, the Carmelites saw their best way as serving the people of God, by providing devout, well-trained friars in the towns, and other centres of population. Hence, talented individual friars could find themselves in all types of apostolates, frequently travelling in England and overseas, doing their best to use their talents as Christ would want.

One of those who found his future, far different from what he had expected, was John Mepsale. He joined the Carmelites in London, and was ordained a priest in St Paul's cathedral on the April 8th, 1368. Nothing more is known about his early life as a young priest. It is not until the early 1380s that his name appears in the records as the chaplain to Catalina, the younger daughter of John of Gaunt, the Duke of Lancaster, born in 1372. It is likely that Mepsale was recommended for this position by his fellow Carmelite, Walter Disse*, who was the confessor for John of Gaunt, his wife Constance, son Henry and elder daughter Blanche.

In 1386, Catalina travelled with her parents when John of Gaunt launched his expedition to claim the Spanish throne. John of Gaunt believed that he was the heir to the throne of Castile through his Spanish wife. Catalina, of course, was accompanied by her spiritual director, John Mepsale.

Gaunt's invading force set out from Gascony and landed at La Coruña in northwest Spain in July. They quickly gained control of the surrounding area of Galicia, but any further advance was frustrated, as King Juan I of Castile refused to engage in battle with the English army, and Gaunt did not have the resources needed to advance further into central Spain. In November, Gaunt negotiated with the Portuguese king, João I, for a joint invasion into Spain and so, after spending the winter in the city of Ourense, 70 miles south of La Coruña, the combined English and Portuguese forces launched their attack in March 1387. The combined English and Portuguese forces met with some initial success but the Spanish army proved to be much stronger and so the English and Portuguese were forced to retire.

It is worth noting that the Constable, who led the Portuguese forces in this invasion, was Nunio Alvares Pereira, a devout man who founded the Carmelite house in Lisbon in 1397. After his retirement as Constable, Nunio joined the community there in 1423 as a lay brother, where he gained a reputation for holiness. He died in 1431, and was canonised by Pope Benedict XVI in 2009.

Before retiring from Spain, John of Gaunt accepted a proposal for his daughter Catalina, to marry Enrique, the son and heir of King Juan of Castille, who was 9 years of age: Catalina at this time was 16 years old. The text of the marriage settlement survives and, as this was the period of the papal schism, the settlement contained the provision that Catalina was given permission to remain an adherent of Pope Urban VI, whom the English supported, and to worship in a private chapel of her own. During this period the Spanish supported the anti-pope Clement VII. The marriage settlement was formally agreed at Bayonne in Gascony on July 8th, 1388. Then, on August 5th, Catalina declared that she freely entered into this marriage and accepted the treaty arrangements.

The marriage took place in Palencia cathedral in northern Spain. Following the marriage, Mepsale as her chaplain remained in Spain with his mistress, and served in her private chapel.

Little is known for certain about Mepsale's later years in Spain but there is a curious account in the St Alban's Chronicle, describing the pressure which was brought to bear on Catalina to change her allegiance to the anti-pope Clement VII. This chronicle was composed by Thomas Walsingham in the early 1400's, and in it, Mepsale is accused of betraying his mistress's trust:

> "We have decided at this point to insert the following remarkable story about the queen of Spain – daughter of the duke of Lancaster and Constanza, who was herself daughter of Pedro the previous king of Spain – lawfully married as she was with the consent of her parents, to the son of the Bastard, the usurper of that kingdom.
>
> An agreement had been made, amongst other terms previously mentioned in connection with that marriage that the said lady should be permitted to remain loyal to our pope, without interference from her husband or others who supported the anti-pope. Also that, by her father's command, and because of her own personal devotion, she would observe that loyalty in her own chapel without the presence of schismatics; that she would in no way want to attend their places of worship, or to take part in their solemn rites, even if urged constantly to do so. However, the lords of that country decided in the following way to ignore the conditions she had made. They bribed a Carmelite brother of her chapel with promises of reward, promising him the first bishopric which fell vacant if he was successful in achieving what they wanted. So he composed a fictitious letter to her, purported to come from her parents, sent to her through pilgrims travelling to St James, and he presented it to his mistress as a genuine letter. The gist of it was that she should not allow any of the previous conditions to prevent her from acquiescing in the wishes of her husband and magnates of Spain, and should conform with their rites in every respect. However, she said she would not believe this letter until it had been more fully confirmed by more trustworthy emissaries, and by that she meant members of her father's household, of whom there were a large enough number, she asserted, for him to have sent such important instructions. Meanwhile emissaries arrived from her father with letters addressed to her which contained nothing at all of this matter in them, nor did the emissaries make any mention of them by word of mouth. She accordingly expelled the perpetrator of this deceit with ignominy from any association with her.
>
> Not long after this man was restored to his former position at the insistence of the duke of Benavente, uncle of the king, his chief counsellor, and main instigator of the said ruse, because of the treasonous action of the friar and through the intervention of his lord and lady, the one aspiring

> nefariously to be the next heir to the kingdom. The treachery was discovered before action was taken, and the duke of Benevente was arrested and locked up in a very strong prison with his fellow traitor. However, with the help of the keeper of the prison, he later escaped from it, and for two days hid in a cave in a vineyard not far from the prison. By the efforts of the friar and a serf belonging to the vineyard who knew of his secret plots, he was brought food from the nearby town.
>
> When the duke's account was learned about, a public proclamation was made that anyone who could apprehend the duke, would receive, if a serf, his freedom and what is more would be handsomely rewarded; if a nobleman, he would be given possession of a hundred pounds worth of land to hold in perpetuity. The serf, delighted by this proclamation and goaded by his wife, betrayed the traitors to suffer the punishment they deserved. And so it was that loyalty and filial obedience was duly rewarded with a small endowment and a generous portion of every kind of favour: as the Apostle says, 'the unbelieving husband is saved by the faithful wife'; and the father in England was not only honoured as the pious recompense of all, thus repaying his alms, but also wonderfully saving from evils that appeared unavoidable both for himself and his own family, who were living far away."

There are some puzzling inconsistencies in the above account, and no confirmation of it has been found in any of the other contemporary chronicles, so it is difficult to know how much credence to give to it. Certainly, the nefarious actions of the duke of Benevente and the Carmelite John Mepsale, reported in the chronicle, seem to be at variance with a later document. This document, preserved in the archives of the Castel S. Angelo in Rome, contains a declaration made by Catalina, on March 27th, 1390, in Guadalajara, Spain. Written in Spanish, the text reports that the Princess Lady Catalina, daughter of John of Gaunt, duke of Lancaster, and husband of Lord Henry, eldest son of the king of Castille, recognises Clement VII as the true pope after being advised by her spiritual director and confessor, John Mepsale, together with the archbishop of Toledo, don Pedro, and the bishops, Alfonso de Zamora, and Juan de Siguenza. Furthermore the princess renounced her previous adhesion to the rival pope, Urban VI.

The Duke of Benavente mentioned in the St Alban's chronicle was Fadrique de Castilla (1360-1394) and he did, in fact, die in prison in Almodóvar del Rio in 1394. However, from the above declaration, it appears that Mepsale acted more honourably than Thomas Walsingham claims. The declaration of Catalina's allegiance to the anti-pope Clement VII evidently took place only two years after her marriage and would seem to be the result of pressure brought to bear on her from the archbishop of Toledo and other Spanish bishops. As the wife of the heir to the throne of Castille, the Spanish would have wanted her to have the same papal allegiance as her husband, and the other members of the royal family. Mepsale would appear to have seen the inevitability of this and lent his support to her transference of allegiance.

What happened to Mepsale after this date is unknown, and his name vanishes from the records. Whatever took place during his final years, it would be nice to think that Mepsale served the Lady Catherine to the best of his ability, leaving his native country behind to be at her side, as she took up her duties as the wife of the heir to the throne in the Spanish court. Mepsale may not have been without any faults, but surely he deserves to be recognised for his life of service.

Catalina's husband succeeded to the throne in 1390, as Henry III, but, due to his youth, he began to reign only in 1393. Catalina bore him three children, Maria in 1401, Catalina in 1402 and the future Juan II in 1405. Catalina was noted for her religious devotion and dedicated herself to religious patronage. Her husband, King Henry III, died in 1406, and she served as joint regent with her husband's brother Fernando. She died in Valladolid on June 2nd, 1418, and was buried in the Toledo Cathedral.

**References:**

*BRCEW* 188-189.

Thomas Walsingham, *St. Alban's Chronicle: The Chronica Maiora*, ed. Raylor, Child & Watkins, (Oxford Medieval Texts, 2003), 948-951.

# 15

# NICHOLAS OF LYNN

## (†1390+)

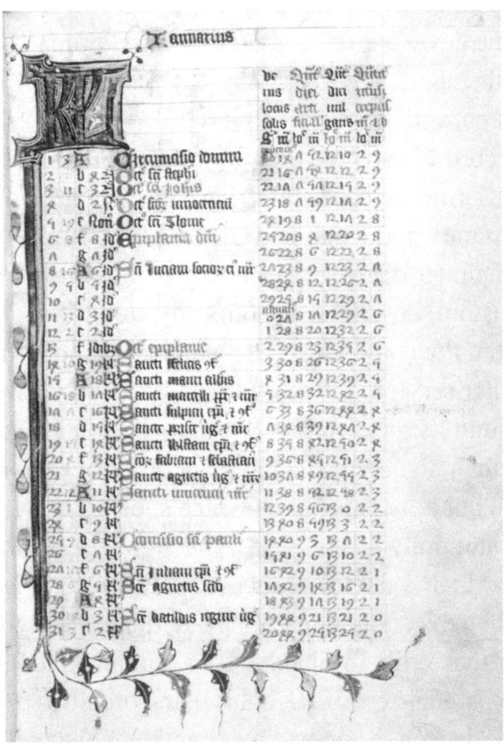

Page from Nicholas of Lynn's Astronomical Calendar for January

For a religious order in the medieval period, the majority of whose members were ordained priests, it is to be expected that its writers would focus their studies and researches on the Bible, theology and philosophy. This was certainly true for the Carmelites and in the chapters of this book the reader can encounter some of the outstanding scholars in the Order, most notably John Baconthorpe* and Thomas Netter*. But there were still some Carmelites who excelled in other disciplines. The study of history attracted some, such as Roger Alban*, who found time in his labours as a copyist, to compile an impressive genealogical descent from Adam down to the King Henry VI of England and, most notably, the best known of Carmelite historians John Bale*, whose careful recording in his notebooks of all the records he could find of the Carmelite Order, has been acknowledged in the many of the entries in this book. In the field of music, there was John Hothby*, who features in a later chapter of this book. However, modern readers will expect to find some mention of notable Carmelite scientists, but it needs to be remembered that the study of experimental science was only just beginning in the medieval period, and was focussed primarily on describing the natural world, mathematics and astronomy. It was in this last field, that one Carmelite achieved fame, and this was Nicholas of Lynn.

The earliest record of Nicholas occurs on September 29th, 1376, when, as a member of the Carmelite community in King's Lynn, he signed a contract between the community and Hugh and Cicely Elyngham, who wished to retire and spend the remainder of their days living within the Carmelite walls. This was a common custom, described as a corrody, and offered the couple a suite of rooms, food from the community kitchen, and the opportunity to attend the daily mass and other services in the community church. All the clerical members of the community signed the legal contract, and, as in official functions, processions, etc., their signatures would be in order of seniority. Nicholas' signature comes sixth out of twenty-three, which shows that he was a fairly senior member of the community at this date. The signature of the prior, John Honygge, comes first, then a doctor of theology, Peter Wysebech, two bachelors of theology, and then the community led by William Spaldyng and Nicholas of Lynn. It is known that William Spaldyng was ordained c1350, but there is no record in the bishops' registers of Nicholas being ordained to any of the clerical orders, subdeacon, deacon, or priest. This can be explained if Nicholas did all his theology studies in the Norwich diocese. Uniquely, in this diocese, all ordinations of members of the religious orders were recorded in a separate register, and, sadly, this register was lost at the Reformation. Hence, we can assume that Nicholas was ordained sometime after William Spaldyng, in the 1350's. As will be seen below, Nicholas was given the title of *lector* which indicates that he took the advanced course in theology, which led to a Licentiate in Sacred Theology (S.T.L.). This two-year course qualified the student to teach theology to Carmelite students who were studying for the priesthood, and was provided in the senior house in each distinction (region). As the Carmelite house in Lynn was in the Norwich distinction, it would be logical for Nicholas to take the course in the Carmelite house in Norwich.

There would have been no doubt about Nicholas' intellectual ability but, at some time, he must have impressed his teachers with his mathematical skills and his interest in astronomy. As a consequence, he was sent to Oxford where he continued his studies under Walter of Elveden, who was one of a number of scholars there studying astronomy, many of them at Merton College. Nicholas would appear to have arrived in Oxford around 1360, and his signature on the document in Lynn would have been made whilst he was visiting his home community for a break from Oxford, or for some other reason. It seems to have been a short stay as his signature is not on another agreement the following year, on April 30th, 1378, nor was it on an earlier agreement on February 19th, 1367.

At Oxford, Nicholas appears to have done well in his studies, and would probably have given classes in astronomy and mathematics in the Carmelite house there. He must have gained a good reputation, as he was asked to prepare a calendar for the coming years. Walter of Elveden had compiled a calendar for John of Gaunt for the years up to 1386, which gave the dates for all the movable liturgical feasts, such as Ash Wednesday, Easter, etc. as well as the phases of the moon, eclipses, and other astronomical events. Nicholas was evidently asked to prepare a similar calendar for John of Gaunt, the Duke of Lancaster, for the years from 1387 onwards to 1463. As he explains in his preface to his calendar:

> "'For Jesus Christ, the mediator of God and men, by his own testimony is Alpha and Omega, the beginning and the end, who is, who was, and who is to come'. *Apocalypse*, chapter 1.
>
> From him, according to the blessed Augustine in his first homily on John, all created things take their origin and beginning, and to him, as to their end, all things should be directed and led back. For that reason, to the glory and splendour both of him and of his blessed Mother, Mary the chaste virgin, the special patroness of our order, as well as at the request and friendly interest of the most illustrious prince, Lord John, King of Castile and Leon and Duke of Lancaster, did I, Brother Nicholas of Lynn of the Order of the Blessed Mary Mother of God, of Mount Carmel, unworthy and least among the licentiates of sacred theology, compose the present calendar in the year of our same Lord Jesus Christ 1386, for the four Metonic cycles immediately following. And this calendar will begin with the ending of the calendar of the reverend Master Walter of Elweden, namely in the year of Christ 1387, on the first day of the month of January, this being the first year of the Golden Cycle. And it will last for seventy-six years, namely until the year of our Lord 1463."

Nicholas' calendar is a very impressive work and its major part is a set of calendars for the months of the year. Each month occupied a full page divided into columns which gave the number of the day, the position of the moon, the Roman calendar, the saint(s) for the day and then the position of the sun, the length of the day (sunrise to sunset), the length of the day (including morning and evening twilights), and the lengths of the morning and evening twilights. These are followed by columns showing the new and full moons for each of the Metonic cycles (lunar phases of 19 years, i.e. 1387-1405, 1406-1424 & 1425-1443) and then Nicholas' own shadow scales (the length of the shadow cast by a man six feet tall).

These are followed by a series of tables for the solar eclipses, complete with sketches of each eclipse and then the same for the moon's eclipses. After these, there are tables for the signs of the zodiac and the ascendant, and the beginnings of the celestial houses and other aspects such as the reign of each planet, etc.

Next, there is a table for calculating the dates of the movable feasts, Septuagesima Sunday, Easter and Pentecost. This is followed by further tables for discovering the motion of the sun and the planets and other heavenly bodies.

Finally, these are followed by twelve canons. Ten of these contain a series of rules which Nicholas used to make his calculations. In the last two canons, Nicholas turns his attention to medical matters. The first canon contains advice for physicians on the times when blood-letting should take place. Medieval physicians believed that in the four humours, that is blood, phlegm, yellow and black bile, which controlled the health of the body. These humours could be balanced by blood-letting, but this needed to be done when the moon was in the right position. So, Nicholas gives rules for the physician on how to calculate when the moon is in a favourable position for blood-letting, and other advice. In the second medical canon, Nicholas gives advice on the administering of medicine, especially laxatives. Here it may be interesting to quote Nicholas' own words at the beginning of this canon:

**CANON 12: CANON FOR GIVING AND RECEIVING MEDICINE**

In order to know what time a laxative medicine should be given, or any other no matter what kind it might be, it is to be noted that in a man's body there are four natural powers, namely attraction, retention, digestion and expulsion. Now the power of attraction flourishes with heat and dryness, and for that reason those things which strengthen it should be given when the moon is in a hot and dry sign without impediment. And similarly, those which strengthen retention should be given when the moon is in a cold and dry sign, because that power flourishes in cold and dryness. Those things which strengthen digestion [should be given] when the moon is in a hot and wet sign. But those things which strengthen the power of expulsion should be given when the moon is in a cold and wet sign. And if the physician should neglect to look at these things when giving medicine, he will be deprived very often of the effect necessary for a cure, because the power of heaven will work to the contrary. Thus if anyone tries to help expulsion by giving a laxative medicine, the power of heaven will occasionally operate through the influence of the moon to strengthen the retentive power, and the same is true for other [powers]. For that reason, if any physician wishes by his art to improve retention, he should choose a time when the moon is in a cold and dry sign, such as Taurus or Virgo. Let him take care, also, that the ascending sign should be of the same complexion. In addition, to make it more useful, let the preparation of such medicine take place in a similar constellation, the reason being that it will work more efficaciously and better because of the power it receives at the time of preparation from the heavenly influence. …

If, therefore, anyone wishes to strengthen expulsion, he should give his medicine when the moon is in a sign that is cold and wet, or at least wet, as when the moon is in Cancer, Scorpio, or Pisces. And let him see to it that such a sign is ascending, that is to say, the cold and wet sign. And besides that, such mixtures should be prepared in a similar constellation, as has been said. And because different planets refer to different humours, when a certain humour ought to be discharged, a time should be chosen in which a planet referring to [the humour] is located in a bad position or is weakened, and then let the physician take action to evacuate that humour because then the effect of the planet does not resist the effect of the medicine. Thus, when one wishes to get rid of melancholy, let Saturn be weakened; if choler, Mars; if blood, the Sun, Jupiter, or Venus; if phlegm, let the moon be weakened. In addition it is to be noted that according to Ptolemy in his *Centiloquium*, in Proposition 19, no one should take purging medicine when the moon is visible with Jupiter. Haly explains the reason for this in the commentary, saying: “The effect,” he says, “of medicine is not natural to the body, that is to say that by attracting humours it overcomes the natural powers [of the body] by its own force; and thus the effect of corporeal nature, which is natural to the body, is contrary to the effect of medicine.” And thus whatever promotes strength in one weakens the strength of the other, just as is evident with two contestants in a fight. According to the astrologers, therefore, since Jupiter strengthens natural things because he is a friend to all nature, the one who wishes to evacuate a humour when the nature of the humour is strengthened by the influence of Jupiter himself, has his work cut short and his effect minimised. Haly gives an example, saying: “Pleasant odours,” he says, “strengthen nature and for that reason in the very impact of the medicine weaken its effect, and this is why the

> constituents that are foetid to the nose and bitter are to be included in many medicines."

Nicholas' calendar is an impressive composition and it quickly became very popular. The calendar is mentioned by Geoffrey Chaucer in his *Treatise on the Astrolabe,* and also in his *Canterbury Tales.* Twenty-eight manuscripts with all or parts of the calendar survive, other copies existed but are now lost. Interestingly, the last two canons on blood-letting and administering medicines were frequently copied apart from the calendar.

John Bale* lists a number of other works composed by Nicholas, but only one, *Astronomy on the Natural World,* survives in two manuscripts. Nothing further is known about Nicholas. It is claimed that he died and was buried in the Carmelite house, in King's Lynn, but no date is given.

There is one final interesting mention of Nicholas. In the sixteenth century, Gerard Mercator (d.1594), wrote that a certain James Knox of Bolduc:

> "...reporteth that a certaine English friar, a minorite of Oxford, a Mathematician, hath seen and composed the lands lying about the Pole, and measured them with an astrolabe, and described them by a Geometrical instrument."

This story was taken up by Richard Hakluyt (d.1616) who added extra details, such as the fact that the friar sailed from King's Lynn, made five further journeys and that he wrote a work called *Inventio fortunata* which he presented to King Edward III. Hakluyt went on to claim that the friar in question was Nicholas of Lynn, and this identification was quickly picked up by later historians. It was not until 1923, that the historian R. Gunther showed that there was no reason for identifying the Franciscan friar with Nicholas of Lynn. However, M. Seymour, an American, claimed to have found a fragment of the work *Inventio fortunata* and wrote that it described what is now Long Island in the U.S.A. is Other authors have continued to believe in Nicholas "the explorer", including a doctoral thesis by the Russian S. Varshavsky in 1964. Fortunately Nicholas' calendar gives sufficient evidence of his ability without the need for any imaginative voyages to the Polar Regions.

**References:**

*BRCEW* 264-266: *ODNB*

*The Kalendarium of Nicholas of Lynn*, ed. S. Eisner, (London: Scolar Press, 1980).

Cornelius O'Boyle, "Astrology and Medicine in Later Medieval England: The Calendars of John Somer and Nicholas of Lynn", *Sudhoffs Archiv*, 89 (2005), 1-22.

Richard Copsey, O.Carm., "Two Carmelite Astronomers at Oxford: John of Avon and Nicholas of Lynn", *Carmelus*, (awaiting publication)

# 16

# RICHARD OF MAIDSTONE

(†1396)

The Carmelite Cloisters at Aylesford where Richard Maidstone is buried.

In the second half of the 14th century, the writings of John Wyclif began to arouse great controversy in the English Church. In some respects, Wyclif's criticisms of the Church were justified.His attacks on the privileged status and wealth of the senior clergy, and his argument for a translation of the Bible into English, so that all could read it, were long overdue reforms. In fact, Wyclif himself completed an English translation of the Bible in 1384, which was widely welcomed. However, as Wyclif developed his theological views and argued in favour of predestination, against the veneration of the saints, transubstantiation and the concept of the papacy, his writings swiftly aroused opposition from the bishops and the clergy.

Among those who preached against Wyclif and his followers, the Lollards, there were a number of Carmelites who occupied a prominent role in defending the Catholic position.

One of the first Carmelites to preach and write against Wyclif, was Richard of Maidstone. He was born in Kent c.1352, probably in the county town of Maidstone, and joined the Carmelite community in Aylesford, which was just three miles away. He quickly gave evidence of his intellectual ability, and so was sent to study in the Carmelite *studium generale* in London. He was living there in 1376, when he was ordained priest on December 20th, at Merton Priory in Surrey. After ordination, he was sent to do higher studies in Oxford University.

It was whilst he was at Oxford that Maidstone wrote what was to become his best known work, a paraphrase in verse of the seven Penitential Psalms. His authorship is confirmed by the inclusion in a few manuscript copies of this work, of the following lines:

> By friar Richard Maidstone
> In Mary's Order of the Carmel
> That bachelor is in divinity.
> She bore Jesus in womb and bosom
> That mother is and maiden free,
> To that child then in her arm
> Which for us hung on rood tree,
> That he for wroth do us no harm,
> Him to whom these psalms say we.

The work became very popular both among the clergy and devout laity, as is witnessed by the survival of twenty-seven manuscript copies of the text. The following extract, in modernised English, gives the preface and the beginning of the paraphrase of Psalm 6:

> **PREFACE**
>
> For love of God, who bought us dear,
> To whom we ought to make our cry
> Because of sins committed here
> In youth and age, so many, aye;
> The seven psalms are often sought
> To purge us of our faults committed,
> And into English they've been brought
> So sin in man may be repented.

**PSALM VI**

*Domine, ne in furore tuo arguas me, neque in ira tua corripias me.*
Lord in thy anger reprove me not
And in thy wrath do not blame me,
For certain, sin me thoroughly sought
So I'd be lost – no help but thee.
The wantonness that I have wrought,
Forget it Lord, for thy pity,
That I be not from heaven brought
To a place where pains shall be.
*Miserere mei, Domine, quoniam infirmus sum; sana me, Domine, quoniam conturbata sunt omnia ossa mea.*
Have mercy, Lord, for I am ill;
Heal me, for bruised are all my bones,
My flesh is frail, still more my will,
My soul is heavy with mourning groans.
But when my corpse is cast in creek
And dead is laid under the stones,
Jesus Lord, merciful, meek,
Lose none that the Father owns.

On March 24th, 1390, Maidstone was licensed to preach and hear confessions in his home diocese of Rochester. Then, he returned to Oxford, where he incepted as a doctor of theology the following year. As a newly promoted doctor, Maidstone would have had to serve his year as *magister regens* (senior lecturer), when he not only gave lectures but also served as the senior theologian for the community in any public debates, etc. In fact, Maidstone soon found himself in a public debate with another theologian, doctor John Ashwardby, the vicar of St. Mary's church in Oxford. Ashwardby was preaching sermons in which he criticised the friars and their practice of mendicancy, that is, living off the offerings of the laity. Maidstone was provoked to preach sermons in defence of the Carmelites and friars in general. His defence of the friars culminated in his major theological work, *Protectorum pauperis* (In defence of poverty) in which he defended evangelical poverty, and the way of life of the mendicant friars.

After this, Maidstone's fame as a preacher spread. Not only was he a well-respected preacher in the university, but was also invited to preach before some of the leading nobles in the country. His fame led him to being appointed as confessor to John of Gaunt, the Duke of Lancaster.

Maidstone's skill in writing poetry led to another of his major compositions. In 1393, a quarrel broke out between the king, Richard II, and the city of London.

The two sides were quickly reconciled, and to celebrate their agreement, King Richard II made a triumphant entry into the city of London in August 1392, amidst great scenes of pageantry and feasting. Maidstone was present on this occasion, probably staying in the Carmelite house in the city, and he felt inclined, or probably was persuaded, to write a poem in Latin celebrating the event. This poem still survives and has now been published, accompanied by an English translation. The poem is very long, and the following lines represent only a short excerpt:

Be now prepared, O Londoners, to meet your king:
   Let him now see how welcome he is to you all.
Let all the clergy of the church proceed in front,
   And every order bear their crosses held before.
Let every city guild be quite distinct, and then
   On horseback cross the river in a splendid style.
Let all that's good in London be displayed," he said,
   "And on that day rejoice, for then will peace be yours."
Emboldened by these words the company drew close,
   And dressed itself in all the best array it could;
Meanwhile, each city square put on its finery:
   The city shone with countless gilden draperies.
The city squares smelled sweet with varied scented blooms,
   And purple buntings hung throughout in every home,
Cloth stained with gold and white and cocchineal dye
   Had here displayed a canopy with aiding skill.
No tongue could tell the labours or the great expense
   That Londoners had undergone before these days.
But look, the day goes by, I mustn't hesitate:
   All rush from town to meet the king and his young bride.
Who could recount the number of that countless crowd
   That flows from London, thicker than the heaven's stars?
On horseback twenty thousand young men could be seen;
   Of those on foot no number could contain them all.
The warden goes before with twenty-four in train,
   For these are London's aldermen, of noble rank.
(Like Rome, the city's ruled by them, as senators,
   And over them the mayor, elected by the folk.)
These were arrayed in finery of red and white,
   Distinguished from the rest by robes of double hue.
The warden goes before, the city's keys in hand
   And, too, the city's sword; the nobles walk behind,
Then after this a decked-out troop from every guild.
   Their suit proclaims that each one is quite separate:

A goldsmith, a fishmonger, and after him
  A mercer bent on trade, a seller of fine wine,
A grocer, baker, painter, and a stonemason,
  A knife-maker, a barber, and an armorer,
A carpenter, a shearer, tailor, shoemaker,
  A skinner, dyer, shop monger, a smith as well,
And here the bowmen, butchers, and the thatchers too,
  The lorimers and drapers too, they came along;
A sheather, girdler, were here, a weaver there,
  A chandler and a waxmaker were there as well;
A brewer and a stirruper, a joiner too,
  As well there was a fruiterer and poulterer.
Among these guilds a welcome "A" stands on an "R"
A glover, pursemaker, a taverner, a cook:
  From each one's suit of clothes, his craft was clear to see.
No one, I think, who saw these crowds, could hesitate
  To say that here he saw the forms of angels stand.
On such support the martial warrior relies
  When he goes forth to war and fears no battle fray.
There each and every guild was granted its own troop;
  The route was packed along the way for four full miles.

After this, Maidstone's career seemed set for great things; he was a friend of royalty, he had achieved fame as a preacher, as a theologian and as a poet. The Carmelites must have been expecting that he would enter royal service and possibly become a bishop, etc. Sadly this was not to be the case. In 1396, Maidstone went down to his own community at Aylesford and, during his stay, he became ill and died on June 1st. He lies buried in the cloister there.

**References:**

*BRCEW* 312-315: *ODNB* 36, 164-165

Valerie Edden, *Richard Maidstone's Penitential Psalms*, Middle English Texts 22, (Carl Winter, Universitätsverlag: Heidelberg, 1990). (Modernised English by Johan Bergstrom-Allen)

Richard of Maidstone, *Concordia (The Reconciliation of Richard II with London)*, with a verse translation by A.G. Rigg, ed. David R. Carlson, TEAMS Middle English Texts Series (Kalamazoo, Michigan: Medieval Institute Publications, 2003).

# RICHARD NORTHALIS

## (†1397)

Richard Northalis, archbishop of Dublin 1395-1397

Of the twenty English Carmelites who became bishops before the Reformation, Richard Northalis was the only one to have been promoted to archbishop. Northalis was born of wealthy parents in London, in the early years of the 14th century, and it has been suggested that he was the son of John Northale, sheriff of London in 1335-36, who died in 1349.

Northalis joined the Carmelites in London and, after his initial formation, he was ordained a priest. He was clearly a talented student although there is no record of him attending university. He proved to be an inspiring preacher, and, probably thanks to his family connections, he preached regularly before King Richard II. Northalis' royal connections led to him being given other tasks. On

February 6th, 1385, he was sent to Rome with John Bacon, the king's secretary, and Sir Nicholas Dagworth for "certain secret negotiations", with the Roman Curia and King Wenceslaus IV, the King of the Romans and Bohemia. Their commission was to obtain agreements with the principal towns in Tuscany, Umbria and Romagna, and with Charles Durazzo, the King of Naples, who was a friend of Pope Urban VI. The group left England on May 7th, 1385, and headed for Genoa, where Pope Urban VI had taken refuge. Soon after their arrival, in November, John Bacon, the king's secretary died, and it seems that Northalis returned to England soon after, possibly bringing the news of Bacon's death, and a report on the progress of the mission.

Then, late in 1386, Northalis was proposed for the bishopric of Ossory in Ireland. He was formally provided to the diocese some time before February 17th, 1387, and consecrated later the same year. From 1386 onwards, Northalis was frequently employed by the king on royal business. He was away from his diocese on royal business in February 1387 and then, on February 6th, 1388, Pope Urban VI requested that Northalis should come to Italy as an ambassador to discuss a concordat between England and the Roman Curia. Northalis arrived at the Roman Curia in Genoa in July, but he was there only a short time as he was back in London by December 14th, when he performed ordinations for the bishop of London, in the chapel of his manor in Stepney. After Christmas, Northalis made preparations for his return to Genoa and for a longer stay there. Then, on February 22nd, 1389, he appointed a Carmelite, brother Thomas Fitzpiers, and John Stopham, as his attorneys in Ireland for two years. Soon after that, he left England and is recorded, on June 15th, being given permission to receive all the temporalities of his diocese, as he was abroad again on the king's business. Northalis was back in England again by November 13th, 1390, when he complained that, in spite of the king's order, two-thirds of the diocesan revenues had been held back by the king's officers. An order was issued granting him the full revenues from his diocese until August 1st, 1391.

Then, on August 29th, 1390, Robert Wikeford, the archbishop of Dublin, died and Northalis was appointed as one of the custodians of the temporalities of the See. He remained as a custodian until July 27th, 1391, when the Augustinian Robert Waldeby was appointed archbishop. On February16th, 1391, Northalis was licensed to bring "corn, horses, falcons, goshawks, fish, gold and silver from Ireland into England and Wales for the purposes of gain". Exactly what Northalis was involved with and why he needed this permission is unclear, but it did allow him to trade and so increase his income. Then on February 20th, 1391, he received a commission with others:

> "... to assemble and meet in some one place or in different places, as they shall think fit, the better, more sufficient, discreet and fit prelates, lords, magnates and commons of Munster, Leinster, Meath, Uriel and Ulster, as well as other parts of Ireland, and enquire, by oath of good and lawful men thereof touching the state of Ireland and the defaults, damages, grievances and losses thereof, the causes and origin of the same, and how a remedy might be applied; also touching the capture of Neel, the elder son of Neel O'Neel, the rebel Irish chief of Ulster, by whom, how and for what ransom he was released, and whether to the king's advantage or loss, and of the capture and release of all other Irish prisoners and rebels since the coming of John Stanley, justiciary of Ireland; also touching the number of the said John's retinue since his last coming into Ireland and its continuance, and whether he has duly observed the covenants touching his stay in Ireland contained in the indentures between the king and him, how many men-at-arms and archers from England he led into Ireland, and how many he had from Ireland; the true yearly value of the revenues and profits of Ireland whilst he was justiciary and how much thereof he received to his own use; further to examine in the king's name all rolls, records and evidences of the Exchequer and other courts of the king there, the behaviour of the king's ministers and officers, etc. and to certify the same into the Chancery in England."

Because of Northalis' increasing royal duties, the king gave him a licence on March 23rd, 1391:

> ... in consideration of his being ordered to attend for business nearly touching the king, for the bishop of Ossory to go to and return from his bishopric as often as he pleases during the next three years, and to have all the profits of the bishopric during that period, whether he is absent or not.

Later that year, on August 4th, Northalis was commissioned as deputy-justice for the county of Kilkenny, and authorized to negotiate with the Irish rebels there. In this role, he attended the meetings of the Royal Council during 1392-1393, and then, on May 29th, 1393, he was appointed Lord Chancellor for Ireland, an office which he held for just over a year. As Chancellor, he was commissioned by the King on June 1st, 1393,

> "... to enquire touching the concealment by the king's officers and others in Ireland of old debts, revenues and profits, and to levy the same when found to the king's use."

During the absence of the Lord Justice, James Butler, Third Earl of Ormond, Northalis as Lord Chancellor, engaged in negotiating with the Irish rebels. His duties even included accompanying the Lord Justice on an armed expedition into Munster. On April 26th, 1394, Northalis was given a grant of £20, as his income as Lord Chancellor did not cover more than a third of his expenses. In fact, he left the office of Lord Chancellor later that year, and the following year, on April 7th, 1395, he was summoned to attend the king at a council meeting in Kilkenny.

Then, on October 25th, 1395, Northalis was translated to become Archbishop of Dublin and he was granted the temporalities, i.e. control over the finances of the See, on February 4th, 1396. As archbishop of Dublin, he also became the dean of Penkridge Collegiate Parish Church (near Cannock, Staffordshire). In 1396, the king granted to Northalis and his successors, that they should exercise the office of admiral or water-bailiff within the manor, lordship and port of Dalkey, and receive all the fees thereunto. This was a lucrative appointment as Dalkey was, at that time, the only safe anchorage for vessels bringing cargoes to Dublin. Probably because of his continuing royal duties, Northalis obtained leave on April 1st, 1396, to be absent from Ireland during the next 5 years without incurring any penalties.

Sadly Northalis did not live long enough to make any significant impact as archbishop. He died in Dublin on July 20th, 1397. A small rectangular limestone slab, the matrix for a lost memorial brass, survives in the north transept of Christ Church Cathedral, Dublin. This has been dated to c.1400 and it has been suggested that it covered the tomb of Richard Northalis. There is no record that Northalis left any written works, and his memorial lies rather in his life and especially his dedicated service to the Church and to his King, Richard II.

**References:**

*BRCEW* 318-320: *ODNB* 41, 125-126

Roderick O'Flanagan, *The Lives of the Chancellors and Keepers of the Great Seal of Ireland*, (London, 1870), i, 63-71.

18

# JOHN SWAFHAM

## (†1398)

Bangor Cathedral where John Swafham was bishop 1376-1398

Nothing is known about John Swafham's background before he joined the Carmelite community in King's Lynn, sometime around 1328. The town of Swaffham from which John takes his name lies 16 miles southeast of King's Lynn. From his later career, it would a reasonable assumption that he came from a prosperous and well-connected family. It has been suggested that he was related to Walter of Swafham, dean of Bangor (1389-before 1396) and William Swafham, archdeacon of Anglesey (1395-1398?) and of Bangor (1398-before 1411).

After completing his basic formation, Swafham was sent to continue his studies in Cambridge University where, eventually, he was awarded a doctorate in theology. Swafham is recorded as being licensed to hear confessions, in the diocese of Ely, on December 7th, 1349. As the Black Death was spreading rapidly through England, during this year, he was doubtless being recruited to fill the gap left by another priest who had died of the plague. Fortunately Swafham survived the perils of the Black Death, and became a noted preacher and an effective critic of John Wyclif and his followers.

The Carmelite historian, John Bale*, claims that Swafham quickly came to the attention of King Edward III, and was a frequent preacher at court, delivering his sermons before many of the great men of the kingdom. On March 1st, 1363, he was appointed bishop of Cloyne in Ireland, and the temporalities of the See (its property and revenues), were granted to him on July 14th. Swafham seems to have been unusual among Englishmen who were provided to bishoprics in Ireland, in that he actually went to Ireland and spent most of his time there. This was possibly the intention of the king, who may have hoped that Swafham would become a trusted administrator in Ireland. The only reference to Swafham, in his early years as a bishop, is when he returned to England in 1368, to attend the funeral cortege of the Duchess Blanche, the wife of John of Gaunt, Duke of Lancaster, which took place in St Paul's Cathedral in London after her death on September 12th.

It was during his early period as bishop of Cloyne, around 1364, that Swafham commissioned the compilation of the Pipe Roll of Cloyne, which listed all the property belonging to the diocese, and the rents and leases granted to tenants. On February 10th, 1370, Swafham was appointed attorney in Ireland, for Sir William Fitzwalter. Then, on January 7th, 1372, Swafham attended the Irish Parliament, which met in Kilkenny, and during the course of which, he was appointed as one of the auditors for the accounts of Sir William de Windsor. On June 8th that year, Swafham attended a meeting of the Council of Ballyhock as the assessor for his diocese. Around this time, Swafham wrote a report, for King Edward III, on the state of Ireland, which he sent from Cloyne on January 1st. (year unknown).

On September 20th, 1373, Swafham was appointed as a member of a commission which was sent to England, by the Irish Parliament, to report to the king on the difficulties being faced in Ireland. Their remonstrances had an effect, and the king ordered the Earl of March to go there as soon as possible. In the interim, Sir William Windsor was appointed custos (guardian). Swafham remained in England for some time. He is recorded as being commissioned to reconcile the chapel of Stanford-in-Lyminge, near Hythe in Kent, which had been polluted by a murder.

On June 8th, 1376, Swafham was present in Westminster Palace at the deathbed of the Black Prince, and the episode is described in a contemporary chronicle:

> "… Swafham said: "Now, without doubt, death is at hand, and you are to go wherever God has appointed, therefore I counsel you, my lord, now to forgive all those that you have offended, for it is clear that you have offended both God and many men. Therefore, first, ask God for forgiveness; and secondly, all men whom, by direct purpose or ignorantly, you have willingly offended". To which he answered, "I will"; and the bishop said it was not sufficient to say only 'I will', but whilst you have the power, to declare the same by words, you ought to ask pardon"; but he answered nothing else, but only "I will"; and when he had often times done this, the bishop said, "I suppose some evil spirits to be here present that has his tongue, whereby he cannot express his mind with words", &, taking the sprinkler, he cast holy water to the four corners of the chamber where he lay, and behold, suddenly the prince with joined hands and eyes lifted up to heaven, said, "I give thee thanks, O God, .. I humbly beseech thy mercy…' When he had spoken these words, he gave up the Ghost."

Soon after this event, on July 2nd, 1376, Swafham was translated to become bishop of Bangor in Wales. The temporalities were restored on October 28th, and Swafham made his profession of faith on November 22nd, before the archbishop of Canterbury, and was installed in office. Once again, Swafham's appointment to Bangor seems to have had political connotations, as there was continual unrest in North Wales, and Swafham's cathedral in Bangor had been destroyed in 1360. A few days before taking up his appointment to Bangor, on November 19th, Swafham gave the sacrament of confirmation to Edmund, the second son of Edmund, the Earl of March, whom Swafham would have met in Ireland.

Swaffham went into action quickly in his new diocese, and in 1380, he launched a legal action against the Countess of March, who had claimed ownership of certain diocesan lands. Although Swafham obtained a judgement in his favour, the dispute lingered on and finally Swafham had to abandon his suit through lack of money. A major diocesan undertaking was the rebuilding of the cathedral in Bangor, and Swafham set about this with his usual vigour. However, when he had completed half of the project, he was forced to appeal to the new king, Richard II, for some relief from his taxes and from the subsidies, which were levied due to his increasing debts. On June 26th, 1386, he was granted relief from all subsidies and from the tenths (taxes), until November the following year. On the same day, he was granted permission to appropriate two parishes to the cathedral, in order to support four more chaplains there. This meant that the income of these two parishes would go to pay for the four chaplains, apart from the salaries for two curates, who would be appointed to provide the pastoral care in the parishes. In return for the king's generosity, towards the rebuilding of the cathedral, Swafham with the agreement of the dean and chapter, established on July 25th, a perpetual daily mass to be celebrated in the cathedral for the king:

> "John bishop of Bangor, the dean and chapter to the king. Grant, for his devotion to the church of Bangor founded by the king and his forefathers, and for benefits received, that a mass of the Virgin Mary shall be celebrated there for ever, with the prayer *Quesumus omnipotens deus ut famulus tuus Rex noster Ricardus qui in tua miseracione suscepit regni gubernacula etc.*, [We beseech thee, Almighty God, that your servant, our King Richard, who has been entrusted with the government of this kingdom…] for the king's welfare during his life, and after his death for his soul and the souls of his forefathers, and of the faithful departed, with the prayer *Inclina domine aurem tuam etc.* [Incline O Lord your ear, etc.] Dated at Bangor, on the feast of St. James the Apostle 1386."

Swafham travelled down from Bangor to Osney near Oxford, where he delivered the document in person to the king on August 6th, 1386. The following year, on August 25th, Swafham was present at the King's Council, which met in Nottingham. His signature occurs as a witness on the judges' manifesto, which condemned the impeachment of Michael de la Pole, the Earl of Suffolk, in 1386. On November 6th, 1387, as work on the cathedral continued, Swafham received further relief from all the tenths, subsidies and other sums due to the king. Sadly, the results of all Swafham's efforts to rebuild the cathedral did not last long, as the building was burnt down again in 1402, by the Welsh forces led by Owen Glendower.

In 1390, Swafham ran into another serious problem with Aberconwy Abbey, when he instructed the abbot to collect the levy of a tenth for the king from the clergy of his diocese, a tax which had been agreed by the clergy of the archdiocese of Canterbury. The abbot wrote to the king and complained that this was unjust as his abbey was in the diocese of St Asaph, and not Bangor. King Richard II agreed and wrote to Swafham instructing him that he should not lay this burden on the abbot. However, Swafham pursued his case and argued that the abbey was originally founded in his diocese, and was only moved outside it at the time of King Edward I in 1283. He added that the abbey still had three parishes and extensive possessions in the diocese of Bangor, and that it had become the custom for the abbot to collect such tenths and other subsidies. The final result of Swafham's appeal is unknown.

In June 1392, Swafham was present at the trial of the Irish Cistercian monk,

Henry Crumpe, for heresy at Stamford. Crumpe had argued against the pastoral privileges granted to the mendicant friars. Judgement was given against Crumpe, and he was suspended from teaching at Oxford. He returned to Ireland where he continued to preach against the friars.

In 1394, Swafham appears to have accompanied King Richard to Ireland, as his signature occurs as a witness on a document issued by the king in Dublin, on January 5th, 1395. Then, on June 26th, 1395, Swafham was released from a debt of £96 7s 8d, which he owed to the king for "divers tenths, subsidies and other issues due to the king". Finally, on July 26th, 1396, Swafham was given a pardon:

> "… for all felonies, trespasses, extortions, misprisions, negligences and ignorances, whereof he is indicted or appealed, and of any consequent outlawries".

This was probably a consequence of Swafham's plea which he had launched against "false accusations of the people of North Wales". Two years later, Swafham made his final escape from all these problems when he died on June 24th, 1398.

Many people imagine that monks and friars spend their time in the chapel saying their prayers and working quietly or reading pious books within the monastic enclosure. Whilst, in the medieval period, this may have been true for the majority of religious, there were others with particular talents or capabilities who were called to serve the king or members of the nobility. At that time, the king did not have the finances to support a comprehensive civil service, and so employing clergy or members of a religious order meant that, rather than pay them a salary, they could be rewarded with a clerical appointment, such as a parish, a canonry or as a bishop. Swafham was certainly intellectually gifted, as his doctorate in theology attests, and probably well-connected through his family or influential friends, so he was an ideal choice by King Richard II, to serve in the troubled situation in Ireland, and then, later, in another troubled region in North Wales. By making him a bishop, Richard avoided paying any onerous salary, and Swafham repaid the king by playing his role in the government of the region, ensuring that the king's rule was obeyed, and that any disturbances were kept in check. Perhaps this was not the future that Swafham had anticipated when he joined the Carmelites in Lynn, but he played a valuable role for his king and country and, hopefully, his religious beliefs. His way of life and preaching were influential in bringing those under his care into a closer union with the God who loved them.

**Reference:**

*BRCEW* 221-222

# 19

# JOHN KYNYNGHAM

## (†1399)

An unnamed Doctor of Theology in a window from the Carmelite House, Cambridge

As has been mentioned earlier, the latter half of the fourteenth century was marked by the influence of John Wyclif, whose writings challenged the established Church both in the abuses and its failure to live in accordance to the Gospel precepts, but also in the truth of some of its central theological beliefs. Wyclif was born in Yorkshire, where his family were landowners, and came to study in Oxford around 1345. So Wyclif started his studies just before the Black Death, which arrived in England in June 1348, and reached Oxford towards the end of the year. It is estimated that around 60% of the population died.

This had a significant effect on Wyclif, who saw the plague as a punishment from God on the Church, and all the wealth it had accumulated.

Wyclif gained his M.A. in 1356, and then proceeded to do further studies in theology. He was ordained and gained his doctorate in theology in 1372. In 1374, Wyclif wrote his first major work called, *On Civil Dominion*, which argued that the Church be divested of all its property, and live a life of poverty. In his later works, Wyclif argued against payments to Rome, the idea of purgatory, clerical celibacy, transubstantiation and the mendicant friars.

The Carmelites were quick to argue against Wyclif's ideas, and one of the first of them was John Kynyngham, who was studying in Oxford around the same time as Wyclif. Kynyngham was born in Suffolk and joined the Order in Ipswich. After his initial formation, he was sent to Oxford where he was studying for his doctorate around the same time as Wyclif. Kynyngham's first known composition is a short litany, written whilst he was a student, which begins:

> "Rise up, Lord God, and free your servant from all evils, past, present and to come. May your power defend me lest I fall in the face of my enemies. May your wisdom instruct me so that I may not go astray in my studies. May your abundant grace save me lest I perish through my mistakes. Guard me, Lord, carefully in all my movements, going and coming, in every place and at every moment; for I confess that I am able to do nothing without you. Therefore I commend myself, above all, to you, who live and reign, God for ever and ever ..."

Kynyngham then continues with petitions to various saints from the Old and New Testaments, male and female, including the following:

> "... Most holy fathers Elijah and Elisha, most appropriately, you are the ones to pray for me so that, living faithfully our religious life, I may be found worthy to attain the reward of the beatific vision. Amen."

And the litany ends with:

> "... All you saints of God who, having left this sinful world, now enjoy the supernatural delights of the celestial kingdom. Because of your own joy, I beg you will extend your pity and bend down to listen to the tearful voice of a poor sinner lying in this lake of misery so that, at least, you will deign to remember me and be my advocates with the divine majesty when I appear before the door of judgement. Then, I shall rejoice, trusting firmly that, as I can achieve nothing by myself, I shall be presented before the omnipotent Lord by such mediators whose delight is to bring salvation to petitioning souls. May he who is God, one and three, living and reigning for eternity, bring me to salvation through your intercession. Amen."

Around 1363, Kynyngham wrote a scholarly response (*Ingressus*) to John Wyclif, entitled, *The response of John Kynyngham, Carmelite, against Wyclif.* This is the earliest surviving work of Kynyngham, and it begins:

> "In this work, I intend to do two things; firstly I will argue, to a certain higher person, what was said and described in my last thesis (*determinacio*) against my reverend Master Wyclif; secondly I will pursue the argument mentioned in the text of the first article where I intended to go further but shortness of time did not permit. ...

This reference to a "last thesis" indicates that Kynyngham had already held a debate with Wyclif, possibly as an academic exercise in the university. However, it is not until a few years later, when both Kynyngham and Wyclif had incepted as doctors, that Kynyngham launched his three significant theses (*Determinaciones*) against Wyclif. In these, Kynyngham describes both Wyclif and himself as masters, indicating that they were now both recognised lecturers in the university, and hence establishing their reputations through public presentations, where they answered difficult theological questions. In Kynyngham's three *Determinaciones*, he argues against Wyclif's claim that all intelligible being is present in God and against the extremely literal interpretation of the Bible which Wyclif adopts.

Kynyngham's future, though, did not lie only in the academic halls of Oxford. In June 1375, he attended the Carmelite general chapter held in Le-Puy-en-Velay in France as a definitor for the English Province. Later, in 1382, Kynyngham was one of the Doctors of Theology who were invited to attend the Church Council, which met in the Blackfriars convent in London on May 17$^{th}$, and 18$^{th}$ & 20$^{th}$ June, in order to consider the writings of John Wyclif. The council condemned 24 propositions taken from Wyclif's works, and it must have been with some satisfaction, that Kynyngham preached the sermon, when the conclusions of the council were announced. As a contemporary chronicle describes the event:

> "And in witness thereof, on the sixth day of Whitsun week [30$^{th}$ May, 1382] next following there was a general procession through the city of London, and all, both clergy and laity, of whatever degree, went barefoot to testify. And the bishop of London presided, with many other distinguished men, and after the procession a friar called [Kynyngham], a doctor of divinity, of the Carmelite order, preached, and in his sermon, upon the archbishop of Canterbury's order and commission which he showed there, publicly pronounced all those conclusions false and condemned, some as heresies and some as errors, and by

> the commission which he had shown denounced as excommunicate all those who thereafter taught, and held, and preached, or nurtured or adhered to those conclusions, and all those thereafter who heard them preached or taught."

Kynyngham was probably still teaching in Oxford during the 1380's as the Carmelite historian, John Bale, lists ten of his works complete with incipits (the opening words, which usually indicates that Bale had seen these works). Among these works, there is a lecture on the *Sentences*, some works on the Bible e.g. on the *Lamentations of Jeremiah*, the prophet *Ezekiel*, and the *Letter of St James*, as well as works on theology, e.g. on angels, the birth of Christ, the Passion of Christ, and the Holy Spirit – as well as two collections of his sermons.

In 1392, Kynyngham appears again on the national scene, when he was present at the trial of the Irish Cistercian Henry Crumpe, at Stamford on May 28th. Crumpe studied at Oxford and was initially very anti-Wyclif. He had attended the Council in London in 1382, alongside Kynyngham. However, he became very antagonistic towards the pastoral activities of the mendicant friars, and denied their right to act as confessors. His views were condemned at Stamford, and Crumpe was forced to leave the university and return to Ireland. Around this time, Kynyngham was appointed as the confessor and secretary to John of Gaunt, and he resided in Gaunt's household. Kynyngham's reputation as a preacher grew and he was invited to preach before King Richard II on All Saints' Day, 1392.

In 1393, following the death of Robert Witheved, Kynyngham was elected prior provincial of England, and this was confirmed at the general chapter which was held in Frankfurt, at the end of May that year. Kynyngham continued to serve as John of Gaunt's confessor, and he was signatory to the duke's will on February 3rd, 1398.The following year, he was invited by the king to attend a council held in Oxford on January 27th, and he was called to advise the king concerning the papal schism. At the end of May 1399, there was a general chapter of the Carmelites held in Le Selve, Tuscany, where Kynyngham was confirmed as provincial, and appointed as vicar-provincial for Ireland, where he was to arrange the election of a new provincial by the members of the province, or by other means, if he deemed it wise. Sadly, Kynyngham was not present at the chapter to hear these decisions as he had died in York a few days earlier on May 12th.

Kynyngham was recognised as a devout, holy man, very learned and respected. In some of the early Carmelite liturgical calendars, he was listed as a "venerable" with his feast day on May 6th. John Bale describes him as:

> "This venerable father was greatly respected for his learning, exemplary conduct, gentleness, as well as for his friendly nature and humility."

**References:**

*BRCEW* 174-175: *ODNB* 31, 297-298

An English translation of Kynyngham's litany will be published in *Early Carmelite Documents*.

# 20

# RICHARD OF LAVENHAM

## (†1401)

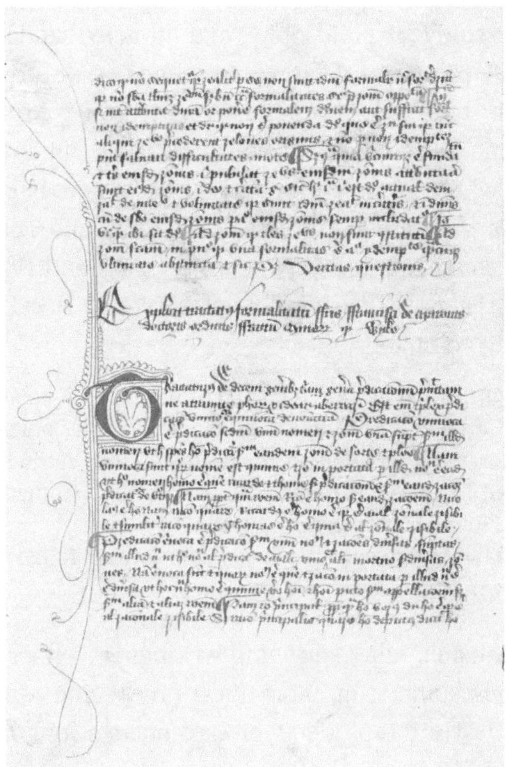

Page from Richard of Lavenham's treatise on the Seven Deadly Sins

The latter half of the fourteenth century saw a number of very talented Carmelite scholars of whom one of the most prolific was Richard Lavenham. We know little about his early life but it is claimed that he came from Lavenham in Suffolk, and joined the Order in Ipswich. His talents were quickly recognised and he was sent to Oxford for his higher studies. After gaining a doctorate in theology, Lavenham spent some years lecturing in Oxford, before being transferred to teach in the Carmelite *studium generale* (international study centre) in London. Lavenham's name first occurs in contemporary records when, as prior of London, he presented three friars from his house for ordination in Fulham parish church, on September 20th, 1399.

Lavenham's major legacy lies in the seventy or more manuscripts which he is recorded as having written, thirty-seven of which have survived. The majority of these are short works on logic and philosophy, and were probably written for Lavenham's students in Oxford and London. The London *studium generale* specialised in the study of philosophy, and attracted students from many of the other Carmelite provinces, who would spend two or three years in London before going on to study theology at a university. It was probably due to some of these students making copies of Lavenham's works, before returning to their home provinces, which accounts for Lavenham's texts being found throughout Europe, e.g. in Venice, Dublin, Basel, Eichstätt, and Turin. In philosophy, Lavenham wrote commentaries of Aristotle's *Ethics* and *Physics*, and it is his commentary on Aristotle's *Physics*, now preserved in Basel University, which bears the following colophon:

> "… And this is the end of this collection of brother N[icholas] Laniham of the Order of Carmelites of Mount Carmel on the eight books of Aristotle's *Physics*, to the praise and honour of Almighty God who with his blessed Virgin Mother, be praised for ever and ever Amen. [Copied] by me John Heynlin 1452 in the University of Leipzig."
>
> [The mistake in Lavenham's first name is also found in another of Lavenham's works preserved in Vienna]

Many of Lavenham's other surviving writings are either collections of excerpts from various authors, or short tracts on specific aspects of logic, etc. Again these are clearly the products of Lavenham's long career in teaching. Some of Lavenham's longer, more developed works, probably date from Lavenham's time in Oxford, and are based on lectures which he gave whilst he was in the University.

Lavenham's works, however, were not limited to logic and philosophy. He is known to have written a series of commentaries on various books of the Bible, e.g. on Isaiah, Tobit, the Epistle of Titus, as well as a Biblical Dictionary. In fact, Lavenham's reading extended much wider than the Holy Scriptures. He compiled a list of excerpts taken from Venerable Bede's *Ecclesiastical History of the English People*, another collection of passages from St Jerome's *Letters*, and excerpts from the Carmelite, John of Hildesheim's *The History of the Three Kings*. His *Determination* on some questions from the book of St Bridget's

*Revelations* was probably taken from some lectures that Lavenham gave whilst he was in Oxford. Lavenham also wrote a short work *On the Foundation of the Carmelite Order*, which was noticed by the prior general Jean Grossi, who saw the work when he visited England in 1413-1414. Grossi described it as a major work on the history and spread of the Order. Sadly it has not survived.

At Oxford, Lavenham was another Carmelite who became involved in the controversy with Wyclif and his followers, the Lollards. His *Determination against the Lollards*, probably dates from his time at Oxford. Lavenham continued to argue against individual Lollards for many years and shortly after 1400, he compiled, *The heresies and errors of Master John Purvey, priest, taken from his heretical book.*

Purvey had been a friend of Wyclif and stayed with him when he left Oxford and retired to Lutterworth. He assisted Wyclif in revising his translation of the Bible and then, after the death of Wyclif in 1384, Purvey moved to Bristol and began preaching. However, he was soon accused of heresy and in 1387 he was forbidden to preach by the bishop of Worcester, but he ignored this edict. In 1390, Purvey was imprisoned by Archbishop Arundel. Whilst in prison, Purvey continued writing and he was finally brought before a convocation of the Canterbury archdiocese. Rather than be condemned, Purvey made a public confession of his errors at St Paul's Cross in 1401. Lavenham appears to have compiled his list of Purvey's heresies between 1400-1403, probably as an aid in the campaign of the English Church against the Lollards.

Among the other known Lavenham works, there was a collection of sermons now lost but the one composition for which he is best known was called, *A Little Treatise on the Seven Deadly Sins* written in English. This work survives in fourteen copies and was intended for priests hearing confessions, but it was clearly a popular text and must have proved helpful to lay persons who were preparing for confession, or who used it as devotional reading. It begins:

*"Christ that died upon the Cross for man's salvation,*
*Grant us grace so as to escape the cunning attacks of the devil*
*Lest, through sinning, we lose our final reward.*

Two things I have tried, through God's grace, to do in this little treatise. First to give briefly a general explanation of the seven deadly sins, in general, by description and by example. And afterward to describe by words and by order, what branches and boughs grow out of them in particular. As touching the first matter, a holy man wrote in his book, "According to some, it is St Thomas [Aquinas], or St Albert [Magnus] according to others" in the *Compendium of Theology*, book 3". "The seven deadly sins," he said, "are like seven sundry beasts, as Pride to the lion. Covetousness to the hedgehog. Wrath to the wolf. Envy to the hound. Sloth to the ass. Gluttony to the bear. & Lechery to the swine." Of which figures and examples, I hope to deal with in each of the seven deadly sins by itself.

"Pride is nothing else but a corrupt desire for great respect", as Saint Augustine writes, and this is in book 14 of the *City of God*, chapter 13. Therefore I compare a proud man to a lion, for just as the lion expects that all other beasts should look up to him, fear him and bow down to him, just so a proud man expects all other men should look up to him, fear him and bow down to him. And therefore, it may truly be said of a proud man as it is written in Holy Writ: "Look, pride rises up like a lion, Jeremiah chap. 49, v.19. Look, says the prophet, and take heed how, like a lion, he shall be caught up in his pride. This is a sin that destroys all the virtues and most grieves God above all other vices. In taking whereof Lucifer, that was sometime the fairest angel in heaven, is now for his pride become the foulest fiend in hell. And if you would know wherein, he showed his pride, I shall answer you and say in this that he desired for his beauty to be the equal of God, for as I said beforehand "Pride is naught else but a bad desire for high worship". And this manner of desire would never have arisen in a man's heart but for three reasons; either it is for gifts of nature, or for gifts of fortune, or else for gifts of grace. The gifts of nature being nobleness of kindred, gentleness of blood, plenty of children, advancement by inheritance, strength, beauty and comeliness of person. The gifts of fortune being lands, rents, gold, silver, treasure, possessions, clothing, horses, harness, jewels, patronage, worship and friendship. The gifts of grace are the different virtues that God gives a man, such as eloquence in speaking, skill in the craft of singing and others similar. These three types of gift are the only reason why a man becomes proud when he ought to be meek, and therefore his sin is so much the more. Saint Gregory said: "and it is in book 34 of *On Morals* [Exposition of the Book of Job] near the end. "Pride", he said, "is the root of all vices for this reason; if the root of the tree were not hid in the earth, no branch would grow out of it, so if pride were not first rooted in a man's heart, no branch of sin would spring out of him."

Out of Pride grow eight branches which have been given titles as:
*Presumption, Vainglory, Disobedience, Boldness, Hypocrisy, Indignation, Shamelessness, Obstinacy."*

There is some confusion over exactly when and where Lavenham died. In his earliest notebook, the Carmelite historian, John Bale*, claims that Lavenham died in 1382 then, in a later notebook, he notes that he was prior in Bristol, and died there in 1383. Bale's contemporary, the historian John Leland, wrote that Lavenham died in Ipswich, whilst in Polydore Vergil's chronicle, written in the early 1500s, there is the following account of the assault on the Tower of

London during the Peasants' Revolt in 1381, where some have judged there is a reference to Lavenham:

> "Here, at their first assault, contrary to right and law, when Simon Archbishop of Canterbury, Robert Hales, the Master of the Order of Knights of St. John, and a certain Carmelite monk named Richard, the king's confessor, were sent to them, they seized them and in a trice beheaded them in a yard underneath the Tower, rejoicing and bawling they had punished the men who had done the most to harm them."

Many later writers seized on this reference to a Carmelite "Richard" and claimed that he was Richard Lavenham. In fact, it was an error and the friar executed was a Franciscan William Appleton, Richard II's physician.

In reality, Lavenham lived on for another twenty years or more. It is recorded that he was prior of London on 20 Sept 1399 when he presented three friars from his community for ordination in Fulham parish church. Then, as noted above, Lavenham composed his book against Purvey sometime between 1400-1403. So, it would appear that he died sometime in the early 1400's.

Lavenham had served the Order faithfully during his life, teaching, writing and using his considerable talents to help young Carmelites in their formation, and also playing his part in countering the spread of the Lollards. He was evidently a noted preacher and his one work in English on the seven deadly sins, was a popular aid for priests and laity alike. His reputation was such that his name was included as a "venerable" in some early Carmelite calendars, with his feast day on $27^{th}$ June.

**References:**

*BRCEW* 305-311: *ODNB* 32, 718-719

There have been a large number of articles on Lavenham's works on logic, e.g. P. V. Spade, "Five Logical Tracts by Richard of Lavenham", in R. O'Donnell, ed., *Essays in honour of Anton Charles Pegis,* (Toronto, 1974), 70-124.

For an edition of Lavenham's treatise on the seven deadly sins, see *A Litil Tretys on the Seven Deadly Sins,* ed. J. Zutphen, (Rome: Institutum Carmelitanum, 1956).

# 21

# WALTER DISSE

## (1404)

Carmelite House in Lisbon in 1745
(The house was destroyed in the earthquake of 1755)

It is quite common in history books for Carmelites to be described as monks, but this is not simply a confusion in terms but also it fails to realise that there are significant differences between the vocation of a monk and that of a friar. Hermits and monks emerged early in the Church's history, and the main source of inspiration for many of the monastic Orders was St Benedict (†547). For Benedict, the monastery was primarily a retreat from the temptations and distractions of the everyday world. It was a place of refuge where a monk could live a life of prayer and work, dedicating his whole life to the service of God, well away from the centres of population. The *Opus Dei* (the work of God) was primarily the worship offered in the monastic chapel, that is the mass, the divine office and the quiet times of prayer and adoration. Having been founded in the feudal period, a monastery had a hierarchical structure, parallel to the secular authorities with the abbot (as lord of the manor), the prior (the warden or seneschal) and the various offices such as sacristan, bursar, etc. filled by the choir monks. The lay brothers, not knowing Latin, and many of them illiterate, were excused from saying the divine office, and served the community doing mostly menial tasks. When monks joined an individual monastery, they took a vow of stability, and they expected to spend their entire life there.

The friars came much later, in the early 1200's, when the culture had changed considerably. By this time, there were large towns and cities, with merchants trading goods, and travelling from one centre of population to another, plying their trade. Hence the friars did not take a vow of stability, nor did they look to make foundations away from populated areas. They saw their role as serving the people, preaching the love of God, and providing spiritual guidance. It is worth noting that St Francis of Assisi was the son of a merchant and hence he saw the role of the Franciscans as being "spiritual merchants", travelling around in order to reach the people, and bring Christ into their lives. So, a friar joins, not a monastery but a province or region, and, although he has a sense of belonging to the house where he joined, he lives at the disposal of the provincial and the province, going where he is needed and serving in whatever role is required.

In some cases, the friar's life of service can involve long periods away from his own community. One such case was that of Walter Disse who joined the Carmelite Order in Norwich, and like other talented students, he was sent to do his higher studies in theology at Cambridge University. His name first appears in the records there when he was ordained deacon on February 16th, 1353, in St Mary's church, Ely. He would have been ordained priest a few months later, and then continued his studies towards a doctorate in theology.

Disse's ability soon came to the attention of some of the leading political figures, and he served as the confessor to the Duke of Lancaster, John of Gaunt, and his wife Constance from around 1374. In the accounts of John of Gaunt, there are regular payments to Disse for his services and the expenses he incurred. As for example:

> "Dated 12 Jan 1375: 'John, etc. to all those etc. Let it be made known that we, for the great affection that we have for our dear brother in God, Walter Disse, and as a work of charity, we have granted to the said Walter Disse ten pounds sterling taken from the proceeds of our manor of Gimingham, in the county of Norfolk in the hands of our receiver whoever that is at

> the time or will be at the times of the terms of Easter and of Saint Michael by equal portions , for the time that he will be our confessor, In witness, etc. Given, etc. at Hertford the 12th day of January, the 48th year [of King Edward III]…"

As the confessor for such an important family, Disse had a secretary/assistant and three or four stableboys to look after his horses and his baggage.

From 1376-1379, Disse appears to have had a break from his duties as John of Gaunt's confessor, as his name does not feature in Gaunt's accounts. In 1376, Disse was the prior of the community in Norwich, and his signature occurs on an agreement between the community and the Benedictine monastery, over the sharing of stipends, when the Carmelites were asked to bury a parishioner from any of the parishes around the monastery.

Disse was back serving as the Duke of Gaunt's confessor in 1380, and his name appears regularly in the accounts again. In 1382, Disse attended the sessions of the council summoned by the Archbishop of Canterbury, to examine 24 propositions taken from the writings of John Wyclif and three of his followers. The council met in Blackfriars, the Dominican house in London, in five sessions between May 21st to June 1st. Initially, John of Gaunt looked favourably on Wyclif's ideas but, by 1382, Wyclif's writings had become more extreme, and Gaunt withdrew his support. Having his confessor on the panel of theologians advising the archbishop would have kept Gaunt abreast of affairs without being directly involved.

However, John of Gaunt's ambitions soon took a new direction when he sought to claim the crown of Castile, in virtue of his marriage to Constance of Castile (see Chapter 14). In 1386, John of Gaunt planned an armed expedition to enforce his claim and, as this was the time of the papal schism, the expedition took the character of a crusade. Spain gave allegiance to the antipope Clement VII in Avignon, whilst England followed Pope Urban VI in Rome. Disse became involved with efforts to raise funds to support Gaunt's expedition. In company with the bishops of Llandaff, Hereford and Dax in Gascony, Disse was given the power by Pope Urban, to re-consecrate all churches, cemeteries, etc. which had become polluted in England and Spain. These four nuncios were also given the authority to create 50 papal chaplains, 50 papal notaries, and to appoint to priestly orders all those who suffered any impediment due to being born outside of a legal marriage, etc. Obviously, such powers were to be dispensed in return for a generous donation to support Gaunt's expedition. The consequences of these faculties and indulgences aroused much opposition as, it was claimed that many of these faculties were granted to very unworthy persons. The appointment to a papal chaplaincy, for instance, gave great freedom to individual monks and friars. The appointment released the individual from obedience to his religious superiors, and conferred the right to be absent from his community. In one instance, the Augustinian friar, Peter Pateshull, celebrated receiving a papal chaplaincy by going to London and trying to incite a mob to burn down the religious houses there as dens of iniquity!

At the general chapter held in Brescia in May 1387, Disse was appointed titular provincial of Spain, but there is no evidence that he accompanied Gaunt on his expedition into Spain. Gaunt's venture in Spain was a failure as the King of Castille refused to meet his army in battle, and Gaunt's soldiers were left scavenging for food and many of them died of disease. Gaunt was in Gascony, late in 1387, and remained there for a year. During that time, Gaunt signed a peace treaty with Spain, and arranged for his daughter Catherine to marry Enrique, the recognised heir to the throne of Castle. Interestingly, she took the Carmelite friar, John Mepsale*, with her as her confessor.

Following the failure of Gaunt's expedition, pope Urban VI, on January 16th, 1389, withdrew the privileges which he had granted to Disse and the three bishops. However, some time before 1391, Disse was appointed the papal nuncio for England, Castile, Léon, Navarre, Portugal and Aragon. There is a claim by an eighteenth-century Portuguese chronicler that Disse visited Lisbon in 1397, having been sent there as papal nuncio and legate *a latere* by Pope Boniface IX. The Constable of Portugal, Alvares Pereira Nuño, ordered that he should be accommodated in the newly founded Carmelite house in Lisbon. This house had been financed by the Constable himself and, on his retirement a few years later, he entered the community there as a lay brother. He lived a very holy life and has been beatified. Pereira claims that, during his stay, Disse impressed everyone by his devout life, his eloquence and his learning. Many people came to consult him, and all were sad to see him depart.

Disse was back in England by April 1399, when he is recorded as being present at the trial of William Sawtrey in Norwich. Disse seems to have spent the remaining years of his life in the Carmelite house in Norwich, and he would have been there in September 1401, when the Archbishop of Canterbury stayed in the house, whilst settling a dispute between the bishop of Norwich and the monks in the cathedral priory. Disse died in Norwich on January 21st, 1404 and was buried in the chapel there. He was remembered as a generous donor to the

Carmelite house in King's Lynn. He was listed as venerable in some old Carmelite calendars with a feast day on January 20th.

Disse left behind a number of works. There was a collection of *Determinations* (public disputations) which he conducted against the followers of John Wyclif. These were probably given during his time in Cambridge. He composed a lecture on some of the Psalms, which was given either in Cambridge or Norwich. In addition, he composed three collections of sermons, and a collection of theological questions, again probably debated at Cambridge. Sadly none of these has survived.

**References:**

*BRCEW* 446-449: *ODNB* 16, 301-302

# 22

# WILLIAM SOUTHFIELD

**(†1414)**

Remains of the Anchorite Cell, Carmelite House, Norwich

During the years from their arrival in 1242, up to the dissolution of the Order in 1538, the English Carmelites produced only one recognised saint, Simon Stock (see Chapter 2). His cult and popular devotion to the scapular vision, emerged during the fifteenth century, without any formal canonization process. However, this does not mean that there were not numerous holy and devoted Carmelites in the early centuries. One who deserves to be remembered was William Southfield, who joined the Carmelite community in Norwich, in the late 14th century.

All that is known about Southfield comes from two sources. The first is the Carmelite historian John Bale*, who entered the same community in Norwich in 1507. Although all those who had known Southfield were dead by the time

Bale joined the Order, there would have been stories circulating in the community about him, and it is likely that Bale had access to some written records about his holy life and remarkable deeds. The historical details in Bale's own account of Southfield's life may be questioned but he gives a very attractive portrait of Southfield which is worth quoting in full:

> "At this time, there was living in the monastery at Norwich the worthy and holy man of God William Southfield, who was born in the county of Norfolk. Received into the Carmelite family in early youth, after his sacred initiation, he gave himself diligently and wholly to the study of divine law and the sacred ceremonies. He was a man of great simplicity and gifted with tremendous devotion; excelling the devoted with his devotions and the pious with his piety and compassion. He neglected nothing that would help him to attain the highest state of life. Both in his lifetime and after his death he worked miracles. He was a truly venerable man, of lively countenance, with a revered and kindly expression. He was pleasant and measured in his speech, and dressed in simple, rough clothes. Placing all his trust in God, he gave himself wholly to the demands of the faith and of his devotion to the mother of God, to whom he said the angelic salutation [the angelus] a thousand times each day. Nor was he content with these, but had this prayer always on his lips and it seemed that he could never say it enough. He observed all the fasts, gave himself wholly to prayer, kept watch over all his actions, was of proven virtue, and, as a result, was granted wonderful visions.
>
> Mary, the Mother of Christ often came to speak with him, and was so gracious to him that she was often seen and heard, through chinks in the walls of his cell, saying the divine office with him. Especially he cultivated humility of heart and bodily mortification. It is recorded of this good William, that he once rescued the monastery from fire, fanning the flames with his scapular, which caused the strength and direction of the blaze to retreat. He did many other notable things, which it would take too long to relate."

Our other source is unique in that it comes from a woman who actually met William Southfield. This was the famous mystic Margery Kempe, a housewife from King's Lynn, who experienced some very intense religious experiences, which led to her weeping and crying out loud in church. Margery had consulted a Carmelite in the King's Lynn community, Aleyn Warnekyn of Lynn*, who supported and encouraged her. However, Margery Kempe aroused some mixed reactions among church authorities, so Aleyn Warnekyn was rebuked by his provincial, Thomas Netter*, and forbidden to speak with her for a while.

Sometime between 1410-1413, Margery Kempe travelled to Norwich to consult with the anchorite Julian of Norwich. She also met with Richard Caister, the vicar of St Stephen's church and with William Southfield. In her autobiography, Margery describes her meeting with William Southfield as follows:

> "This creature [Margery herself] was charged and commanded in her soul that she should go to a White Friar, in the same city of Norwich, who was called William Southfield, a good man who lived a holy life, to reveal to him the grace that God had wrought in her, as she had done to the good Vicar before. She did as she was commanded, and came to the friar one morning and was with him in a chapel for a long time, and told him her meditations and what God had wrought in her soul, in order to know if she were deceived by any delusions or not.
>
> This good man, the White Friar, all the time that she told him of her feelings, held up his hands and said: 'Jesus, mercy, and thanks be to Jesus'.
>
> 'Sister', he said, 'have no fear about your manner of life, for it is the Holy Ghost plentifully working his grace in your soul. Thank him highly of his goodness, for we are all bound to thank him for you, who now in our times inspires you with his grace, to the help and comfort of all of us who are supported by your prayers and by others such as you. And we are preserved from many misfortunes and troubles which we should deservedly suffer for our trespasses, were there not such good creatures among us. Blessed be Almighty God for his goodness.
>
> 'And therefore, sister, I advise you to dispose yourself to receive the gifts of God as lowly and meekly as you can, and put up no obstacle or objections against the goodness of the Holy Ghost, for he may give his gifts where he will, and the unworthy he makes worthy, the sinful he makes righteous. His mercy is always ready for us, unless the fault be in ourselves, for he does not dwell in a body subject to sin. He flies from all false pretence and falsehood: he asks of us a low, a meek, and a contrite heart, with a good will. Our Lord says himself: 'My Spirit shall rest upon a meek man, a contrite man, and one who fears my words.'
>
> 'Sister, I trust to our Lord that you have these conditions either in your will or your affections, or else in both, and I do not consider that our Lord allows to be endlessly deceived those who place their trust in him, and seek and desire nothing but him only, as I hope you do. And therefore believe fully that our Lord loves you and is working his grace in you. I pray God increase it and continue it to his everlasting worship, for his mercy.'
>
> The said creature was much comforted both in body and in soul by this good man's words, and greatly strengthened in her faith."

Southfield died on Aug 26th, 1414, and was buried in the Carmelite church in Norwich under a marble tomb. Bale claims that his body stayed incorrupt for a long time after his death. The epitaph on his tomb was:

> "Come to the aid of those who pray to you, kind father William".

**References:**

*BRCEW* 470-471:

# 23

# ROBERT MASCALL

**(†1416)**

Plaque commemorating the site of the Carmelite Friary, Ludlow where Robert Mascall became a Carmelite

In the second half of the 14th century, as England was recovering from the ravages of the Black Death, the Carmelite Order flourished, and it attracted some outstanding scholars and gifted preachers. Among these was Robert Mascall. He was born in Wales, probably to a wealthy family, and joined the Carmelite community in Ludlow, where he made his profession in 1366. His intellectual ability soon became evident and, after his basic formation, he was sent to Oxford, the senior house in that Carmelite distinction or region, to undertake further studies in theology. He completed the two year course in the house of studies there, and was awarded his licence in theology (S.T.L.), an internal award of the Order which qualified him to teach theology. It appears that he then returned to Ludlow to teach the young students there, for a few years before returning to Oxford to continue his studies for a doctorate.

In 1381, Mascall's qualities had become known to his higher superiors and, at the general chapter held in Verona at Pentecost that year, "lector Robert Maracher" was appointed as the bachelor in theology, at the Order's General Curia in Rome. The wording suggests that Mascall had been continuing his studies at Oxford, and was on the brink of qualifying as a bachelor in theology. Once this degree was awarded, he departed for Rome, where he was to assist in the teaching of the students there in the newly re-established General Curia, following the transfer of the papal residence from Avignon to Rome in 1377. Another consequence of the transfer to Rome, was the loss of access to the student house in Paris, as the Carmelite friars in France gave their allegiance to the anti-pope Clement VII, who now resided in Avignon.

Exactly how long Mascall remained in Rome is uncertain, as the post of bachelor in the Curia, was not mentioned in the Acts of the next General Chapter held in Bamberg in 1385, and the position was given to another in the following General Chapter, which was held in Brescia in 1387. What seems likely is that Mascall, after serving for some years in Rome, took the opportunity to return to Oxford, to complete his studies for the doctorate. He could have secured a doctorate from the Order whilst he was in Rome, but such awards were frowned upon by the authorities in Oxford and Cambridge, and not generally recognised in England. Mascall had completed his studies for the doctorate, passed his year as *magister regens* (principal lecturer) in the Carmelite house in Oxford, and returned to Ludlow as prior before 1393, because he is recorded as being one of the doctors in theology who were present at the trial of the Lollard – Walter Brut – held in Hereford in October of that year.

At this point, as a respected doctor in theology, Mascall's career began to flourish. On February 2nd, 1396, he preached before King Richard II, in the Carmelite church in Nottingham, for which he received the princely sum of 40s. After the deposition of Richard in 1399, Mascall quickly moved to support the new King Henry IV. He was appointed as confessor to the king, and, in preparation for the new king's coronation on September 30th, he was granted:

> "Of a similar gift for this occasion, to Brother Robert of the Carmelite Order, the Confessor of our Lord the King, and to his companion, that is to the said brother, eight ells of blanket cloth long, and to his companion, four ells of cloth, for making up."

This gift was to ensure that Mascall and his companion might be suitably attired for the coronation ceremony. Mascall served as confessor for the king for the next few years and, on November 6th, 1401, he was given a royal grant of £69 10s 6d. per year to cover his own expenses:

> Grant to Robert Mascal of the order of Friars Carmelites, the king's confessor, whom the king has charged to stay continually about his person for the safety of his soul, for the maintenance of himself and his fellow and his men and servants within the household and four horses and one 'hakeney', of 3s. daily, amounting to £54 12s. yearly, for the wages of each of four grooms keeping the horses 1½d. daily, amounting to £9 2s. 6d. yearly, and for other small necessaries 116s. yearly, all of which sums amount to £69 10s. 6d. yearly, to be received yearly at the Exchequer from the day of the coronation so long as he shall be the king's confessor, as William Syward, confessor of Edward III, had."

Sadly, Mascall's tenure as the king's confessor came to an abrupt end, on January 4th, 1404, when Parliament demanded the dismissal of various members of the king's household, including Mascall. Shortly after, on February 9th, Mascall and two other royal servants appeared before Parliament to answer for their behaviour but, although King Henry disagreed with the order for their dismissal, he was forced to accept it.

A few weeks later, on March 29th, the bishop of Hereford, Thomas Treffnant. died and King Henry decided to put Mascall's name forward as the next bishop. However, there were other candidates proposed for the See, so Mascall set off for Rome, in order to plead his case in person before the Holy See. His efforts there were successful, and he was provided to the diocese on July 2nd, 1404, and he was consecrated bishop in Rome on July 6th.

Unfortunately, while returning to England in late August, Mascall encountered some unexpected difficulties. As he was crossing the Channel, the ship in which he was travelling was seized by Flemish pirates, who imprisoned the passengers and crew in Dunkirk, and held them for ransom. This action was in response to an attack by English soldiers on the island of Wulpen, on August 14th, where they had pulled the church down, set fire to the houses and robbed the inhabitants. In order to secure his release, King Henry IV had to write a letter to the Duchess of Burgundy on September 10th:

> "Be pleased to know that it is come to our notice by a relation made to us by men worthy of credit, that your subjects of Flanders, who are lying in ambush along the sea coast with a view to committing all the evil that they are able upon our lieges, have just recently captured a ship, in the which our most dearly beloved in God, Brother Robert Mascall, lately our Confessor, was proceeding on his way from Middleburgh towards our realm; and after that your said subjects had thrust all hands out of the ship

> into the sea, they sent away the said Brother Robert to Dunkirk within your said lordship; and there they detain the same Robert as their prisoner, and will not deliver him out of their custody without his paying them a sum of money and a ransom, to the final destruction of his poor estate, as it is said. Whereof we have great cause to wonder, since at the urgent instance and desire of the merchants of your said lordship, and especially of the three towns of your country of Flanders, and on the suggestion of your friendly letters, recently sent as well to us, as to our commissaries at that time residing at our town of Calais, a treaty was arranged between your commissaries and our own, which is still pending, whereof I hope God may give a good conclusion, in case such outrages and attempts be not a cause for the contrary and for the rupture of it. – Therefore we pray you with all affection, and require you, high and mighty Princess, that you would command your said subjects that they give the said Robert his liberty without compelling him to pay his ransom, or doing him any other damage, even as you would desire that we should do to you in a similar case. For of a truth, high and mighty Princess, we cannot and will not endure such horrible proceedings any longer. – High and mighty Princess, be pleased to certify to us, as soon as you possibly can, that which you deem it right to do out of regard for us in this behalf. And may our Lord be pleased to have you always in his holy keeping. Given under our signet, at our Castle of Tutbury, the 10th day of September."

There were three of the king's ambassadors in Calais at this time, negotiating a treaty with the Duchy of Burgundy. These forwarded the king's letter to the duchess, on September 16th, and added their own pleas for Mascall's release, as well as for the English fishermen who had been seized with him. They sent a second letter on September 28th, and then addressed a third letter on October 1st, which was addressed to the Four Members of Flanders. (The Four Members of Flanders were the towns of Bruges, Ghent and Ypres together with the Franc of Bruges, which was an area outside of Bruges. The four formed a medieval parliament and were a powerful body in Flanders). Another letter was sent to the duchess on October 3rd, seeking Mascall's release. The duchess replied to these letters on October 6th, from Arras, protesting that she had forbidden her subjects from harming the English, but their actions had been provoked by the attack on Wulpen.

Meanwhile the ambassadors wrote to the archbishop of Canterbury on October 6th, and to the king on October 11th, giving an account of their efforts to secure Mascall's release. One of the ambassadors, Nicholas Rysshetoun, returned to England, where he consulted with the king, who was in Coventry where Parliament was meeting, and from there, on November 2nd, Rysshetoun sent a further letter to the duchess. Rysshetoun, however, was out of touch with the latest developments, as it appeared that Mascall had been released some weeks earlier, and was residing in the bishop of Hereford's house in London since October 4th.

Now safely back in England, Mascall spent the next two years staying in his London residence, and serving the king. One of his servants, was appointed to act in his place, in any judicial matters in his diocese. On June 7th, 1406, Mascall was present when Parliament met in Westminster, and his signature occurs among those of the bishops who signed the two acts confirming the coronation of Henry IV, and declaring their loyalty to him.

On October 4th, 1405, Mascall attended a meeting of the Great Council which was held in Worcester. Then, on December 22nd, he was back in Westminster at Parliament, and his signature occurs on two more documents. In the meantime, Mascall's diocese was suffering from raids by the Welsh followers of Owain Glyndŵr; moreover there is a record of a royal grant of £10 towards the costs of repairing the damages, which the diocese had suffered.

From 1406, Mascall took his diocesan duties more seriously, and his register records him travelling between his house in London and his diocese, where he resided in his manor in Prestbury, or his other manor in Whitbourne. Possibly, Mascall was feeling the effects of his increasing years. By now he was in his late 50's, and so welcomed the more restful life he could live in his largely rural diocese. Mascall's register records him regularly conducting ordinations in his cathedral. However, royal and other important duties still demanded his presence elsewhere. From October to December 1407, he attended the Parliament held in Gloucester, where he was appointed as one of the triers of the petitions from England, Wales and Scotland. Also, he was regularly in London, attending, for example, a meeting of the Great Council which was held in Lambeth on March 19th, 1411, and taking his place at the convocation of the clergy, called by the Archbishop of Canterbury, which met in St Paul's cathedral the same year.

Mascall was back attending Parliament and convocation early in 1413, but sadly the routine of the events was disrupted when King Henry IV died on March 20th, whilst Parliament was sitting in Westminster. It is likely that Mascall would have attended the king's funeral rites in London, but there is no evidence that he travelled later in the year to Canterbury for the king's interment in his tomb, in the nave of Canterbury cathedral. However, with the accession of King Henry V, Mascall was probably relieved to see another Carmelite called Stephen Patryngton* being appointed as the king's confessor.

Under the new King Henry V, Mascall's routine continued to be very demanding and he was back in London in November 1414, attending the meeting of Parliament when, this time, he was appointed a trier of the petitions from Gascony. The same procedure was repeated the following year, when Parliament met in Westminster in November 1415, followed by convocation later the same month. Mascall's register shows that he was back in his manor at Whitbourne for Christmas 1415, and remained there until the end of January. Then he was, once more, travelling the 130 miles, through the cold and rain, to London. He attended the meetings of convocation on April 1st and May 7th. He was in St Paul's cathedral again on May 31st, where he assisted at the consecration of John Wakering as bishop of Norwich.

Soon afterwards, Mascall made his way back to his diocese, where he is recorded as conducting a series of ordinations from June 12th until September 19th. However, he did take a pleasant break in the middle of August, when he attended the Carmelite provincial chapter, which was held in his diocese at the Carmelite house in Ludlow. The choice of Ludlow was special as it allowed the chapter delegates to celebrate Mascall's golden jubilee (50 years), as a Carmelite. There was a solemn mass at which the prior provincial, Thomas Netter* preached the sermon, which began:

> "A jubilee blessing on you, lord father, and with your permission, brother..."

Doubtless after the mass, there was a suitable celebratory meal. In spite of his increasing ill-health, Mascall was soon back on the road to London, where he was present in Parliament on October 19th, when his signature appears as one of the guarantors of a loan. Then, on October 27th, he was able to obtain a special pardon for his steward, Thomas Berkeley, a canon in the cathedral, who had been indicted before the King's Bench in Worcester, for the murder of John Milleward, a yeoman. Sadly, Mascall's health deteriorated further and, on November 23rd, he composed his will, and then added a further codicil on December 16th. He died on December 22nd, 1416. In his will, Mascall asked that he should:

> "... be buried in the vault (*arcum ecclesie*) of the church of the Carmelite friars in Ludlow..."

However, his wish was not followed and Mascall was interred in the Carmelite church in London.

Mascall was not a great writer and, according to John Bale*, he left behind him only some collections of sermons and speeches, now all sadly lost. However, his bishop's register survives and has been edited by the Canterbury and York Society. Apart from his formal acts as a bishop, his register contains a number of letters, addressed to various persons in his diocese. One example is a letter which he wrote to his clergy, on September 22nd, 1410, forbidding the superstitious worship of a well in the parish of Turnaston:

> "Robert, to the Dean of Hereford our official and all the Clergy in our county and diocese, greeting etc.:
>
> Although it is provided in the divine laws and sacred canons that all who shall adore a stone, spring or other creature of God, incur the charge of idolatry, it has come to our ears, we grieve to say, from the report of many credible witnesses and the common report of the people, that many of our subjects are in large numbers visiting a certain well and stone at Turnaston in our diocese where with genuflections and offerings they, without authority of the Church, wrongfully worship the said stone and well, whereby committing idolatry; when the water fails they take away with them the mud of the same and treat and keep it as a relic to the grave peril of their souls and a pernicious example to others. Therefore, we suspend the use of the said well and stone and under pain of greater excommunication forbid our people to visit the well and stone for purposes of worship. And we depute to each and all of you and firmly enjoin by virtue of holy obedience, to proclaim publicly in your churches and parishes that they are not to visit the place for such purposes.
>
> Given at Wormsley Sept. 22 in the year aforesaid."

During his life, Mascall maintained contact with his Carmelite brethren, and one of his generous acts was to finance the rebuilding of the Carmelite church in Ludlow. Nor did he forget the problems faced by the Carmelites studying in Oxford, his own university, and he sold some land to provide two pensions one of £4 per year and one of £3 to help Carmelite students in Oxford. These pensions were still being paid until 1538, when the prior sold them.

Robert Mascall was a good example of someone who placed his life at the service of others. Entering the Carmelites, he devoted his life to God, using his talents, first in his studies, then in the service of the prior general, and the king. In his later years, he was noted by his care for his diocese. His travels alone give witness to his great energy and dedication, and he set an example which hopefully inspired his fellow Carmelites.

**References:**

*BRCEW* 344-347: *ODNB* 37, 138-139

Ann Rhydderch, "Robert Mascall and John Stanbury: King's Confessors and Bishops of Hereford", M.A. thesis, University of Wales, University College of Swansea, 1974).

Robert Mascall's register as bishop of Hereford was published by the Canterbury & York Society in 1917.

# 24

# STEPHEN OF PATRYNGTON

**(†1417)**

Portrait of Stephen Patryngton, as Bishop of Chichester

One of the most notable Carmelites in the late 14th century was Stephen of Patryngton. Born in Yorkshire around 1345, he joined the Order in York. His name first occurs in the records, when he was ordained acolyte, in St Leonard's Hospital chapel, York, on 19 December 1366. Patryngton continued his studies in York and was ordained priest on June 8th, 1370, in Bishopthorpe manor chapel. After ordination, Patryngton was sent to pursue further studies in theology in Oxford.

In Oxford, Patryngton's qualities as a leader were soon recognised, and he was listed as prior there on November 24th, 1373, when he received a licence to hear confessions in the diocese of Canterbury. He had gained his B.Th. and was back in office as prior on June 12th, 1382, when he attended the second session of the Council, convened by Archbishop Courtenay, at Blackfriars in London, to examine a number of propositions taken from the writings of John Wyclif and his followers. At this period, Patryngton was frequently absent from the university on royal duties and so on July14th, it became necessary for the king to issue an instruction to the chancellor and proctors of the university, not to censure him for his absence.

Patryngton probably incepted as a Doctor of Theology sometime around 1384-1385,and from then on his reputation began to spread, and he was in demand as a preacher and confessor. On January 14th, 1390, he was licensed to lecture and preach in Lincoln cathedral, as the deputy for the chancellor of the university. Then, during the 1390's, Patryngton served as the confessor for John of Gaunt, the Duke of Lancaster, and his wife, replacing another Carmelite, Walter Disse*. On 26 April 1399, Patryngton was given a grant of £10 per year for life, for his "good service to the Duke and his Duchess".

In 1396, Patryngton wrote to Thomas Arundel, Archbishop of Canterbury, protesting against a petition which was to be presented to Parliament, forbidding religious orders to accept any one below the age of twenty years. In the event, after many protests from all the religious orders, Henry IV reduced the age level to 14 years, and this was approved by the Commons, when they met in October & November that year.

At the provincial chapter held in Sutton, near Plymouth, in August 1399, Patryngton's career took another direction, as he was elected provincial for the English province. One of his early acts occurred in 1402 when he was summoned to attend Parliament. King Henry IV had ordered the leaders of the four mendicant orders to present themselves before Parliament and swear an oath that they and their successors would henceforth observe the statute about not accepting applicants who were less than 14 years of age. Then, later that year, on Christmas Day 1402, Patryngton preached before the King and the royal family at Windsor Castle.

Patryngton appears to have been an active and effective provincial and a number of his letters survive. Three of them are appeals to the king, asking for the arrest and return of friars who had run away. There are also three letters of confraternity, signed by Patryngton which were granted to prominent patrons of the Order. These letters appointed the recipients as *confraters*, that is "brothers" of the Carmelite family, who would share in all the graces and blessings derived from the prayers, good works, fastings, etc. which were performed by the Carmelite friars. When they died, the recipients would have masses said, and prayers offered for them, just the same as was done on the death of a friar.

In 1412, Patryngton is recorded as being present in Winchester College, when a feast was held to mark the reaching of an agreement between the College authorities and the local Carmelite community. The Carmelite house stood alongside the College and, following the suppression of all the religious orders in 1538, the property was granted to the College. The College infirmary was built on the site and remained there for many years.

At the end of 1413, Patryngton was appointed as chaplain to King Henry V. This was an important position, which was reflected in Patryngton's salary. He was paid 3s. per day for himself and one companion as his assistant, but he had to live in the king's hostel, wear the king's livery and keep four horses for riding and a hackney for pulling a cart. Each horse had a groom who was paid 1½d. a day. The total annuity paid to Patryngton amounted to £69 10s. 6d. However, Patryngton's royal duties meant that he could no longer serve as provincial, so he resigned his office in 1414. Then, on February 1st, 1415, Patryngton was appointed as bishop of St. David's, in Wales, and he was consecrated by the Archbishop of Canterbury in All Saints' Church, Maidstone on June 19th, 1415. King Henry V was present and so was the newly elected Carmelite provincial Thomas Netter*, accompanied probably by friars from the nearby Carmelite community in Aylesford.

Although a bishop, Patryngton's first priority was still to serve the king and so, after his consecration, he returned to London where he appointed two vicars-general, who were to look after the affairs of the diocese in his absence. Four folios of Patryngton's episcopal register survive so it is possible to trace some of his movements. Patryngton remained at the side of King Henry V as preparations were made for the king's expedition to France. He accompanied the king as Henry made his way down to Southampton. On July 1st, the royal party stopped at Winchester. Patryngton remained there for three weeks, collecting details of the clergy who would be available for the defence of the country, during the king's absence. Then, Patryngton hastened to join the king in Southampton, when he acted as a witness to the King's will. In the will, there was a generous bequest to Patryngton:

> "Item. We leave to the reverend father Stephen, bishop of St. David's, the better altar from our private room, together with its chalice, paten, cruet and gold pax."

From Southampton, Patryngton accompanied the King to Portchester Castle, near Portsmouth, where the troops and ships were gathering. He was there on July 27th, and remained at the King's side for two weeks until the expedition set sail for France. Then, he returned to London.

Just before the king departed for France, the bishop of Chichester had died in June 1415, and Patryngton was keen to be transferred to the now vacant and much richer diocese of Chichester. It seems that King Henry V gave some indication that Patryngton would be a suitable candidate and so, whilst he was in Portchester, Patryngton appointed two proctors to further his suit in Rome. Unfortunately, Patryngton's suit quickly ran into difficulties as Pope Gregory XII had died on July 4th, and hence any papal decision had to wait for over a year until the election of Pope Martin V on November 1st, 1417. Patryngton's selection, though, as the new bishop, must have been seen as a foregone conclusion, as his petition to have the income from the see during the vacancy, was granted by the king on August 25th, 1416.

On September 4th, 1416, Patryngton was present at a meeting in the Carmelite house in Sandwich, together with King Henry V, the Archbishop of Canterbury, the Bishop of Durham and other nobles. At this meeting, the Bishop of Winchester handed over the great seal, before he departed with the King for Calais. It is possible that Patryngton accompanied the king to Calais, where there was a meeting between King Henry V, the Holy Roman Emperor Sigismund and John I, the Duke of Burgundy, where they agreed to form an alliance against France.

The following year, Patryngton was engaged in a round of duties. On April 18th, 1417, he was in Windsor Castle chapel, where he took part in the consecration of Edmund Lacy as Bishop of Hereford. Then on May 1st, he was in St Paul's Cathedral, London, when Lord Lestrange and others were indicted for attacking Sir John Trussell in St Dunstan's Church on Easter Sunday.

Later that year, it appears that Patryngton received orders from the king to accompany him abroad and, on November 6th, 1417, he received a licence to hear the confessions of those on service in the king's army abroad, and to grant absolution even in specially reserved cases. Then two days later, on November 8th, he was granted letters of protection, before going overseas with the king to the Council of Constance. Finally, on December 15th, Patryngton received the long-awaited papal bull authorising his translation to the diocese of Chichester. On December 21st, the Pope wrote to the Archbishop of Canterbury authorising him to receive the oath of fealty from Patryngton. All was now ready for

Patryngton to be appointed to the most senior diocese ever entrusted to an English Carmelite. Sadly, providence intervened as Patryngton fell ill in November and died on December 22nd, before he could be installed as the new bishop in Chichester. Patryngton's will was dated November 16th, and in it he made cash bequests of over £80. He left his mitre and pastoral staff to his cathedral in St David's, and two silver basins and two silver candlesticks to the cathedral in Chichester. Strangely enough there are no bequests to his Carmelite brethren, and even the Carmelite church in London, where he was buried, was specifically excluded, as he had *"specially donated other goods of mine to those of this house and convent."* Fortunately, our Carmelite historian, John Bale*, has preserved the epitaph on his tomb:

> Here lies the body of brother Stephen of Patryngton,
> He left a reputation as a father, exemplar of the rule,
> Leader of the Carmelite body, doctor, prior of the English;
> Confessor of Henry V, a famous king and
> his companion, and also bishop of St David's,
> May Christ, for him, change his cap into a golden one,
> For he was made to hold together, well employed,
> The mitre of a bishop and the title of a doctor.

Sadly, most of Patryngton's writings, which date from his time teaching in Oxford, have been lost. Apart from official letters and documents, mentioned above, there is a collection of disputed questions, which were debated at Oxford, which has been attributed to Patryngton. Finally, there are some theological notes which were collected by Patryngton, when he was a student at Oxford. These survive is a notebook, giving an interesting glimpse into the syllabus covered by theology students in the 14th century. The text ends with the attribution:

> "Thus ends the collection of articles by magister Stephen of Patryngton that he collected together in Oxford and elsewhere before he was awarded his doctorate."

**References:**

*BRCEW* 427-429: *ODNB* 43, 968

Leonard Kennedy, C.S.B., "A Carmelite 14th Century Theological Notebook", *Carmelus*, 33 (1986), 70-102.

# 25

# THOMAS PEVEREL

## (1419)

Worcester Cathedral where Thomas Peverel was bishop from 1407-1419.

A wide range of candidates entered the Carmelite Order during the Middle Ages. Most of them came from very humble backgrounds, and their parents worked as farm labourers, or were workers employed in the towns. Some were from the better-off merchant families in the towns, or from the families of local officials, who were employed by the town or who held crown appointments. Finally, a small but significant number of vocations came from wealthy or noble families, and one of the most notable of these was Thomas Peverel. John Bale* claimed that he was born in Suffolk, and joined one of the communities in the Norwich Distinction.

Peverel's name first occurs in the records on September 29th, 1377, when he is listed among the friars in the community at King's Lynn, who signed an agreement over a corrody, for Hugh and Cecily Elyngham. A corrody was a practice whereby an elderly person, or husband and wife, could spend the remainder of their years living in a religious house. In return for a substantial donation, the individual or couple would be given suitable accommodation or pay for it to be built, and they would be provided with food each day from the community kitchen. They would be able to attend the daily community mass, and the divine office, if they desired. The agreement for Hugh and Cecily Elyngham stated that they would be provided with a hall with two rooms, so these were arranged, one above the other, complete with two chimneys, and two toilets at the main end of the hall, near the friars' refectory. At the other end of the hall, there was to be a lower room, which served as a store, and a second for food and other necessities. A further room, above the two lower stores, contained a small stove with a chimney. All were to be built and constructed by the prior and community, attached to the second cloister between the refectory and the new infirmary, and with free access to the nearby gate. There is no record of what the financial contribution of the Elynghams was, to cover the cost of the building, their food and maintenance, whilst in the priory.

At this period, King's Lynn served as the study centre for the smaller houses in the Norwich distinction, where students could be sent prepare for the priesthood. However, Peverel seems to have stayed there only for a short period and, as a particularly talented student, he was transferred the following year to Norwich, to complete his studies. Then, he was sent to Oxford for higher studies, and he became a bachelor in theology by May 1392, when he attended the council convened by the archbishop of Canterbury, in the Carmelite house in Stamford, for the trial of the Cistercian monk, Henry Crumpe, a follower of John Wyclif.

However, Peverel never completed his doctorate at Oxford. The Carmelite Prior General, Giovanni da Rhò, conducted a visitation of the province in 1391-139, and became aware of the talented student at Oxford. It is possible he met Peverel sometime during his visitation, and hence when the next General Chapter met in May, the following year in Frankfurt, Peverel was appointed as second *socius* (assistant) to the Prior General. Peverel occupied this position for two years and evidently made a good impression as, on October 25th, 1395, he was appointed to be bishop of Ossory in Ireland. On the same day, Pope Boniface IX wrote a letter to King Richard II, asking the king to take Peverel into his favour. The Pope's letter appears to indicate that Peverel's future lay in royal service, rather than in the pastoral care of his diocese. Following Peverel's return, on May 19th, 1396, he was granted a licence to reside in England, whilst receiving the income from his diocese. He named two clerics to act as his attorneys in Ossory.

Peverel's service to King Richard II was evidently appreciated and, after two years, he was transferred to be bishop of Llandaff in South Wales, and, on July 2nd, 1398, the bishops of London and Carlisle were ordered to receive the oath of fealty from Peverel, for his new diocese. The following year, on March 17th, 1399, Peverel was appointed as chancellor to Queen Isabella, the new wife of King Richard II. She was only 9 years old. However, in July that year, Henry, son of John of Gaunt, returned from exile to lead a rebellion against Richard II. As Richard was away in Ireland, Henry quickly seized control of England, and Peverel gave him his support. On October 23rd, 1399, he was one of the nobles who agreed to the secret custody of Richard II. Following Richard's death. Henry was crowned as King Henry IV, and Peverel appears to have retreated to his cathedral in Llandaff. However, in the summer of 1402, a rebellion broke out in Wales, led by Owain Glyn Dwr, and this forced Peverel to flee from his diocese. On August 12th, 1405, Peverel was granted protection for one year on going into Wales with King Henry IV. However, Llandaff remained too dangerous a place, especially as Glyn Dwr was planning to set up a rival episcopate, owing allegiance to Clement, the anti-pope in Avignon.

On June 27th, 1406, Peverel added his seal to the act which bestowed the English crown on the male heirs of both Henry IV and Henry V. Then, on July 4th, 1407, Peverel was appointed as bishop of Worcester. It seems likely that he was named to this important diocese as a reward for his continued support of Henry IV. In the event, Peverel proved to be a very pastoral-minded bishop. His increasing age, now over fifty years old, probably prevented him from much travelling. From his register, which still survives, it can be seen that Peverel remained mostly in his diocese, travelling around and attending to diocesan matters and the needs of his people. Still, Peverel's support for both Henry IV and his son Henry V continued and he is recorded as lending them large sums of money.

On May 31st, 1416, Peverel was in London, and is recorded as being one of the Principal Co-Consecrators, when John Wakering was consecrated as bishop of Norwich in Saint Paul's cathedral, London.

An interesting glimpse into the personality of Peverel is recorded in June 1417, when he was staying in his manor at Henbury, near Bristol. The mystic Margery Kempe was passing through Bristol, and describes in her autobiography, her meeting with the bishop:

> "And immediately afterwards, she was summoned to appear before the Bishop of Worcester, who was staying three miles outside Bristol. She rose early the next day and went to the place where he was – he still being in bed – and happened to meet one of his worthiest men in the town, and so they

talked of God. And when he had heard her talk for a good while, he asked her to eat with him, and afterwards he brought her into the bishop's hall.

When she came into the hall, she saw many of the Bishop's men in clothes very fashionably slashed and cut into points. Lifting up her hand, she blessed herself. And then they said to her, 'What the devil's wrong with you?'

She replied, 'Whose men are you?'

They answered, 'The Bishop's men.'

Then she said, 'No, truly, you are more like the devil's men.'

Then they were annoyed and rebuked her, and spoke angrily to her, and she put up with it very meekly. And afterwards she spoke so seriously against sin and their misconduct that they were silent, and held themselves well pleased with her talk – thanks be to God – before she left.

Then she went into the church and waited for the Bishop to come; and when he came she knelt down and asked what his will was, and why she was summoned to come before him; it was very inconvenient for her, inasmuch as she was a pilgrim, intending by the grace of God to go to Santiago.

Then the Bishop said, 'Margery, I have not summoned you, for I know well enough that you are John Brunham's daughter from Lynn. I beg you not to be angry, but be pleasant with me, and I shall be pleasant with you, for you shall eat with me today.'

'Sir,' she said, 'I beg you to excuse me, because I have promised a good man in town to eat with him today.'

And then he said, ' You shall both eat with me.'

And so she remained with him until God sent wind so that she could sail, and she was made very welcome by him, and by his household as well. Afterwards, she was shriven by the Bishop, and then he asked her to pray for him to die in charity, for he had been warned by a holy man, who had understood by revelation that this Bishop would be dead within the space of two years. And so it happened indeed. And therefore he lamented to this creature and asked her to pray for him, that he might die in charity.

At last she took her leave of him, and he gave her gold and his blessing, and commanded his household to escort her on her way. And he also asked her, when she came back again from Santiago, to come to him.

Later, on April 18th, 1417, Peverel was in Windsor, when he is recorded as being one of the Principal Co-Consecrators, when Edmund Lacy was consecrated as bishop of Hereford, in the presence of King Henry V.

Sadly, Peverel lived only two years longer and, on March 1st, 1419, he died in his manor of Henley, (two years after his meeting with Margery Kempe as prophesied). He was buried in the Carmelite house in Oxford, where he had been a noted benefactor.

There survives a critical comment on Peverel made by an Englishman, who was in Rome at this time. William Swann, a canon of Chichester, was serving as an official in the papal court, and he wrote the following comment on Peverel in his letter book:

> [Peverel was a man of] "evil life and unseemly conversation who spent his time in the company of lords and ladies".

Swann's comment here needs to be treated with some caution as his letter book covers the years c1408-1415, and Peverel served in Rome only from 1393 to 1395. So it seems unlikely that Swann met Peverel in Rome. It is possible, though, that Swann met Peverel on one of his visits to England or, alternatively, that he is reporting comments that he had heard from others. Moreover, in contrast, among his Carmelite brethren, Peverel left a reputation for having lived a devout and dedicated life. In fact, in some of the early Carmelite calendars, he was described as 'venerable' with a feast day on March 1st.

**References:**

*BRCEW* 427-429: *ODNB* 43, 968

# 26

# EMMA STAPLETON

**(†1422)**

Illustration of an Anchorite being enclosed in her Cell.

The Carmelite Order was very slow to to open membership of the Order to women and lay people. This can be partly explained in the early years by the dangerous situation on Mount Carmel, where the first hermits were open to attacks by the surrounding Arab forces. Even after their migration to Europe, the Carmelites found difficulty in being formally recognised and, as has been mentioned earlier, the Order was nearly suppressed at the Second Council of Lyons in 1271. However, towards the end of the 13th century, informal groups of lay persons began to establish links with individual Carmelites churches. This was especially true in Italy where, in a number of towns, individual lay persons made vows to the local Carmelite community. For instance, in 1283, Bonaventura di Misano, made a solemn vow of chastity to the

Carmelite community in Messina, giving all her goods to the community, and receiving a small portion of the income from them for her own personal needs. In Bologna in 1304, Benvenuta Venturoli promised obedience to the Carmelite community there and gave them all her goods. She became a *conversa* or oblate, and the prior put her under obedience to reside in her own house as the taking of religious vows involved being linked with a fixed place of residence. Other examples of lay people taking vows occur in Florence in 1309 and 1343, and Pisa in 1390.

In Florence, lay people wishing to demonstrate their Carmelite links, took part in the public processions on feast days, wearing short white cloaks, to show their devotion to Our Lady of Mount Carmel, and their attachment to the Carmelite community. This practice spread to other Carmelite churches and participants began to group together in recognised groups or confraternities. It is worth noting that the Lay Carmelites in Florence continue to wear short white cloaks during religious ceremonies to this day.

In the course of time, small groups of devoted women, single or widowed, came together, living in common, and to all extents and purposes, acting like professed religious although they could only take private or personal vows, without any formal ecclesiastical approval.

Lay confraternities were also flourishing in other countries, where the Carmelites had communities. In Toulouse, in the late 1270's, there was a confraternity linked with the Carmelite church, numbering thousands of members. Sadly, financial and other problems brought this organisation to an end after a few years. In Bayonne, in 1350, the confraternity of Our Lady of Mount Carmel was founded by the Carmelites, and this lasted for many years.

In England, there is no record of any explicitly Carmelite confraternities, but Carmelite churches hosted many other confraternities and guilds, which used the local Carmelite church. These were independent groups, who were not formally linked to the Carmelite Order, even though many of them would make use of the services of individual Carmelite priests. Apart from providing a chapel or altar, the Carmelites would also make available a space for such groups to meet and even for them to have a monthly meal together. In Coventry, there is evidence that the novices would sing for the members of the confraternity as they dined. One example of such a guild is the Gild of the Conception of the Blessed Virgin Mary, which was founded c.1365. This was described in an official return in 1389 as having been founded:

> "Out of the devotion of certain poor men in honour of the Conception of St. Mary and All Saints. All attend mass on the Feast of the Conception and find 10 candles to burn on festivals before the image. They pay the Carmelites 10s. a year for celebrating for souls, etc. Thirty masses for a dead brother are said at expense of the gild.
>
> Each brother and sister pays 3d. quarterly to the common box. In infirmity or detention in prison or other adversity, 7d a week is given from the box. At death if a brother's goods do not suffice he shall have burial at the gild's expense."

It was not until 1452, that the Carmelite Order obtained a papal bull, *Cum Nulla*, which allowed the Order to establish a Second Order of Carmelite nuns, and a Third Order for lay people. This led to the formal approval for the groups of devoted women, such as those who lived together in community in Florence and elsewhere, and also for the acceptance into the Carmelite Order of some of the Beguines, who were groups of lay women, mostly in the Low Countries.

However, in England, there were no similar groups of devoted lay people living in common, and popular devotion had taken a different path. Devout individuals over the years had chosen to live as hermits or enclosed as anchorites in a local church. With the encouragement of the Provincial Thomas Netter*, the Carmelites granted space for anchorites in a number of their churches. There is evidence for the existence of anchorite cells in the Carmelite houses in Norwich, Cambridge, King's Lynn, and Northampton. Among the anchorites who lived in these cells, the names of only five men and six women have survived. Also, several Carmelite friars lived as recluses or hermits for a period. Richard Misyn* spent time as a recluse in Lincoln in the 1430's at the same time as Thomas Scrope* was doing the same in Norwich. Another Carmelite, Thomas Sylvester, a member of the community in Blakeney, chose to transfer to the Carthusians, where he was granted permission to live as an anchorite in 1493. Other Carmelites such as William Southfield*, were noted for devoting their lives to prayer and contemplation in their cell without any formal rule of enclosure.

Among the women, Alice Wakeleyn and Margaret Hawten are recorded as living at different periods, in the cell in the Carmelite church in Northampton. Other anchorites which are known were Agnes in Ipswich, Joanna Catfelde in King's Lynn, Alice Gransetter in Cambridge and Emma Stapleton in Norwich. These six women anchorites are the only known manifestation of women choosing to live a form of the religious life under Carmelite inspiration in England. Such a choice was, of course, a major undertaking, and the Church laid down strict prescriptions before anyone was allowed to be enclosed. Apart from possession of the necessary spiritual motivation and maturity, an anchorite needed some financial security, particularly for a woman. Normally as she could not leave her cell, a woman recluse would need two servants to take turns, bringing food, running errands and removing any rubbish and excrement from the toilet. Thomas Netter* also took care to ensure that any anchorite had the appropriate spiritual guidance and regular confession, etc. However, for most of these anchorites, the records contain little more than their name and the place in which they had their cell.

However, fortunately, our Carmelite historian John Bale*, belonged to the community in Norwich, and so was able to preserve a little more information about one of the anchorites who lived in the cell there. This was Emma Stapleton and she came from a wealthy family who lived in Ingham in Norfolk. She was born around 1390, the daughter of Sir Miles Stapleton. One of her ancestors, Sir Miles Stapleton of Haddlesey, the cousin of her grandfather, fought in the crusade which was led by King Peter of Cyprus and attacked Alexandria in October 1365. He would have known the Carmelite saint, St Peter Thomas, who was the papal legate who accompanied this crusade.

Following the death of her father in 1419, Emma decided to become an anchorite in the cell at the Carmelite house in Norwich. What led to this decision is unknown, but Emma would doubtless have been influenced by the example of Julian of Norwich, who lived as an anchorite in Norwich from the 1390s until her death sometime after 1416. Another person who possibly influenced Emma was the Carmelite William Southfield*, who was noted for his holy life and spiritual guidance. He was consulted by the visionary Margery Kempe who "...was much comforted both in body and in soul by this good man's words, and greatly strengthened in her faith". He died on August 24th, 1414.

Emma was formally enclosed on April 1st, 1421 by the Carmelite provincial, **Thomas Netter**. It is claimed that she occupied the chamber under the Holy Cross chapel, which was reserved for women. Netter took great care over her spiritual care, and he appointed a select group of Carmelites as her spiritual directors and guardians. The members of this group were *magister* William Thorpe, the prior of the house, his brother *magister* John Thorpe, *magister* Adam Hemlington, the subprior Bartholomew Acton and brother Adam Hobbes. The choice of five friars was probably cautionary, as Netter would have been aware that these talented friars would be in demand elsewhere as well, so the number ensured that there would always be one of them there for Emma to consult if she experienced any problems.

Sadly, Emma only lived as an anchorite for just over a year,and died on December 2nd, 1422. (Some modern authors state that she died in 1442, but this is due to a misreading of Bale's notes, and a misprint by the nineteenth-century historian of Norfolk, Francis Blomefield).

Unlike her predecessor and close neighbour, Julian of Norwich, Emma Stapleton did not leave any record of her life as an anchorite, or her spiritual experiences. However, alongside Thomas Scrope's* translation of Felip Ribot's *Ten Books…*, John Bale* copied the *Rule of St Linus*, which was intended for anchorites, and which probably served as a guide for Scrope, during his time as a recluse in the Norwich house. There is a good chance that this may also have been used by Emma, a few years earlier as a pattern for her life. The *Rule* is not by St Linus (†c76), the second pope, but it is a medieval composition written in Middle English for anchorites.

**THE RULE OF ST LINUS**

Linus, our holy father in Rome, ordained this rule for all solitary men that adopt the life of a hermit: he commands them thus to spend the night and the day in the loving of God.

The beginning of the day is at midnight and a hermit shall rise at midnight from Holy Rood day until Easter Day and from Easter Day until Holy Rood day [14 Sept], he shall rise at the dawn of the day. For Matins, he shall say 40 Our Fathers, 40 Hail Marys and 3 Creeds. And for Lauds, 15 Our Fathers, 15 Hail Marys and 1 Creed. And for Prime, 12 Our Fathers, 12 Hail Marys and 2 Creeds. And when he has said Prime, he shall hear Mass. And after Mass, he shall say for every hour [Terce, Sext & None], 10 Our Fathers, 10 Hail Marys and 1 Creed. After that, he shall go to his oratory and meditate on the Passion of Christ or on some other holy theme. For midday, he shall say 10 Our Fathers, 10 Hail Marys and 1 Creed, and then go to eat. After he has eaten, he shall say 30 Our Fathers, 30 Hail Marys, 3 Creeds and the Psalter of Our Lady [Rosary] for all his benefactors. For Evensong, he shall say 40 Our Fathers, 40 Hail Marys and 1 Creed. For Compline, he shall say 10 Our Fathers, 10 Hail Marys and 1 Creed. After Compline is said, he shall keep silence.

He shall fast every day in Lent, Advent and on the Apostle's Fasta that is to say from Holy Thursday until Whitsunday. He shall go to confession and receive communion three times in the year, at Christmas, Easter and Whitsunday. He shall fast on Fridays and Saturdays throughout the year: on Fridays with bread, beer and soup only. He shall eat no meat except on Christmas Day, Epiphany, the feasts of St. Paul, the first hermit, St. Anthony, all the feasts of Our Lady, Ascension, Whitsunday, the feast of the Trinity, Corpus Christi, the Nativity of John the Baptist, the feast of St. Peter and St. Paul, of the Angels, All Hallows, the feast of the saint of his cell, and the day of the dedication of the cell.

Also he shall go to bed in his habit, girded with a belt or with a cord. He shall wear a hair shirt but if he is weak then he may leave it off. He shall wear shoes without socks. And when he dies, he shall be buried in the habit that he wore during his life.

The total of Our Fathers said each day is 187, and as many Hail Marys, and also 14 Creeds, besides the Psalter of Our Lady.

This is the rule of a hermit's life.

The Apostle's Fast, as observed by Orthodox Christians, normally runs from Pentecost/Whit Sunday until the Feast of St Peter and St Paul (20 June).

**References:**

*BRCEW* 36:

27

# THOMAS NETTER

**(†1430)**

Thomas Netter of Walden, provincial

Thomas Netter was born around 1372, in the village of Saffron Walden in Essex, to a couple called John and Matilda. Around 1386, when he would have been 14 years of age, he entered the Carmelite community in London. At that time, the community numbered around 80-100 friars, some of whom were from other provinces on the continent, as London was a *studium generale* (international study centre) for the whole Order for students studying philosophy. The provincial at that time was Robert Ivory, but when Netter joined, Ivory was an old man, and he retired from any active role in 1390.

Netter completed his studies for the priesthood in London, and was ordained a priest on September 23rd, 1496, in Holy Trinity priory, Aldgate. Whilst a student in London, Netter appears to have made the acquaintance of the Franciscan theologian, William Woodford, who wrote several works arguing against John Wyclif. Netter himself had initially been attracted by some of John Wyclif's ideas but, as he later admits, it was his friendship with Woodford that led to him seeing the errors in Wyclif's theology.

After his ordination, Netter was sent to pursue higher studies in theology at Oxford, where he was promoted to be a bachelor in theology, c.1403. As a bachelor of theology, Netter was then required to give a series of lectures on the Bible, and on Peter Lombard's *The Sentences*, the standard theology textbook. A bachelor in theology also had to give a number of prescribed sermons, and here Netter appears to have excelled. In 1409, he was named as *regius orator* (royal preacher), and was sent as one of the king's delegation to the General Council being held in Pisa. This Council had been called to resolve the papal schism, caused by two popes, Gregory XII and Benedict XIII, claiming to be the rightful pontiff. Netter is listed as one of the theologians who were invited by Cardinal Peter Philargi, to a meeting in the sacristy of the Franciscan church on May 28th, to give their opinion on whether there were grounds for the cardinals to depose a reigning pontiff. At the meeting, Netter gave his opinion in writing which began:

> "Reverend doctor, as the wise heart knows the time and the way to respond to all matters, it is the right moment and opportune ..."

Sadly, the full text of this tract has been lost. However, in the discussions following this meeting, the Council Fathers voted to depose both claimants and elected a new pope Alexander V.

Netter had returned to Oxford by the end of 1409, when he became involved in the deliberations of a committee set up by the University to produce a list of Wyclif's heretical propositions. Soon after, Netter incepted as a Doctor of Theology, probably in 1411, and then he became the *magister regens* (principal lecturer) in the Carmelite house for the following year. It was whilst he was in this post that he was involved in a confrontation with the Lollard, Peter Clerk, a follower of Wyclif. Netter himself describes the occasion when he and his fellow Carmelite William Ufford (who had accompanied him to the Council of Pisa) challenged Clerk to a debate:

"I felt these provocations: then, all at once, through a certain nobleman, I was chosen together with my brother in religion at the University of Oxford William and challenged to a battle by one of the boldest of them, called Peter Clerk, to dispute over pilgrimages, the Eucharist, religious life and voluntary mendicancy. We came, we were ready, but as those who were present know and still declare, before we could come to blows, Peter Clerk took himself off, rendered speechless by his own silliness."

Netter's reputation as a theologian was now widely recognised and he was took part in a number of trials for heresy. On March 5th, 1410, he was present at the trial of the Lollard, John Badby, in St Paul's cathedral, London. During this trial, an amazing event occurred which Netter himself witnessed:

"I will recount the episode which I saw with my own eyes, being present in person in St. Paul's cathedral in London, when the venerable bishop of Canterbury of happy memory, Thomas Arundel, son and brother of the duke, sat in judgement, assisted by the bishop of Norwich, Alexander, and other diocesan bishops. Arundel interrogated a certain tailor from the Worcestershire area, who had fallen into heresy and questioned him on his belief in the Eucharist. However, he was completely unable to persuade the tailor of the true faith for he was not willing to call or believe that the most blessed sacrament was anything but "blessed bread". At length, when ordered to do reverence to the host, the tailor replied, blaspheming: "truly, it would be more just to do reverence to a spider." And immediately there descended from the highest point of the roof an apparition of a huge and horrible spider, which followed its thread straight down to the mouth of the blasphemer and, while he was still speaking, it made great efforts to enter through his soiled lips. Despite the intervention of many hands, it could only just be prevented. That illustrious prince Thomas, duke of Exeter, at that time chancellor of the kingdom, was present and saw the monster. Then the archbishop rose up quickly with the other [bishops] and explained to all the people gathered there what the avenging hand of the Lord had done to the blasphemer.

Not to delay: he who prefers a spider to the most precious body of the Lamb, has consigned his sinful flesh to be devoured by the flames, as were the remains of the more detestable spider. Witness the foul and distasteful belief of those who go astray, who reduce the most holy sacrament to such a comparison, and worse they bring their idol from the roof, in the coming of a spider."

Netter also took part in the trial of Sir John Oldcastle on Monday September 25th, 1413, and some of his exchanges with Sir John can be found in an account of the trial by the Carmelite historian John Bale*. The following year, Netter was present at the provincial chapter held in Yarmouth. This chapter was probably held early in the year, as the provincial, Stephen Patryngton* had indicated that he wished to resign because of his royal duties as confessor to King Henry V. The prior general, Jean Grossi, was in England at the time conducting a visitation and so he was able to preside at this chapter, and to confirm the election of Netter as the next provincial. He and Netter became close friends and wrote frequently to each other.

Netter was to remain in office as provincial for the next sixteen years, until his death in 1430. During this time, he was in contact with many important figures and his letter book, now sadly lost, contained the texts of 164 of his letters. Fortunately, John Bale* copied a number of these letters into one of his notebooks, and they provide some interesting glimpses into the problems faced by a Carmelite provincial at this period.

In 1414, a General Council was convened at Constance, in order to resolve the schism caused by the existence of two rival popes. Netter was asked by King Henry V to be a member of the English delegation and to attend the Council. He received a letter of recommendation signed by the king himself. The Council began on All Saints Day, November 1st, 1414 but the official English delegation was delayed and did not arrive until January 1415. In fact, Netter appears to have made his own way to the Council. He travelled to Rome first before making his way to Constance. As his name does not appear in any of the official records of the Council, it is likely that he was only there for a short time. Whilst in Rome, Netter made the acquaintance of a young German Carmelite, Conrad Ernst, who was studying there. Ernst was impressed by Netter and he asked if he could accompany him to the Council. Afterwards, he travelled with Netter back to London, where they arrived early in 1415.

On his return, Netter was invited to preach at St Paul's Cross, the open-air pulpit in the grounds of St Paul's cathedral. John Bale* describes this event in his history of the province:

> "When [Netter] became aware that the English people were being led astray by certain Wycliffites, with their false theories of the sacraments, and that nobody was lifting a hand against them, he rebuked the king and the nobles of the kingdom at St. Paul's Cross, London, as being supporters of heresy; and so put himself in mortal danger. However, everyone was full of admiration for the man and for his zeal for fallen souls, especially the king himself, Henry, the fifth of that name, who not only employed him as the keeper of his conscience but reverenced him as a father."

Soon after this sermon, Stephen Patryngton* was appointed as bishop of St David's, and resigned his role as the king's confessor. The king, Henry V, then turned to Netter and asked him to be his confessor and advisor.

As provincial, Netter was responsible for convening a provincial chapter each year as was customary. However, when Netter was away on the king's business, the provincial chapter did not meet and instead, there were meetings in each of the four distinctions (regions). In 1416, there was a celebration of special significance during the provincial chapter. The provincial chapter met in Ludlow that year, so as to celebrate the golden jubilee of Robert Mascall*, bishop of Hereford. Mascall had been a Carmelite for fifty years and so the chapter provided a suitable occasion for the province to celebrate this achievement. Netter himself preached the sermon at the mass and his opening words addressed to Mascall were:

> "Lord father, and with your permission, brother, a jubilee blessing …"

Sadly, Mascall did not live long after this celebration as, soon after returning to London, he fell ill and died on December 22nd. The following year, Netter convened the provincial chapter to meet in Nottingham in August. Earlier that year, King Henry V had launched his invasion of France and, on September 4th, the English troops captured the town of Caen in Normandy. Soon afterwards, the king wrote to Netter:

> "… Besides that, in our town of Caen (which, during the siege by our army, was rendered to us by the special grace of God without any great loss of life) there is a convent of your Order which still remains undamaged. We wish and we beg you, dearest father, with all the speed that you are able, to select and send some brothers of your Order, well suited individuals, to dwell in this house, sufficient in number so that they can sing the divine office."

Netter quickly set about recruiting a group of Carmelites to send to France, and soon he was able to write to the king:

> "On receiving your extremely gracious letter, I was not a little surprised to find united, at the same time in one person, attention to the winning of battles and to the poor in Christ's churches. The meek David did not behave like this, nor did the wise Solomon. David fought courageously but he did not rebuild the temple. Solomon built the temple, but did not fight wars. Therefore God is to be praised who has endowed you with the double spirit of our fathers, for fighting battles courageously and for meditating humbly on the service of Christ.
>
> There are coming to you, O most kind prince, about thirteen of your servants, our brothers, among whom are some who have already left for those parts. Also, there are coming from us someone who was prior of Sandwich for ten years, an *inceptor* in theology, and a third who was formerly the subprior in London, all reputable preachers, as well as other junior priests

for celebrating the office, whose names I have added to the superior's commission. Following them will be a doctor of theology. All of them, in my judgement, are trustworthy men in their way of life and capabilities.

Finally, prostrate at the feet of our most godly prince, I beg that he will protect the prior of this convent, so that the brothers with him may dwell safely in peace, and so that they may not be taken away from their cloister in the service of lords and royal officials, and thus withdrawn from the worship which they owe to God."

In 1419, Netter was appointed by the king as a member of a delegation to go to Poland to negotiate a peace treaty between Wladyslav II, King of Poland, Vitold, Duke of Lithuania and Michael Kuchmeister, the Grandmaster of the Teutonic Knights. A second delegation, led by two bishops, was sent by the pope and the Holy Roman Emperor, Frederick III, sent the Archbishop of Milan, Bartolomeo della Capra. Netter travelled to Poland, accompanied by Conrad Ernst and, on their way, they stopped at Vienna. Whilst he was in the city, Netter met with some members of the Jewish community there and he asked them questions about their customs concerning confession and penance. Later, he described this encounter:

"Now, while I was on a journey to Vienna, a beautiful city in Austria, in fact when I had reached there, travelling to the king of Poland, as a nuncio of the illustrious king of England, Henry V, I met with a crowd of Jews in the street, travelling in the middle of friends, a good number of whom then joined with me. I asked and urged one of them to tell me if they still had the custom of making oral confession to a priest. Then he replied very carefully, that it was so, especially in three cases that is of adultery committed secretly, also murder done in secret, and hidden blasphemy against the name of the great God or his law. I questioned whether a priest would add a penance if I confessed such a sin? He said yes, and for every sin, its own penance. And so, would this custom have been preserved for such a long time in captivity, if it was not of great significance to them from long practice of their law; especially as they had already made many sacrifices, due to the trials of their captivity, of things which the law ordered them to fulfil?"

From Vienna, Netter and Conrad Ernst made their way to Grudziadz in Poland where they met the other delegates in July 1419. With Netter playing a significant role, the negotiations in Poland soon came to a fruitful conclusion, and the warring parties were persuaded to sign a new truce agreement. Early in August, Netter and Conrad Ernst were free to set off for England. They made a detour whilst in France, in order to report on their mission to King Henry V, who had just captured Rouen. The two of them had arrived back in England by the middle of November 1419.

Netter's actions as provincial did not always meet with the approval of the members of the province. He was noted as a strict superior, who set high standards, and his expectations aroused some resentment. Whilst he had been a student in London, Netter had become friends with a fellow student, a Carmelite from Bordeaux, William Costall. At this time, the region of Gascony was under English control, and there were many English merchants living in Bordeaux. Having finished his studies, Costall returned to France and, by 1421, he had been appointed prior of of the community in Bordeaux. In February of that year, Costall wrote to Netter warning him that some of the friars in the English province were making complaints to the prior general about his conduct. They accused Netter of ruling too severely, and claimed that his strictness had caused a hundred friars to flee the Order. These friars also protested that Netter was ignoring some of the permissions granted by the prior general, and that he was disrespectful of the person of the prior general himself. One of the leaders of these complaints was John Orwell, a Carmelite priest in the community in Ipswich. The accusations prompted Netter to act quickly. First, he consulted with his council, and they decided that John Keninghale* should be sent to Rome to put their response to these accusations to the prior general, Jean Grossi. In the meantime, Netter wrote to Grossi as follows:

> "... There remains something else that I consider should not be passed over, for much earlier this year, around the Feast of the Purification, I received a letter from my venerable and beloved, from the depths of my heart, *magister* William Costall, the prior of Bordeaux, informing me of some unfavourable rumours which accuse me of a complex crime before your holiness, that, through the excessive severity which I use, I have already caused around one hundred brothers to leave and follow Satan, and that I violently and indiscriminately trample on and remove the permissions that your grace has granted to the brethren, and that, to my own scandal, I treat badly your authority and dignity. If John Orwell has such influence at the level of your paternity, that he should dare and succeed in making such accusations without any legal proof, then I am sorry that I have become so little respected by such a distinguished master.
>
> Now I have never been convinced of anything more certainly than that one has to suffer continually from the attacks of the malicious. For if I had sought to please such persons I would not have been the servant of Christ. Now if there are no lawbreakers, no audacious or frequent apostates, if there were no notorious thieves and robbers, and if those who do such things are not corrected in prisons in almost every place for their wickedness's, or lack of control, or filthiness, I should be a failure in their sight and they would rejoice avidly at my misfortunes. Yet if I should deal leniently with

> all these, I fear that that I might bring their impunity down on my own head.
>
> If, out of innate prudence, you lend credence to rumours such as these, I am amazed why you hold back from accusing me, your son, and you do not wish to hear the evidence of other more trustworthy fathers in order to learn the exact truth. If you do not believe them, then what have I done wrong that I cannot avoid such widespread disgrace? But far be it that such can come easily before your most worthy paternity. Now you know that it is the custom of our brethren to criticise, to complain as they undergo their punishments, but I do not wish to be considered as one like these, nor I hope as hard-hearted. I would like, reverend *magister*, for you to listen to other voices and then, perhaps, you may see that I have always held your letters in great respect, and those which were cancelled I did so on your instructions. God knows those who left through apostasy but I do not know if, because of the exactions from my faults, I deserved such sorrow. But I know that it was not because of my severity but because of their fickleness that they have made their complaint. Also I know that not so many have apostatised in my period of office as used to in other times and how many after old crimes committed in those days have returned to the penance of the Order, and been received with joy as others say. And when you learn how many talented young men have entered the Order, then you will rejoice in the Lord. I see myself accused before your holiness, and whatever I may say in my favour, I have declared openly but the works which I do, they will bear witness for me."

The complaint that over one hundred friars had left the Order due to Netter's strictness is demonstrably a wild exaggeration. The surviving records, although incomplete, contain details of only seven friars who absconded from the Order during Netter's period was provincial. However, there is evidence of some difficult friars in the province who created problems for Netter. In his letters, there is a mention of one friar from Sandwich who was very difficult to control and led to Netter having to write an explanatory letter to the prior general, dated March 8$^{th}$ 1421:

> "Now there is one of our brothers, Lawrence Clerke from the convent of Sandwich who, because of the increasing plague in our convent in London, in which 24 have died this year, was directed, by a letter from our provincial chapter at Ipswich, to help out the community there. But he, without any other communication coming from our side, giving him instruction by word of mouth or letter, after having waited 11 weeks for a written letter of obedience finally, as his prior has related, having stirred up trouble among the local people, inciting them to kill the prior and burn down the convent, he left as an apostate. And, as he has written a letter to you, we will be most surprised if such a one is allowed to return unpunished. At the least, you should do nothing until you have received

> a complete report for, unless there is a very pressing reason, such a great outrage cannot be allowed by us to go unpunished."

Unfortunately, Lawrence Clerke appears to have got in first because, on the same day as Netter signed his letter to the prior general, Pope Martin V granted Clerke "a dwelling for life" in the house in Sandwich. Evidently Clerke had got his petition to Rome in early, but how this matter was finally resolved is not known.

There is one other entry concerning a dissatisfied friar in Netter's letter book. This friar, John Boxhole, complained not about Netter's strictness but that the religious observance in the province was too lax. He wanted to transfer to a stricter Order, the Carthusians at Sheen. Once again, Netter felt such an accusation was unfounded and he wrote a heartfelt letter to the prior of the Carthusians on March 24th, 1415 in which he claimed:

> "... How many holy fathers have there been so far, and were there before us, and only our John could not be good among us? But let our brother answer: where did he overcome his juvenile passions, where did he overcome the urge for illicit things, was it not with us? Where did he learn to have a taste for the saintly life, where to despise the world, was it not with us? Where, I ask, did he begin to love chastity and to exercise sanctity, if not with us, he who from his adolescence lived with Carmelites? No other witness will I cite to bring against my brother John except myself: how many complaints we uttered in contempt of the world, what tears we shed in holy and daily confessions, what hours he devoted in the middle of the night to prayers and when overcome with sleep his frozen limbs rested on the frigid marble or at least on hard boards. And thus formed by our men he does not hesitate to say: with you I have not been able to be good. Pardon me, I beg of you, for I feel wronged. I say to you, reverend fathers and dear fellow brothers, let our brother John not be disturbed; for his sake I give you thanks, for you may be able to make him good, who, and I use his own words, could not be good among us. As for the rest, if you give your assent and lighten our burden, I shall send you forty brothers that you may make them better, none of whom is inferior to our John, none is worse."

One of the notable developments during Thomas Netter's period in office was the encouragement of women who wished to be associated with the Carmelites (see the previous chapter, Emma Stapleton*). Papal permission to accept women formally into the Order was not received until 1452, but Netter anticipated this by welcoming individual women to live as recluses or anchorites in cells attached to Carmelite churches. Netter sought to ensure that these recluses received wise guidance and support and, as described in the previous chapter, the list of the Carmelites who were entrusted with the spiritual care of Emma Stapleton* still survives.

In 1422, Netter received a summons from King Henry V, to join him in France and, on March 25th, he was granted £10 to cover his travel expenses. Netter spent the summer with King Henry, and was present at Valenciennes on August 31st, when the king died. Netter, then, accompanied the king's body as it made its way slowly back to England. The cortege spent some days in Rouen, waiting for the arrival of Queen Catherine who reached the town on September. From there the funeral procession proceeded to Calais and across to England. It entered London on November 5th, and, on the following day, Netter preached the sermon at the king's funeral mass in St Paul's cathedral.

Netter retained his place as the royal confessor and served the new king, Henry VI. However, he must have spent a significant part of his time completing his major theological work, *The Doctrine of the Ancient Catholic Faith of the Church against the Wycliffites and Hussites (Doctrinale)*. This work was a comprehensive analysis and refutation of the writings of John Wyclif and his followers. It is divided into six books, of which the first four were probably revised versions of earlier compositions. These are normally bound together in volume one. This first volume was completed around 1425, and a copy was sent to Pope Martin V early in 1426. Book 5, a longer work, treating of the sacraments, was completed in 1427 and became volume 2. Once again, a copy was sent to the pope. Finally Book 6, which covered the sacramentals, was completed and became volume 3. This was sent to Rome some time before 1430. Pope Martin wrote complimentary letters to Netter when he received each of the first two volumes.

Netter's *Doctrinale* appeared too late to stem the spread of Wyclif's ideas throughout England and in the Czech Republic; however, it proved to be a major resource in the theological disputes with the followers of Wyclif, and, surprisingly, it was consulted by both sides. Netter had a wide knowledge of Wyclif's ideas and he quoted extensively from Wyclif's writings in his *Doctrinale*. So, many of those defending Wyclif's ideas were forced to consult Netter's *Doctrinale* in order to learn exactly what arguments Wyclif had used. Netter's work was very widely read and numerous manuscript copies of his *Doctrinale*, survive. The work first appeared in print in the 1520's, but the later edition by Bonaventure Blanciotti, printed in 1757-1759, is now the standard text, although a modern critical edition is long overdue.

Netter's life ended, appropriately, as he placed himself once again at the service of his king. He was summoned to accompany the young King Henry

VI as he travelled to France, where the new king was to be crowned in Paris. Netter was a member of the royal party when they set out from London early in April 1430. They were in Calais on April 23rd,, but had to remain there whilst the English army cleared the French forces from the surrounding area, so as to provide safe passage for the royal party. The road was clear by July 17th, and the king and his escort set off for Rouen, where they arrived on July 29th. Once again, they had to wait while a safe passage towards Paris was cleared. It was whilst the royal party were in Rouen that Netter was taken ill and he died in the Carmelite house there on 2nd November. He was buried at the base of the sedilia, on the left side of the choir near the altar. The epitaph on his tomb read:

> "Here lies the most devout and learned father in Christ, Thomas Walden, English, a Carmelite of London, who in his day was not only a defender of the Catholic faith, but bequeathed innumerable works to posterity for the defeating of heresies. For this reason, everyone called him "the hammer of the heretics". Because of his sublime preaching, he was chosen and appointed the father confessor and councillor of the most Christian kings Henry IV, Henry V and Henry VI. Therefore the family of Carmel rejoices for such a great and renowned man who died in the Carmel of Rouen, with a reputation for holiness, on 2nd November 1430."

Of all the Carmelites in the medieval English province, Thomas Netter was one of the most outstanding. As a theologian, it can be argued that John Baconthorpe* was more original and provided a more comprehensive body of writings. However, Netter was a major figure not only within the Order, but also in the wider national and international world. The Carmelite historian, John Bale* gives a very appreciative description of him in his history of the province written in 1536;

> "There was in this man true genius as well as considerable practical ability. A man of zeal in all that he undertook, skilled in every branch of letters, and so noted for his graceful eloquence that no one of that time was his superior in the art of conciliation, or in prevailing on men to accept his judgement. In negotiating affairs he would take all sides into account, examine all aspects, missing no detail; this he would do not just thoughtlessly or casually but despatching everything with wisdom and authority.
> … the worthiness of his actions and his pleasant conversation began to be so well-known that many of the most distinguished men held him in the highest esteem. Nor did people in the highest positions consider it beneath their dignity to seek his opinion, being well aware of his great wisdom. So much so that there was no question which arose nor any problem, however insoluble or difficult, that he did not resolve by his counsel, his application

and his diligence. He was useful not only to the Order (over which he presided) but also to the chief men (who with the king were troubled and greatly disturbed by many concerns) and also many matters throughout England. During his life, he was always giving gifts to the schools of the mendicant orders in England. He brought an end to rebellions and wars, and quelled heresies and schisms. When he was confessor, counsellor and secret envoy for Henry V and VI, kings of England and France, swearing, frauds, sins of the flesh and other human ills were miraculously almost eliminated from the kingdom."

**References:**

*BRCEW* 414-425: *ODNB*, 40, 444-447

John Bergström-Allen, & Richard Copsey, O.Carm., eds., *Thomas Netter of Walden. Carmelite, Diplomat and Theologian (c.1372-1430)* (Faversham: St Albert's Press, 2009).

Kevin Alban, O.Carm., *The Teaching and Impact of the 'Doctrinale' of Thomas Netter of Walden (c.1374-1430)*, (Turnhout: Brepols, 2010).

Kevin Alban, O.Carm., "Carmelite Identity and Orthodoxy. Thomas Netter and the Doctinale", in *Historiography and Identity. Responses to Medieval Carmelite Culture*, Jens Röhrkasten & Coralie Zermatten, ed., (Zurich: Lit Verlag, 2017), 63-75.

# 28

# ALEYN WARNEKYN OF LYNN

**(†1432)**

The Gateway to the Carmelite Priory in Lynn

The Carmelite name, in the title to this chapter, will come as a surprise to those who have some acquaintance with the medieval history of the English province. Alan or Aleyn of Lynn as he is usually called, was a very talented and industrious Carmelite friar. Recently, though, thanks to the researches of Dr Susan Maddock, former archivist for the town of King's Lynn, and now honorary research fellow at the University of East Anglia, our knowledge of Aleyn's family background and his activities in his home town has grown considerably. Very generously, Dr Maddock has shared her findings with me, and consequently, the following account of Aleyn's life is much fuller and adds considerably to the text published in my *Biographical Register*.

The town records reveal that Aleyn's grandfather, Stephen Warnekyn was an emigrant from the Low Countries or Germany, who settled in Lynn in the second half of the 14th century. He was a tailor by trade and is known to have resided in Jews Lane, in the town from around 1374-1379. He died sometime before 1388. His son Alan Warnekyn, was the father of our Carmelite and a prosperous figure in the town. In 1379, he was a married man employing two servants, and he lived in the Trinity Hall ward of the town from 1375-1394. He was admitted as a burgess of Lynn in 1385.

Aleyn, his son, was born around 1375 and joined the Carmelite community in the town. He was a talented student and, after ordination, he was sent to pursue higher studies at Cambridge, where he incepted as a doctor of theology shortly before 1410. As a doctor of theology and son of a burgess, Aleyn was invited to sit with the mayor of Lynn, and other dignitaries in the town hall on December 12th, 1412, when a new set of ordinances for the governance of the town was approved.

Aleyn remained at Cambridge University for some years, lecturing to university students in the Carmelite house before returning back to his own community in Lynn. At that time, the Carmelite house in Lynn served as a house of formation for the smaller communities in the Norwich distinction (or region), e.g. Burnham Norton and Blakeney. Students came to Lynn to study philosophy and then theology. The more talented friars would be sent to Norwich, where there was an advanced course in theology leading to the award of a Licentiate in Theology (S.T.L.) which entitled the recipient to teach theology. The brightest students would be chosen to continue their studies at Oxford or Cambridge for a doctorate in theology..

Aleyn appears to have spent some years teaching in the study house in Norwich as John Bale* records that he was a prolific writer, learned in both the Latin and Greek Fathers. Bale, a member of the community in Norwich, copied the titles and *incipits* (opening lines), of over fifty compositions by Aleyn, which had been preserved in the library in Norwich. Among these, there were works by Aleyn on the Visions of St Bridget of Sweden, a tract on the Four Senses of Holy Scripture, and also a collection of sermons. However, Alen's major contribution to the library was his compilation of over fifty indexes for the major theological and classical works, which the students used in their studies. These were intended for the young friars preparing for the priesthood in Norwich and Lynn. Among the works for which Aleyn compiled an index were Alexander Nequam's *Commentary on the Song of Songs*, the work *On the Revelations of Birgitta of Sweden*, Giles of Rome's *On the Conduct of Princes*, and works by Bernard of Clairvaux, St Augustine, St Basil, Gerard of Nazareth, and others.

In addition to his teaching duties, Aleyn became a close friend of the mystic Margery Kempe, and he gave her spiritual direction over a number of years. She mentions him frequently in her autobiography, as the following excerpts reveal:

> (i) "It so happened one Friday before Whitsun Eve [9 June 1413], as this creature [Margery Kempe] was in the church of St. Margaret at N. hearing Mass, she heard a great and dreadful noise. She was greatly amazed, very much fearing public opinion, which said God should take vengeance on her. She knelt there, holding her head down, and with her book in her hand, praying to our Lord Jesus Christ for grace and for mercy. Suddenly – from the highest part of the church vault, from under the base of the rafter – there fell down on her head and on her back, a stone which weighed three pounds, and a short end of a beam weighing six pounds, so that she thought her back was broken in pieces, and she was afraid she would be dead in a little while. Soon after, she cried, 'Jesus, mercy,' and immediately her pain was gone....
>
> "A worshipful doctor of divinity, named Master Aleyn, a White Friar, hearing of this miraculous event, inquired of this creature about the whole manner of this occurrence. He – desiring the working of God to be glorified – got the same stone that fell upon her back and weighed it, and then he got the beam-end that fell upon her head, which one of the keepers of church had put on the fire to burn.
>
> "And this worshipful doctor said it was a great miracle, and Our Lord was highly to be glorified for preserving this creature against the malice of her enemy, and told it to many people and many people greatly glorified God in this creature. And also many people would not believe it, but preferred to believe it was more a token of wrath and vengeance, than of mercy or favour."
>
> (ii) [When a Franciscan friar complained that she wept during his sermons]
>
> "Afterwards, a worthy doctor of divinity, a White Friar – a very serious-minded cleric and elderly doctor, and very well thought-of – who had known the said creature many years of her life, and believed the grace that God worked in her, took with him another worthy man, a bachelor of law, a man well-grounded and long practised in scripture, who was confessor to the said creature, and went to this friar as the good priests did before, and sent for wine to cheer him with, praying him of his charity to look favourably on the works of our Lord in the said creature, and grant her his benevolence in supporting her, if she happened to cry or sob whilst he was in the middle of his sermon. And these worthy clerics told him that it was a gift of God and that she could

not have it but when God would give it, nor could she withstand it when God would send it, and God would withdraw it when he willed – for that she had through revelation, and that was unknown to the friar.

"Then he, neither giving credence to the doctor's words nor the bachelor's, trusting a great deal on the favour of the people, said he would not look favourably on her crying for anything that anyone might say or do, for he would not believe that it was a gift of God… Then the worthy doctor and her confessor advised her that she should not go to his sermon, and that was a great pain to her."

(iii) "So our Lord of his mercy, just as he had promised the said creature that he would ever provide for her, stirring the spirits of two good clerics who had for many long years known her conversings and all her search for perfection, made them strong and bold to speak for his part in excusing the said creature, both in the pulpit and outside it, wherever they heard anything moved against her, strengthening their arguments sufficiently with authorities from holy scripture. Of these clerks, one was a White Friar, a doctor of divinity; the other was a bachelor of law canon, a man who had laboured much on the scriptures….

"And then some envious persons complained to the Provincial of the White Friars [Thomas Netter*] that the said doctor was associating too much with the said creature, forasmuch as he supported her in her weeping and in her crying, and also informed her in questions of scripture, when she would ask him any. Then he was admonished, by virtue of obedience, that he should no longer speak with her, nor inform her about any texts of scripture, and that was most painful to him, for, as he said to some people, he would rather have lost a hundred pounds, if he had had it, than her conversation – it was so spiritual and fruitful.

"When her confessor perceived how the worthy doctor was charged by obedience that he should not speak with her, then he, to exclude all opportunity, also warned her by virtue of obedience that she should not go any more to the friars, nor speak with the said doctor, nor ask him any questions as she had done before.

And then her thoughts were very sorrowful and gloomy, for she was excluded from much spiritual comfort. She would rather have lost any earthly good than his conversation, for it was to her a great increasing of virtue.

"Then long afterwards, she happened as she went along the street to meet the said doctor, and neither of them spoke one word to the other, and then she had a great cry, with many tears. Afterwards, when she came to her meditation, she said in her mind to our Lord Jesus Christ, 'Alas, Lord, why may I have no comfort from this worthy clerk, who has known me so many years, and often strengthened me in your love? Now, Lord, you have taken from me the anchorite – I trust to your mercy – the most special and singular comfort that I ever had on earth, for he always loved me for your love, and would never forsake me while he lived for anything that anyone could say or do. And now Master Aleyn is barred from seeing me, and I from him. Sir Thomas Andrew and Sir John Amy have got benefices and are out of town. Master Robert scarcely dares speak with me. Now I have in a way, no comfort from either man or child.'

"Our merciful Lord, answering in her mind, said, 'Daughter, I am more worthy of your soul than ever was the anchorite and all the others you have mentioned, or than all the world may be, and I shall comfort you myself, for I would speak to you more often than you will let me. And, daughter, I want you to know that you will speak to Master Aleyn again, as you have done before.'"

(iv) "At one time, God visited the said doctor, Master Aleyn, with great sickness, so that no man who saw him would promise him life. And so the said creature was told of his sickness. Then she grieved for him, especially because she had had it by revelation that she would speak with him again, as she had done before and, if he had died of this illness, her feeling would not have been true.

"Therefore she ran into the choir at Saint Margaret's Church, kneeling down before the sacrament, and saying in this way: 'Ah, Lord, I pray you, for all the goodness that you have shown me, and as surely you love me, let this worthy cleric never die until I may speak with him, as you have promised me that I should do. And you, glorious Queen of Mercy, remember what he used to say about you in his sermons: he used to say, Lady, that he was indeed blessed that had you for his friend, for, when you prayed, all the company of heaven prayed with you. Now, for the blissful love that you had for your son, let him live until such time that he has leave to speak with me, and I with him, for now we are separated by obedience.'

"Then she was answered in her soul that he should not die before the time that she had permission to speak with him, and he with her, as they had done years before.

"And, as our Lord willed, a short time afterwards, the worthy cleric recovered and went about hale and healthy, and had leave of his Provincial to speak with the said creature. And she had leave from her confessor to speak with him.

"It so happened that the said doctor was to dine in town with a worthy woman, who had taken the mantle and the ring, and he sent for the said creature to come and speak with him. She, much surprised at this, got permission and went to him. When she came into the place where he was, she could not speak for weeping, and for joy that she had in our Lord, inasmuch as she found her feeling true, and not deceptive, that he had leave to speak to her and she to him.

"Then the worthy doctor said to her, 'Margery, ye are welcome to me, for I have long been kept from you, and now hath our Lord sent you here that I may speak with you, blessed may he be.'

> "There was a dinner of great joy and gladness, much more spiritual than bodily, for it was sauced and savoured with tales from holy scripture. And then he gave the said creature a pair of knives, in token that he would stand with her in God's cause, as he had done before."
>
> (v) "And, on one occasion, as she lay at her prayers in the church during the time of Advent before Christmas, she thought in her heart that she wished that God, of his goodness, would make Master Aleyn to preach a sermon as well as he could. And as soon as she had thought in this way, she heard our Sovereign Lord Christ Jesus saying in her soul, 'Daughter, I know very well what you are thinking now about Master Aleyn, and I tell you truly that he shall preach a very holy sermon. And see that you believe steadfastly the words that he shall preach, as though I preached them myself, for they shall be words of great solace and comfort to you, for I shall speak in him.'
>
> "When she heard this answer, she went and told it to her confessor and two other priests whom she greatly trusted. And when she had told them her feeling, she was sorry, for fear as to whether he would speak as well as she had felt or not – for revelations are hard sometimes to understand."

Margery Kempe, writing in 1432, mentions Aleyn of Lynn as still living but it seems that he died not long afterwards. He was a man of great learning, who dedicated a large proportion of his time to preparing material for his students. More importantly, he was a very spiritual priest and, as witnessed by Margery Kempe, he proved a discerning, spiritual guide for her and probably to many others who came to him for counsel and advice.

**References:**

*ODNB* 34, 898-899: *BRCEW* 10-13 (for the revised article, see the latest version of *Corrections and Additions* (on Carmelite website).

Maddock, Susan, "Margery Kempe's home town and worthy kin", in *Encountering the Book of Margery Kempe*, ed. L. Kalas & L. Varnam, (Manchester Univ. Press, 2021), 163-184.

# 29

# JOHN KENINGHALE

**(†1451)**

Council of Florence from *Nuremberg Chronicle* (1493)

Throughout the medieval years, it is striking how many talented friars came from the Norwich distinction or region. This distinction contained only five houses (Norwich, Blakeney, Burnham Norton, Kings Lynn, Yarmouth), and yet it produced 67 doctors of theology and 11 bishops. The other three distinctions were larger; London and Oxford had 10 houses in each, whilst the York distinction had 14 but, in contrast to Norwich, London produced only 65 doctors of theology and 6 bishops, whilst Oxford had 47 doctors and 4 bishops, and York only 42 doctors and 4 bishops.

The productivity of Norwich, with only five houses, was remarkable. However, having only five houses had one great advantage. As the Order was only allowed to put forward one candidate each year for a doctorate at Oxford, and the same at Cambridge, these places were allocated to students from each each distinction in turn. So, a bright student in one of the five houses in the Norwich distinction, had a better chance of being put forward for a doctorate, than any of the greater number of students in, for example, the fourteen houses comprising the York distinction. (For a list of the houses in each distinction, see Chapter 13, "Thomas Brome").

Among the brightest of the young students in Norwich was John Keninghale. The first record we have of him is when he was ordained acolyte on March 8th, 1407, in Norwich cathedral. The officiating bishop was another English Carmelite, John Leycester, titular Archbishop of Smyrna. After ordination as a priest, Keninghale was sent to do higher studies in theology at Oxford University, where he incepted as a doctor sometime between 1421-1425.

Whilst at Oxford, Keninghale undertook a number of important missions for the provincial Thomas Netter*, and he travelled to Rome several times on his behalf. In one of his letters to the prior general Jean Grossi, dated March 8th, 1421, Netter wrote that he was sending Keninghale, a bachelor of theology, to Rome to answer certain criticisms which were being levelled against Netter himself.

Keninghale had incepted as a doctor by 1425, as he was given the title *magister* (doctor) when he was elected to be one of the definitors, for the English province, at the general chapter, held at Pamiers in the south of France, at the end of May. On his return, Keninghale was sent to present a copy of the first volume of Netter's *Doctrinale Fidei Ecclesiae* (The Doctrine of the Church) to the Archbishop of Canterbury, Henry Chichele who, it is written, received it *gaudentur* (with joy) at a meeting of the king's council. Then, early the following year, Keninghale set off on another visit to Rome, where he presented a copy of Netter's book to Pope Martin V, sometime before April 1st. Keninghale's frequent visits to Rome led to him being described by Netter in a letter to the Provincial of the Lower German Province, as his "*nuncio* to the Apostolic See".

As a recognised doctor of theology, Keninghale was appointed as a consultant at a number of trials for heresy. In 1428, he was present at the trial of William White in Norwich. The following year, from March 15-18, 1429, he was present with three other Carmelites at the trial of John Skylly, a miller from Flaxton, held in the chapel of the bishop's palace in Norwich.

Keninghale was the definitor for the province again at the General Chapter held in Nantes, France, on June 4th, 1430. It appears that the provincial, Thomas Netter*, who was in attendance on the new king Henry VI, during his journey to his coronation in Paris, had resigned his office before leaving, probably due to the pressure of his royal duties. Hence, at the General Chapter, Keninghale was appointed as provincial in his place. This appointment was then announced at the provincial chapter, held this year at Hitchin, near London, in August after Keninghale's return.

During the General Chapter in Nantes, the prior general Jean Grossi also retired from office, and he was replaced by an Italian, Bartolomeo de Roquali. The following year, Roquali attended the General Council being held in Basle. He arrived there in March 1432, and ordered all the prior provincials of the Order to be present. However, Roquali's instruction did not meet with any great enthusiasm, particularly as a number of the provincials were unhappy with the way in which Roquali had been elected as prior general. So Roquali was forced to appeal to the Cardinal Protector of the Order, who then formally instructed all the provincials to be present. So, Keninghale had to set out for Basle, where he arrived in October 1432. However, Keninghale's relation with Roquali, the prior general, was not good and, in December, he was forced to make an appeal to the delegates at the General Council, in which he claimed that Roquali was trying to depose him. The delegates upheld Keninghale's complaint and Roquali was made to promise that he would do nothing against the will of the Council, and that he would replace any unfavourable letters which he had written against Keninghale, with favourable ones.

Early in 1433, a delegation of Hussites (the followers of John Hus of Bohemia), arrived to present their beliefs and debate with the Council. On January 26-28,, 1433, Peter Payne, an English follower of John Wyclif addressed the Council and, on January 30th, Keninghale asked for permission to reply to certain remarks of Payne which were injurious to the kingdom of England. Then, on February 4th, Keninghale intervened again, offering to produce a refutation of Payne's arguments, if he was allowed two hours to search through the writings of John Wyclif. Keninghale attempted to do this on February 6th, but, according to a Bohemian, Peter of Zatec, he failed. That same day, though, Keninghale accused Payne of being a heretic and a traitor to King Henry VI. Then, on April 7th, Keninghale produced some conclusions from John Wyclif's *De Blasphemia* (On Blasphemy), that had been condemned by Pope Martin V. Zatec claims that Keninghale had declared that no one could read half a page of that book without finding ten errors or heresies, and that he had called Wyclif a person "of thrice damned memory". However, Keninghale evidently made a good impression on the delegates, as he was asked to preach before the Council on December 20th, 1433. Included among Keninghale's baggage, there was a copy of Thomas Netter's *Doctrinale Fidei Ecclesie* (The Doctrine of Faith of the Church), which Keninghale presented to the papal legate at the Council. The legate quickly had a copy made, which he then presented to Procopius, the leader of the Hussite delegation.

Keninghale returned to England for a short time early in 1434, possibly carrying letters from the General Council and keeping King Henry VI and his Council, abreast of the discussions taking place there. At the Carmelite General Chapter held in May 1434, in Ravensburg, Keninghale and the other Carmelites who had been present at the General Council, were granted funds for their expenses. Keninghale himself served on a number of committees and delegations at the General Council until, in June 1434, he set out to return to England. On July 5$^{th}$, the king granted him £10 for coming from the Council at his request to inform him on what was happening.

In 1438-1439, the Council transferred to Florence, and Keninghale was one of four English Carmelites who attended the Council there. They were the only English theologians present, as Henry IV's delegation and the theologians from the other Religious Orders had been prevented from travelling, due to hostilities between England and Burgundy. It was whilst he was staying in Florence that Keninghale suffered from a severe fever and a painful headache. He was advised to go to the tomb of the newly beatified Carmelite saint, Andrew Corsini, and to beg for his intercession. Keninghale did so and was miraculously cured of his ailment. There is an account of this episode in the life of St Andrew Corsini written a few years later:

> "A reverend master of theology, brother [.....] provincial of the Carmelite Order in England, was suffering greatly from fever, so much so that he cried out day and night, due to the pain in his head, beseeching somebody to put him out of his misery. Then, when all the bells began to peal because of the great crowds of people, the provincial asked why so many bells were ringing. He was told: "Because a new saint has been discovered, and God is working many miracles through him. He is a member of your Order and was the bishop of Fiesole." Then the provincial said: "Quickly, help me for I want to go to the church. Hopefully he will not pass me by but will help me as well so that I do not die from despair." Entering the church, he approached the picture of him and watched the men and women touching this picture and afterwards rubbing their faces, and he asked: "What are they doing?" He received this response: "They are suffering from pains in the head and after this devotion many are cured." Now, when the provincial was told this, he went up to the picture or icon, on which was painted an image of blessed Andrew, and said: "O blessed Andrew, I pray to you and beseech you not to ignore me but to help me, who is one of your Order. See my pain and the agony in my head and bring me relief for I am at the end of my tether." And so saying, he touched the picture, full of faith, devotion and hope, and then he rubbed his head and his face. At that moment, with absolute truth, he was immediately freed from all his pain and fever. Then,

> when he was due to return home, he arranged for a holy picture to be painted of blessed Andrew with some of his miracles. These miracles took place around the time of his translation that is the year 1439 AD."

Keninghale had returned to England by March 5th, 1441, when he wrote to the king, seeking the arrest and return of a fugitive friar. In 1443, Keninghale, together with the provincial of France, Jean Soreth, were appointed commissary-generals by the new prior general Jean Facy, and they presided at an extraordinary provincial chapter of the Lower German Province held on January 7th, 1443, in order to settle some dissension in the province. In 1444, Keninghale, who had held office of provincial for 14 years, resigned because of the demands of "affairs of state".

During his later years, Keninghale, became prior of Norwich, and he had a special cell built for himself there. John Bale* records that, in 1450, Keninghale built "a very beautiful library" in the house. As Norwich was a major study centre for Carmelite students, this new library would have been a welcome addition.

Finally, on April 28th, 1451, Keninghale died and was buried in the chapel at Norwich. John Bale records a number of the works written by Keninghale, but his letter to the king about a fugitive friar, and his sermon delivered at the Council of Basle, are the sole surviving texts. The latter still awaits a modern printed edition.

It has been suggested that Keninghale was the editor of a collection of anti-Lollard documents entitled *Fasciculi Zizaniorum* (Bundles of Weeds), and it is conceivable that Keninghale could have undertaken this project at the request of the provincial Thomas Netter. A copy of the work survives, made by the Carmelite Roger Alban* in 1439. This collection is an invaluable source for the study of John Wyclif, and for the Carmelite responses to his writings. It contains articles and sermons by various Carmelites as well as some accounts of the different inquiries into Wyclif's writings. The Latin text of this collection was published in the 19th century. If Keninghale was the major editor of the collection, then he deserves a heartfelt vote of gratitude from later historians.

**References:**

*BRCEW* 171-173: *ODNB* 31, 223

Margaret Harvey, "England, the Council of Florence and the End of the Council of Basle", in *Christian Unity and the Council of Ferrara-Florence* 1438/39-1989, ed. G. Alberigo (Leuven, 1991), 203-225.

# 30

# ROGER ALBAN

## (†1453+)

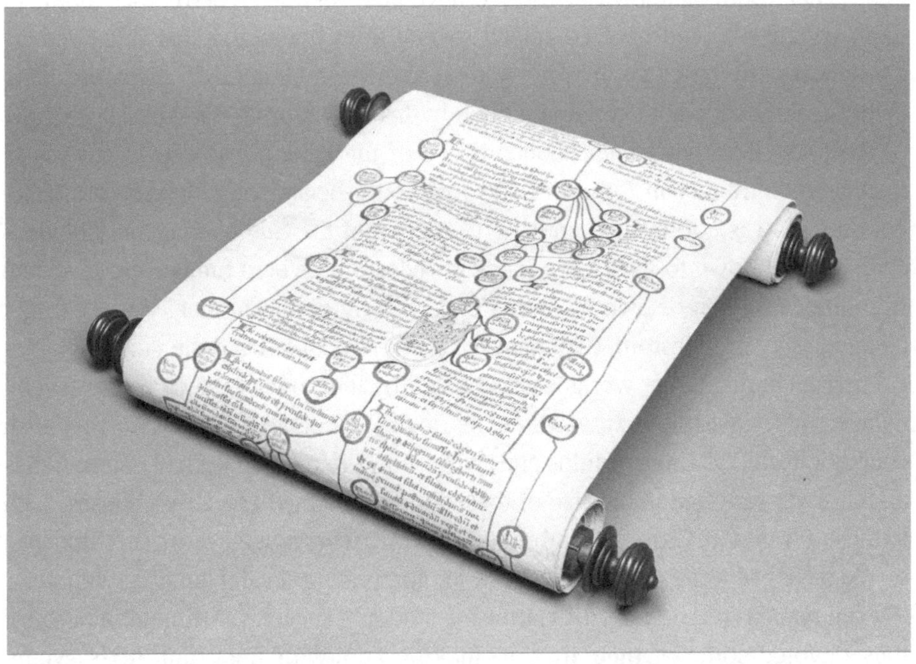

Copy of Roger Alban's Chronicle, *Progenies regum Brytanniae*

Carmelite friars tend to be remembered for a variety of reasons. Some achieve a reputation for living a holy and devout life, some for the positions of authority in which they have faithfully served the Order or the wider world outside and others are remembered for their learning, their sermons or for the books which they have written. However, behind all these outstanding friars, there were others who only registered in the records for more mundane achievements as, for example, Aleyn Warnekyn of Lynn*, described in a previous chapter, who was a dedicated teacher and who spent a large amount of his time preparing indices for many of the theological books, which his students were studying.

In the medieval period, before the invention of printing, one of the major difficulties faced by any Carmelite pursuing his studies in philosophy or theology, lay in gaining access to the major texts which he needed to consult. Of course, each Carmelite house had its own library but the number of books in it was very limited. The catalogue of the library at Hulne Priory in Northumberland, listed 97 books in 1366. At the other end of the country, the library at Aylesford, which was kept in a special room, is known in 1386 to have possessed just 75 volumes. Some of these volumes, would have contained several texts bound together but, even so, the resources in these two libraries were very modest. Of course, new works were being steadily added but copying a book by hand took time. For example, a copy of the *Liber Concordantium* (Concordance of the Bible), was copied for use in the Carmelite library in Aylesford and work on it began some time before 1348, but the task was not finished until 1376. A copy of the *Catholicon* (Latin dictionary), is also known to have been made at Aylesford. Where funds were available from the community's own resources or a wealthy donor, further volumes might be purchased. In Aylesford, two manuscripts were bought from the vicar of the local parish church. Other works were donated by their owners, such as the several manuscripts bequeathed to the Carmelites, in the will of the rector of Hunton parish church in Kent. Of course, Hulne and Aylesford were relatively small communities and this was reflected in the size of their library holdings. The larger houses, such as those at London, Oxford, Cambridge and York, where there were many students, would have had more extensive collections comprising several hundred volumes.

The names of a number of Carmelite students survive, fortunately, because they devoted some of their time to making copies of important texts. Many of them undertook this task in order to provide copies of theological texts for their own use or, at the request of their prior, student master or librarian. Most of these copies would eventually end up in the community library, although some might be intended as gifts to important church officials or patrons of the Order, especially texts which had been written by influential Carmelite authors, such as Thomas Netter*. The names of over twenty friars who had copied manuscripts survive, mostly because they left their names in a colophon (a note added at the end of book) or elsewhere is the text. One interesting example is the colophon left by John Holt, a London Carmelite, who copied a volume of Thomas Netter's *Doctrinale* where he signs himself at the end (in Latin):

> "May the tongue of the reader bless the right hand of the writer. Written by the hand of brother John Holt, Carmelite".

Another copyist, John Langwath, who joined the Carmelite Order in Lincoln, signs himself:

> "Written by Langwath in 1424 A.D., aged 47 years".

Finally, there is Richard Tenet who copied John Baconthorpe's, *Commentary on the Four Books of the Sentences,* and who wrote at the end of Book 2:

> "Here ends the 2nd Book of the Sentences … written during his vacation after ordination by brother Richard Tenet".

This last quote enables us to date the copy to 1422, the year of Tenet's ordination. One particular name occurs in a number of texts, and that is the name of Roger Alban. He is said to have been born in St Alban's in Hertfordshire, and is known to have entered the Carmelite Order in London. He was ordained priest on March 6th, 1406 in St Paul's cathedral, and it appears that he spent a significant part of his religious life, in copying manuscripts, for the use of his brethren. A particular example of his work can be found in the British Library which preserves a copy of St. Bonaventure's *Pharetra* and some other short works (Harley Ms 3138), made by him. At the end of this work, there is the inscription:

> "Here ends the book which is called by its author *Pharetra*. Which was written by Roger Albon, in 1424 A.D., on 22nd day of September, Amen."

Alban copied a number of other works which are preserved in the British Library, notably a concordance of the gospels by Zacharia of Chrysopolis (*B.L.* Ms Stowe 8) and a book called *The Poor Caitiff* (*B.L.* Ms. Stowe 38). Another work in which Alban's hand can be recognised is a commonplace book that is a collection of prayers, short devotional pieces, useful remedies, etc. (*B.L.* Ms Harley 211). Alban's hand can be identified in several of the items copied into this book. Among the texts which Alban copied in this collection, is a tract called *The Seven Deadly Sins,* written by the Carmelite Richard of Lavenham*.

Another major work written in Alban's hand is the extensive collection of anti-Wyclif documents called the *Fasciculi Zizaniorum* ("a bundle of weeds"), which dates from 1439. This collection appears to have been assembled by the Carmelite Thomas Netter* whilst he was working on his major work, the *Doctrinale antiquitatem fidei* (The doctrine of our ancient faith), which he wrote to refute the beliefs of Wyclif and the Lollards. These documents came to the attention of John Keninghale*, who succeeded Netter as provincial in 1430. As many of them were either written by Carmelites or mentioned events at which Carmelites took place, Keninghale seems to have made the decision to preserve them in a more permanent form. He delegated the actual task of the copying of the texts to Roger Alban, who completed his task in 1439.

However, the five surviving manuscripts listed above, represented only a part of Alban's literary activities. Apart from his copying work, there is one large original composition, which Alban wrote himself and which earned him a deserved reputation. This is his *Progenies regnum Brytanniae* (The ancestors of the king of Britain) which begins:

> "Considering the abundance of chronicles as well as the scholarly difficulty about the study of the noble ancestors of the kings of England…"

This is a genealogical work, normally copied in roll form, of which the first part lists the royal genealogy from Adam down to Jesus Christ. Then, the second part continues with a list of the popes and of the Roman Emperors down to the 15th century, together with the names of the kings of England, down to King Henry VI. The work was composed soon after 1453 and is often confused with similar chronologies by other authors. Alban's work, though, survives in twelve copies which indicate that it was a popular text. There are copies in the British Library, in the Oxford and Cambridge University libraries, the Lambeth Palace library, and a very fine copy in Winchester College which contains the heading:

> "Roger Alban a Carmelite in London is the author of this scroll."

This genealogy is Alban's last known work and it seems that he died soon after completing it. The *Progenies regum Brytanniae* certainly made Roger Alban well known, especially among those of the nobility, who would have been able to afford to purchase a copy. However, Alban's quiet work, over the years, copying texts to help his fellow Carmelites in their studies, was probably his greater contribution to the Order. Many Carmelites must have owed him a great debt of gratitude for his patient, careful workmanship.

**References:**

*BRCEW* 359: *ODNB* 1, 567

# 31

# RICHARD MISYN

## (†1462)

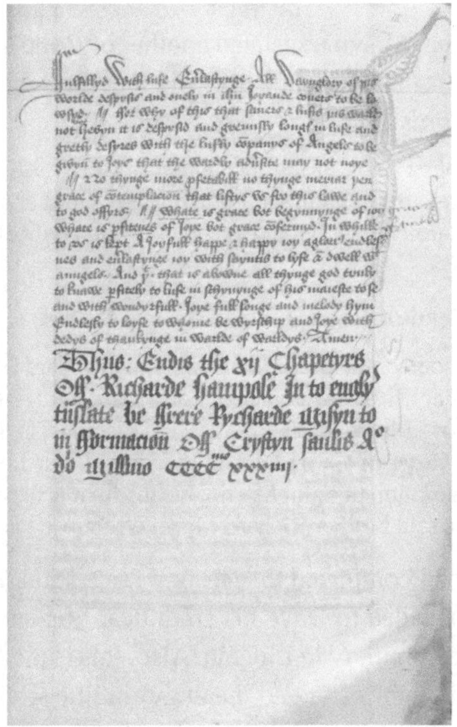

Thus: Endis the xij Chapetyrs Off. Richarde hampole In to englys translate be frere Rycharde misyn to informacion Off Crystyn saulis A° do millmo cccc xxxiiij.

Richard Misyn's translation of Richard Rolle's *The Mendynge of Lyfe*

From among the Carmelites, there was one friar who played a small but significant part in the development of the English mystical tradition. This was Richard Misyn, who joined the Carmelite Order in Lincoln. He completed his theological studies in the Carmelite study centre in York, and, after his ordination in 1422, he was sent to pursue further studies in theology at university, probably at Oxford, where he gained a B.Th.

However, Misyn felt called to a life of prayer, rather than one of study, and so, instead of proceeding to a doctorate, he returned to Lincoln, where he lived as a recluse or hermit for a number of years. During his period in seclusion, he occupied his time in making a translation into English of Richard Rolle of Hampole's *De Emendacione Vitae* (The Mending of Life). At the end of his translation, he wrote:

> "Thus ends the 12 chapters of Richard Hampole into English translated by friar Richard Misyn, for the information of Christian souls, in the year of Our Lord 1434."

The following year, Misyn translated another of Rolle's works into English, the *Incendium Amoris* (The Fire of Love), signing himself at the end of Book 1 this time with the words:

> "Here ends the first book of the *Incendium Amoris*, by Richard Hampole hermit, translated from Latin into English, by brother Richard Misyn, hermit, of the Carmelite Order and bachelor of sacred theology, in the year of Our Lord 1435."

And then, at the end of Book 2, he adds:

> "Here ends the book of the *Incendium Amoris* by Richard Hampole, hermit, translated into English at the request of Lady Margaret Heslington, recluse, by brother Richard Misyn, bachelor of sacred theology, at this time prior of Lincoln, of the Order of Carmelites, in the year of Our Lord 1435, on the Feast of the Translation of Saint Martin, bishop, that is the 4$^{th}$ nones of July [4$^{th}$ July], by the said brother Richard Misyn written and corrected."

By the time he had completed this second translation, it would appear that Misyn had been persuaded to leave his eremitical life, and to accept the position of prior of the community in Lincoln. Also, this is the first time that Misyn signs himself as "bachelor of sacred theology", a title which he uses regularly from now on. In addition, there is the mention that he had completed his translation at the request of Lady Margaret Heslington. Margaret Heslington was an anchoress, who lived in a cell in the churchyard of St Margaret's church, not far from the Carmelite house in York. It is possible that Richard Misyn came to know her while he was studying in York. She must have been fairly old by the time that Misyn made this translation as she died four years after receiving it, in 1439.

By now, Richard Misyn's reputation seems to have spread and soon after completing his translations, he was appointed chaplain to Henry Percy, Earl of Northumberland, one of the leading figures in the kingdom. On November 15$^{th}$, 1441, there is an entry in the papal registers:

> "To Richard Misyn, a Carmelite friar, S.T.B. Dispensation to him a priest and a chaplain of Henry, earl of Northumberland, to receive and hold for life any benefice with cure, wont to be governed by secular clerks, etc."

This permission was given so as to provide Misyn, with an annual salary, during his service for the Earl. Misyn would have received the income for the parish, out of which he would have paid for a curate to say mass, and undertake the other pastoral duties in the parish. On November 18th, 1443, he was admitted as rector of Edlaston in Derbyshire, a living which he held, probably, until 1446. Then on September 8th, 1446, he was admitted as the perpetual rector of Colwich in Staffordshire. Around this period, it is claimed that Misyn was appointed "inquisitor and prosecutor for apostates" by the Carmelite provincial Nicholas Kenton. Exactly what this title involved is not clear, and this is the only appointment of this type ever recorded in the medieval Carmelite province.

On July 29th, 1457, Misyn was appointed as bishop of Dromore in Ireland. Once again, there seems to have been no intention for Misyn to go to Dromore, and his promotion as bishop was made so that he could serve as a suffragan (assistant) for the Archbishop of York, William Booth. The formal commission for Misyn to act as suffragan in the diocese, was issued on the December 1st, 1457. From this time onwards, his name features regularly in the archbishop's registers, as he carried out ordinations, and other episcopal functions, for the archbishop. Misyn's income from his Irish diocese was very small and so, in order to provide him with an adequate income, he was appointed to various, more lucrative ecclesiastical positions. On January 3rd, 1459, he was admitted as rector of West Leake in Nottinghamshire. Then on July 20th, 1459, he was collated as the warden of St John's Hospital in Ripon. Finally he was named as the vicar of Birstall parish in Yorkshire from 1460. In all these positions, Misyn would have appointed another priest to serve as his vicar or curate, and to perform the pastoral duties for him. Meanwhile, Misyn himself appears to have lived in the Carmelite house in York. As a bishop, though, he would have had various privileges. For example, he would have had more appropriate living quarters, where he could entertain visitors, with a servant to care for him, and having control over his own finances, etc.

Misyn was well into his 60s when he was admitted as a member of the Corpus Christi Guild in York in 1461-1462. This was obviously a mark of respect for Misyn, and there is a memorial of his link with the Guild which still survives. A wooden mazer bowl (a silver-coated shared drinking vessel), which had been blessed by Archbishop Richard Scrope (†1405) was presented to the Corpus Christi Guild in 1413, and it was later blessed again by Misyn. The bowl bears the following inscriptions, recording the two indulgences granted to those who drank from this bowl:

> "Richard archbishop Scrope grants to all who drink of this cup 40 days of pardon. Robert Gubsun."
>
> "Bishop Misyn grants in the same form the aforesaid 40 days of pardon. Robert Stensall."
>
> [The names after each grant indicate the leader of the guild at that time].

Misyn died on September 29th, 1462, aged around 64 years, and was buried in the Carmelite chapel in York. His life can be conveniently divided into two distinct parts. There were the early years when he lived as a hermit, devoting his time to prayer and meditation. During this time, his translations of the two works by Richard Rolle, give a glimpse of the spirituality which inspired him, and also how he saw the need for translations of Rolle's works into English, so that they could be read by others living a similar life of prayer, but who lacked any knowledge of Latin. Then, in the latter part of his life, Misyn's talents and his pastoral qualities were recognised, and he served first the Earl of Northumberland as his chaplain, and then, promoted to be a bishop, he served the Archbishop of York, faithfully carrying out the duties of a suffragan bishop for his final five years.

**References:**

*BRCEW* 316-317: *ODNB* 38, 380-381

Tamás Karáth, "Richard Misyn's Transmission of Rollean Mysticism within and beyond the Carmelite Community", *Celebrating St. Albert and his Rule: Rules, Devotion, Orthodoxy and Dissent*", ed. Michelle Sauer & Kevin Alban, ed., (Rome: Edizioni Carmelitane, 2017), 151-182.

# 32

# JOHN HAUTEYN (SCHARYNGTON)

**(†1466+)**

Drawing of Oxnead Manor, Norfolk (after later rebuilding)

Most of the Carmelites featured in these chapters were praiseworthy figures in the history of the Order; individuals who, by their lives, gave a great example of prayer and devotion or of service through their teaching or administrative talents. John Hauteyn, sadly, does not fall into any of these categories; in fact, his life is more an example of how not to be a friar, rather than acting as a model for others to follow. However, by a curious act of fortune, we know more about his personal history and his life in the Order, than of the great majority of brothers, who lived quietly and almost anonymously, throughout their lives as Carmelites. It is worth recording that if a Carmelite in the Order, during the medieval period, wished to be remembered by future generations then, to start, he should be ordained to the priesthood as then his name will be preserved in the episcopal registers. Lay brothers, on the other hand, passed almost unnoticed by future generations. So far, research tracing individual Carmelites in the English Province before the Reformation, has identified the names of around 4,500 friars, but only three of these were lay brothers. Another more secure way of being remembered is to achieve a position of authority either within the Order as a prior, or provincial, or in the wider church as a bishop or other senior ecclesiastical role; then one's name will feature in official documents, etc. A third way is to write, when your compositions hopefully will survive and be quoted by future generations.

A final but less complimentary way of ensuring that one's name will be remembered, is by becoming involved with the law. This can be relatively blameless, if it involves appearing in court as a witness, or as the plaintiff seeking redress for a debt or an injury suffered. The worst case is, as a defendant for a crime, which might involve some sort of sentence. In the medieval period, though, ordained friars could plead "benefit of clergy" and be referred to the bishop's court for trial, where the sentences were more lenient. Whatever the reason, appearing in a royal court meant that a friar's name would be entered in the court records, and so remain for posterity. Fortunately, the Anglo-American Legal Tradition (AALT) based in the University of Houston, has undertaken a massive project of photographing all the early English legal records preserved in the National Archives in Kew. They have photographed nearly 10,000,000 images from the legal rolls, which are freely available online. However, searching these images, written by hand in abbreviated Latin, is difficult and takes considerable skill and time. Fortunately, the AALT team are working hard to produce indices, of the plaintiffs and defendants, which can be searched. So far, consulting these indices and other sources has led to the identification of over 80 Carmelites, who are mentioned in the court records, and these references have significantly helped to extend our knowledge of some of our medieval brethren.

In the case of John Hauteyn, his name and personal details survive, not in the royal legal records, but in the proceedings of an ecclesiastical court, which was held in Norwich and which have survived in a manuscript held in the British Library. The court met, at the command of the pope, to hear the plea made by Hauteyn that he should be allowed to leave the Carmelites, as he was forced to join the Order under the age of 14 years. The contents of this manuscript can be supplemented by a number of other sources, most notably the letters of the Paston family who were a significant family in East Anglia at this time, and who had a particular interest in the case of John Hauteyn. Fortuitously, a large number of the letters between the members of the Paston family have survived, because they were impounded by the State under Henry VIII, and lay untouched in the Tower of London, until they were rediscovered and taken into the care of the National Archives.

The ecclesiastical court record describes Hauteyn's efforts to prove that he was under 14 years of age, when he was compelled by his parents to join the Order in London. The Paston family became involved because, if Hauteyn succeeded in being laicised, he would then be free to pursue his claim to be the rightful owner of Oxnead manor where Agnes Paston lived. Hauteyn believed that he should have inherited this property from his father, but the Paston family maintained that they had purchased the manor in good faith. Fortunately for historians, the Paston family, in their defence of their claim to the title of Oxnead Manor, drew up a document, with the help of the relatives and neighbours of the Hauteyn family, which described Hauteyn's childhood and family background.

According to this deposition, Hauteyn's parents were Haymund and Claricia, and he had an elder brother Robert, four years older than himself. Around 1394, Hauteyn's parents moved from Sharrington in the north of Norfolk, to Swaffham Market which was 25 miles further south, and there, they entered into the service of a certain Thomas Delgate, living in as members of his household. A few years after this move, Hauteyn was born, and in 1399, Haymund Hauteyn recognised the needs of his larger family, and he purchased a separate house for them to live in. Sadly, a few years later, on a visit to London, Haymund Hauteyn was drowned in the Thames. In due course Clarissa remarried and, around 1410, she decided that Hauteyn should be sent to London, where he became an apprentice to a Thomas Brown. This was not a happy arrangement and, after a short time, Hauteyn ran away. He went to the Carmelite house in London where he asked to join the Order. He was interviewed by the provincial, Thomas Netter*, and Hauteyn assured him that he was over 14 years of age. So, Hauteyn was accepted and, in due course, made his religious profession. It was murmured among the Carmelites that Netter grew very fond of Hauteyn who became known as Netter's "beaufitz" (favoured son). However, Hauteyn did not live up to Netter's hopes for him and, after a few years, he ran away from the Carmelites and had to be brought back by his mother. On his return, Netter sent him to Oxford where he spent some time in the community prison cell. In the medieval period, each priory had a prison cell, where offending friars could be detained.

Some months later, Hauteyn was brought back to London, and started his studies for the priesthood. After a couple of years, Hauteyn moved to Maldon where he would have studied philosophy, but he only lasted for a short period there before he ran away again. This time, when he was brought back, he was sent to Norwich where he spent six months in the prison cell in the Carmelite priory there. On his release, Hauteyn completed his studies for the priesthood in Norwich.

After ordination as a priest, Hauteyn was transferred to the small Carmelite house in Blakeney where his uncle, John Aldeburgh, was the prior. He stayed there for four years and, towards the end of this time, his uncle appointed him as collector of alms from the local villages (*terminarius*) and guest master (*hospes*). However, the temptation in these roles proved too much and, once again, Hauteyn ran away. This time, he stole some lay clothes from one of the servants in the guesthouse, and a book belonging to his uncle, which he sold in Aylesham for four and a half marks (£3). (His uncle was forced to repay this amount in order to get the book back).

Arrested and returned once more to the Carmelites, Hauteyn found himself again in the prison cell in Norwich. It was whilst he was there, that he launched an appeal to Rome for a dispensation from his vows, claiming that he had been forced by his parents, against his will, to join the Carmelites when he was under the minimum age of 14 years. On May 16th, 1441, Pope Eugene IV accepted Hauteyn's petition for laicisation, and issued an instruction to John Kelyng, the abbot of St Benet's Abbey at Holme, Norwich, ordering him to assemble an ecclesiastical court which would take evidence and give a judgement. This court met for the first time on September 3rd, 1443, in St Leonard's chapel, in the manor of Heigham near Norwich. After the reading of the papal mandate, it ordered that the first formal hearing of evidence would take place on September 28th, in the conventual church of St Benet's Abbey. As Hauteyn had originally joined the Order in London, and spent some years there, the court ordered that notices of the proposed hearing should be displayed on the walls of St. Paul's cathedral in London, and a formal announcement was made at the high mass on September 15th, asking for interested persons to come forward. Also, the older Carmelites in the London house, who had known Hauteyn, were ordered to make written statements about what they knew of him, under the threat of a fine of £20 if they failed to do so.

It was then that the Paston family, who were an interested party in this matter, compiled their deposition containing evidence from a number of persons who lived in Swaffham or Aylesham, and who had known the Hauteyn family. The Paston family also produced a statement from John Hauteyn's uncle, John Aldeburgh, the prior of Blakeney. These depositions were dated September 8th, 1443.

When the ecclesiastical court met on September 28th, Hauteyn himself produced two certificates, one signed by the "archbishop of London", and the other by the dean of the Norwich diocese. Some of the senior Carmelites from Norwich attended the court, led by their prior, Peter of Saint Faith, a doctor in theology. He was accompanied by two more doctors of theology, Henry Wichingham and John Taverham, a bachelor of theology William Westwyk, a lector in theology, Richard Water, and two other older friars, Simon Castleacre and Robert Carleton. Of these friars, John Taverham was around 70 years of age, Peter of Saint Faith was over 50 years and all the others were 40 years or older, so they would all have known John Hauteyn, and been aware of his escapades. They appear to have given their evidence during this hearing, whilst Hauteyn was told to present his witnesses at the next session, to be held in the parish church of North Walsham.

In the meantime, on October 13th, the London Carmelites who were to give evidence, were assembled, before a public notary, in the chapter room of their house in Fleet Street, London. They were led by their prior Thomas Ashwell, another doctor in theology and he was accompanied by six further doctors in theology, Thomas Wellys, Richard Fyssus, William Terry, Stephen Gansior, Robert Kent and John Lord. The large number of doctors in theology, giving evidence in London, was due to the status of the London house, which was a *studium generale*, where students from the other provinces of the Order came to study philosophy. Those who gave evidence against Hauteyn, were all of a similar age to Hauteyn,and probably were fellow students with him whilst he was in London.

When the tribunal met on the October 15th, in the parish church in North Walsham, the depositions of the London Carmelites were presented, and then Hauteyn called his own witnesses. The first was Robert Hempnale from Aylesham, the village where Hauteyn's mother had moved after the death of Hauteyn's father. In Aylesham, Hauteyn's mother had married Peter Fish, who was blind, and she lived with him for 6-7 years before he died. Then she remarried for the third time to William Punyant who was called as Hauteyn's second witness. Hauteyn called two further lay witnesses, John Mortoft of Iteringham and Walter Herman of Swafield, and an anonymous Carmelite who testified on his behalf. In their defence, the Carmelites declared that they had never accepted anyone under the age of 14 years. Unexpectedly, the proceedings were then stopped by order of King Henry VI.

Hauteyn, however, did not give up his claim, and was encouraged by the fact that the senior member of the Paston family, William Paston, died on August 13th,1444. As a result of this bereavement, the Paston family lost a lot of their influence in the county. So, in 1446, Hauteyn managed to get his case re-opened. This time the Carmelites appear to have abandoned their defence, possibly judging that any further legal action was not worth the expense, and that there was little enthusiasm in the Order to have Hauteyn returned. So, in March 1447, judgement was given against them and Hauteyn was declared to be no longer bound to the observance of his religious vows.

Hauteyn was now free to pursue his legal claim to be the rightful owner of Oxnead Manor. His major difficulty lay in obtaining the necessary legal counsel so, sometime between 1447-1449, he wrote to the Archbishop of Canterbury, John Stafford, Chancellor of England, seeking help:

> *To the most Reverend Father in God the Archbishop of Canterbury, Chancellor of England.*
> Beseeches meekly your gracious Lordship, your own servant and orator John Hawteyn, chaplain, that where he hath divers suits and actions in law to be sued against Agnes, that was the wife of William Paston, of the manor of Oxnead, in the county of Norfolk; and for as much as your said beseecher can get no counsel of men of court to be with him in the said matters, by cause that the said William Paston was one of the King's Justices, and John Paston, son and heir to the said William Paston, is also a man of court; that it please your good Lordship to assign, and most strictly to command John Heydon, Thomas Littleton, and John Oelston to be of counsel with your said beseecher in the said matters, and order that he has to do against the said Agnes and order; and your said beseecher shall content them well for their labour. And that this be done in the reverence of God and way of charity.
>
> John Hawteyn, chaplain.

Hauteyn still had one powerful supporter, the Duke of Suffolk, who had his own problems with the Paston family, and saw Hauteyn as a useful pawn, to use in his attempts to reduce the influence of the Pastons. He realised that Hauteyn had some popular support for his claim to Oxnead manor, and, in an undated letter in the Paston papers, there is an account of Hauteyn bringing a group of his supporters to Oxnead, where he demanded to speak to Agnes Paston, in order to put forward his claim to the property. He was sent away unheard by Edmund Paston. This confrontation must have taken placed between 1447-1449. On March 11th, 1449, Margaret Paston wrote to her husband that there had been a plot among the shipment of Covehithe to put the Pastons out of Oxnead, and to give the property to Hauteyn. In another letter, Hauteyn himself is recorded as going to St Benet's Abbey (16 miles east of Norwich) and around the city of

Norwich, boasting about how he would regain possession of Oxnead manor.

Unfortunately for Hauteyn, a shift in the political climate led to the loss of his most powerful supporter. On February 7th, 1450, the Earl of Suffolk was impeached and banished from the kingdom by King Henry VI. On May 2nd, the Earl took ship for France but, when the crew discovered the identity of their passenger, they seized him and beheaded him on the ship. With the death of the Earl, Hauteyn's suit for Oxnead collapsed and, late in 1450 or early 1451, Hauteyn and the other members of his family released their rights to the property. After this, Hauteyn disappears from the historical records.

In many ways, the case of John Hauteyn is a sad one. As a youth, he probably saw the Carmelite Order as a safe refuge, where he could find a pleasant way of life. When this didn't prove to be the case, he made a series of attempts to escape. In the medieval period, though, religious life was a lifelong commitment, with few possibilities for a dispensation, so whenever Hauteyn absconded, the Order alerted the county authorities, and Hauteyn was arrested and brought back. In Hauteyn's case, he was forced to launch his appeal for a dispensation, on the grounds that he was accepted into the Order under the age of 14 years – some 40 years earlier. The Carmelites, with the assistance of the Paston family and others, initially defended the case and it would probably have been formally rejected, if the king had not intervened to stop the case. When Hauteyn managed to get the case re-opened, it seems that the Carmelites had had enough. After all the trouble that Hauteyn had caused, they must have been relieved to see the back of him. Hauteyn himself, though, was spurred on by the thought that he could regain the family property of Oxnead manor. However, this was an unrealistic dream and, when his efforts failed, he was faced with a bleak future. What happened to him is unknown, but hopefully he managed to get some gainful employment as a priest or otherwise. He was now in his 50's, and it would be nice to think he found some suitable place to pass his final years.

**References:**

*BRCEW* 156-158:

Colin Richmond, *The Paston Family in the Fifteenth Century: vol. 1: The First Phase*, (Cambridge Univ. Press, 2002) 43-47.

# 33

# JOHN STANBURY
## (†1474)

Chantry chapel of John Stanbury, bishop of Hereford

For anyone walking around Hereford Cathedral, a particular delight is to visit the richly sculptured chantry chapel in the north aisle, and to admire its beautiful fan vaulting and stained glass windows. This chapel, completed during the 1480's, contains the tomb of a Carmelite John Stanbury, who was the bishop of Hereford from 1453-1474.

Stanbury was born around 1408, in Stanbury Manor, at Morwenstow in Cornwall, the second son of Walter Stanbury and his wife Cicely. He joined the Carmelites probably at the Carmelite priory in Sutton, near Plymouth, sometime in the early 1420's. After his novitiate and early formation, Stanbury's talents and probably the financial support of his family, led to him being sent to the Carmelite house in Oxford, for higher studies in theology.

The house of studies in Oxford had just been transferred to a new property, which had been acquired by the Carmelites. This was Beaumont Palace, one of King Edward II's royal residences, situated just outside the north gate of the city. It had been given to the Carmelites in 1318 in fulfilment of a vow made by King Edward II as he made his escape from the Battle of Bannockburn in 1314 after the defeat of the English army by the Scots. It must have taken some time to modify the palace so that it would be suitable for a religious community but, by 1321, the Carmelites had transferred from their original friary, which was further down Beaumont Street just beside Worcester College. The site of this first friary was purchased by the Benedictines and now forms part of Worcester College. The transfer was not without its difficulties as the area around Beaumont Palace was used by prostitutes and other "women of ill-fame". The noise and activities of these neighbours, forced king Edward II to issue an order in 1328 that all such persons were to be removed from the neighbourhood if the prior requested it.

When Stanbury arrived in the late 1420's, he would have found himself in a house which was still being adapted and enlarged to cope with a student community of around fifty friars. Extra buildings and land were acquired in 1318, 1324 and again in 1339, to cope with the needs of the community, among which was a cemetery which was blessed in 1320, by the bishop of Bangor. There is a local tradition that, during the building of a suitable chapel, the Carmelites used a side chapel in the local parish church of St Mary Magdalen, but this seems unlikely except for special liturgical ceremonies.

Stanbury enrolled in the University for a bachelor's degree, and then for a doctorate in theology. Normally this course of studies would take 10-12 years after ordination to complete, although not all this time would have to be spent in Oxford. After gaining his bachelor's degree, Stanbury would have been required to give some courses of lectures himself, in the Carmelite *studium*, to both Carmelites and students coming from other orders or colleges. He would have lectured for one year on the Bible, and then two years on Peter Lombard's *Four Books on the Sentences*, the standard theology textbook. These lectures would have been given under the watchful eyes of the Carmelite *magister regens* (senior lecturer). It is known that Stanbury had incepted as a doctor by June 1443, in that year, he was appointed to be one of a panel who were to arbitrate in a dispute between the Junior Proctor of the University, and the members of Trillok's Inn. The Proctors in the University oversee the behaviour of students in the town when they are outside their colleges and this dispute was probably over the behaviour of students from Trillok's Inn, a hostel for students. Again, in 1446, Stanbury is recorded as being one of the three representatives from the Oxford distinction or region of the Carmelites, who were called to discuss the reform of the whole province.

Soon, Stanbury's reputation appears to have reached the royal court, and King Henry VI put forward his name as a candidate, to become the new bishop for the diocese of Norwich, one of the most important dioceses in the country. However, Stanbury was to be disappointed as another more influential candidate was chosen. In recompense, Stanbury received a gift from the king of 20 marks (£13 6s. 8d.) and was then appointed to be bishop of Bangor in Wales. He was consecrated on June 20th, 1448. Stanbury's main duties, though, were to serve the king and he delegated most of his diocesan duties to others. Stanbury is recorded as being in the king's chamber in 1450, when the Earl of Suffolk was ordered to go into exile and, later the same year, he was present at a meeting of the king's council. The affair of the Earl of Suffolk had, as has been mentioned in the previous chapter, a sad ending when he was beheaded whilst on a ship crossing the Channel to France. There was great rejoicing in London, as the earl was very unpopular due to his part in the defeats suffered by the English forces in France, and a contemporary ballad, which caricatured the various lords and clerics around the king, contains the line:

> "I have lifted up my eyes, sayth brother Stanbury".

Stanbury remained close to the king as one of his trusted advisors. In 1453, he was translated to be bishop of the more important diocese of Hereford, and to celebrate this event, a solemn mass was celebrated in St Paul's Cathedral on February 7th, at which the Archbishop of Canterbury, John Kempe, presided. The sermon was preached by one of Stanbury's fellow Carmelites from Oxford, brother Walter Hunt*. Stanbury then travelled to Hereford, where he was formally enthroned in the cathedral on April 25th, 1453, by the Abbot of Gloucester.

Stanbury is recorded as being present at meetings of the Privy Council throughout 1454-1455 and he was also occupied in a number of other tasks, being appointed by the pope as one of four senior clerics to conduct an inquiry into a quarrel, over the offerings made by Robert Wright, and some other parishioners, to some of the London churches. Stanbury was present in Parliament in July 1455, where he took the oath of loyalty to the king, and he was appointed trier of petitions for Gascony, when Parliament re-assembled in November. He was also present at the Great Council held in Coventry on February 14th, 1457, and then attended on the king "for certain special matters" in Westminster on October 11th.

In 1460, civil war erupted again – the War of the Roses – when there was an invasion of England by an army led by the Earl of Warwick. The critical moment came when the king's forces met those of the Earl of Warwick, at the Battle of Northampton, on July 10th. The royal army was defeated and King Henry VI was seized and imprisoned. Stanbury was present with the king, and encouraged him to fight but, after the battle, he himself was imprisoned in Warwick Castle for some months. Following his release, he retired to his manor of Bosbury, from where he sent an appeal to the pope and to the archbishop of Canterbury for protection against his enemies. On the accession of King Edward IV, Stanbury attended his first Parliament on November 4th, 1461, and is mentioned several times in the parliamentary records. But, by now, Stanbury was getting old, and he was no longer in favour with the new king so, on April 21st, 1461, he was given papal permission to resign his see, as he was:

> ".. so old and weak that he can no longer rule and administer the said church".

Stanbury was allowed to retire, and to reserve a pension for himself out of the income of the diocese, provided that it did not exceed "one third of the fruits of the diocese." He returned to his manor of Bosbury in December 1463. Stanbury, though, was not the type to retire and live a life of leisure, although he probably delegated much of the routine administration to his vicar general or others. He spent most of 1464 completing a book with the title, *An Explanation of the Creed.* Then, from 1468, he was much occupied with the suppression of Lollardy in the diocese.

Finally Stanbury died whilst staying in the Carmelite house in Ludlow on May 11th, 1474. In his will, he left £10 to the Carmelite house in Oxford to be used for his obit (funeral mass) and spent at the discretion of the prior, his old friend, Walter Hunt. A chantry chapel was built in his cathedral, and his remains were buried there during the 1480's. The deed of endowment for the newly built chapel was dated August 10th, 1491.

In 1844, during repairs to the foundations, his tomb was temporarily moved. Inside his tomb, there was found a gold ring set with a sapphire stone, inscribed inside with the words "en bon an" ("Happy New Year"), indicating that it was a New Year's gift (possibly from the king). In 1924 and 1929, the chapel was refurbished and stained glass inserted in the windows, picturing Stanbury's enthronement and his supposed association with Eton College. The link with Eton is often repeated by earlier historians, but there is no evidence that Stanbury was involved in any way with the foundation of Eton, nor did he have any significant role there. However, he may have visited the College on formal occasions.

In March 2002, a burglar smashed the window illustrating Stanbury's enthronement, in an attempt to enter the cathedral, but the alarm went off and the burglar took flight. The window was badly damaged but has now been careful re-assembled and put back in place by James Budd, a stained glass specialist.

> These sad marble stones form a tomb for the bones
> Of John Stanbury, a bishop and a Carmelite.
> He was a doctor whose fame spread throughout the world.
> O Christ, we beg you to cleanse him from all sin.
> He presided wisely and with respect over the see of Bangor
> Then, for twenty and one years, he brought lustre to our see.
> Once entrusted with this flock, the wolf fled before him.
> Then death, that savage beast, sank his cruel teeth into him.
> In the year one thousand four hundred and sixty
> Plus four, he was laid low in the church, this Easter season.
> Whoever reads this, pray for our bishop with kind intent,
> So that, all forgiven, there may be a worthy welcome for him in heaven.

Of the nineteen works attributed to Stanbury, none survive. Many of them appear to be collections of his lectures and other academic exercises, which he wrote whilst teaching in Oxford. Other works, designed for his students, included a set of 10 indices for some of the major theological texts. The remaining items are mostly collections of sermons, addresses, etc. from his period as a bishop.

Stanbury stands out in this collection of medieval friars primarily because he was one of the few Carmelites to be appointed to a major English diocese, the others being Robert Mascall* (also Hereford), Thomas Peverel* (Worcester) and Stephen Patryngton* (appointed to Chichester but died before he could be enthroned). Also Stanbury was a faithful servant and close adviser to King Henry VI. Although his royal duties meant that he was absent from his diocese for long periods, Stanbury did not lose contact with his diocese, and for the last ten years of his life, rather than retire gracefully, he continued in office, and was active in seeking to keep his flock faithful to the Catholic faith. His elaborate chantry chapel reflects the esteem in which he was held, a man who sought to serve his diocese, his king and the Saviour who redeemed him.

**References:**

*BRCEW* 216-218: *ODNB* 52, 92

Ann Rhydderch, "Robert Mascall and John Stanbury: King's Confessors and Bishops of Hereford", M.A. thesis, University of Wales, University College of Swansea, 1974).

# 34

# WALTER HUNT

**(1478)**

Carmelite Friar at work

One of the most significant theologians in the Carmelite Order during the fifteenth century was Walter Hunt. According to John Bale*, Hunt was born in the west of England, and so would have joined the Order in Gloucester, Bristol or Plymouth. Evidently his talents were recognised early, and Hunt was sent to study in the *studium generale* in London, where he was ordained deacon on September 24th, 1418, in St Paul's cathedral. He was ordained a priest on March 2nd, 1420, in Ramsbury prebendary church, near Swindon, which was possibly chosen because Hunt's family came from that region.

Following his ordination, Hunt went to Oxford to pursue higher studies in theology. He was there when a provincial chapter was held in the house in 1426. That would have been a major disturbance, as a provincial chapter would be attended by around 80-100 friars, and they would have been there for a week around the Feast of the Assumption on August 15th, Each day, at the daily mass, one of the doctors of theology in the province would have given the sermon (in Latin, of course).

Hunt completed his studies in Oxford and incepted as a doctor in 1434. Following his inception, Hunt would have served as *magister regens* for the next year. During this year, he would have acted as principal lecturer in the Carmelite house, and his lectures would have been attended by students, from other religious orders and colleges in the university. Hunt appears to have been a very competent teacher and he was, in fact, to spend the rest of his life at Oxford. He wrote over twenty theological works, but sadly only a couple of short pieces have survived. These two pieces are *Determinationes*, that is, public presentations on significant theological questions. The two questions which Hunt tackled were – *On the authority and pre-eminence of Peter over the Apostles, and Is the Church only for the predestined.* These two questions were probably selected, in order to argue against the heretical ideas, being expressed by John Wyclif and his followers. In his answers, Hunt uses arguments drawn from the Carmelite Thomas Netter's* *Doctrinale.* Netter had finished lecturing in Oxford before Hunt began his studies there. However the three volumes of Netter's *Doctrinale* were completed between 1426-1430 and so provided a major source for Wyclif's ideas and how to argue against them. Hunt's *Determinationes* appear to have been given at Oxford sometime in the 1450's.

Among the other works which Hunt wrote, there were a number of standard works such as a *Catholic Dictionary, Excerpts from twelve chronicles and histories,* a book *On the virtues* and another *On the vices,* etc. A number of Hunt's writings are clearly written against the Lollards, the followers of John Wyclif. These works have titles such as, *Whether the Religious Orders are a Spiritual Power in the Church Militant, On the Authority of the Pope over the Universal Church,* etc. There are also two works which illustrate how Hunt was a man of his time as they would not be acceptable nowadays. These are, *Against preaching by Women* and *Against Women distributing Holy Communion.* These two *Determinations* were directed against the practices introduced by the Lollards.

However, Hunt's activities were not confined to the University, and in 1438-1439, he was one of four Carmelite doctors of theology, who attended the General Council which met in Ferrara. Then, following an outbreak of the plague in Ferrara, the Carmelite delegation followed the Council as it transferred to Florence. The four English Carmelites were the only English representatives at the Council, as the other members of the English contingent were unable to travel due to an outbreak of hostilities between England and the Duke of Burgundy.

This General Council was called to try and achieve a union between the Latin and Greek Churches. Hunt appears to have been one of the chief exponents of the Latin Church in the negotiations with the Greek Orthodox representatives, and he was complimented on his efforts by Pope Eugene IV.

In 1446, Hunt was one of the representatives for the Oxford distinction (region) who met to discuss the reform of the English province. The following year, on February 7th, the Carmelite John Stanbury* received the papal bull, translating him to be the bishop of Hereford. On that day, John Kempe, the Archbishop of Canterbury, celebrated the mass of the Holy Spirit in St. Paul's cathedral, and afterwards the Archbishop and clergy, with John Stanbury, processed to the chapel of the blessed Virgin Mary, where Hunt preached the sermon on the text from II Corinthians, 6:3, "In order that our service be not brought into disrepute".

In 1450, Hunt was described as chaplain to Cardinal John Kempe, the Archbishop of York, when he was granted permission to hold a benefice for life. This licence was a way of granting a salary for Hunt's duties as chaplain. Two years later, on July 26th, 1452, Hunt was given a further licence to accept a canonry and prebendary stall in a collegiate church, probably in Lower Hall, Leominster. Exactly how long, Hunt was chaplain to Cardinal Kempe in unclear, but his role must have ended when the cardinal died in 1454.

All doctors of theology were entitled to attend Carmelite provincial chapters so, in 1456, Hunt would have been present at the provincial chapter held in Northallerton, where John Milverton* was elected provincial. Afterwards, Milverton is recorded as writing a letter which began:

> "Brother John, humble prior provincial, etc. … As in our last provincial chapter celebrated in Northallerton, Brother Walter Hunt …"

Unfortunately, the remainder of the letter has been lost, so one will ever know what Hunt did or said. Later that year, on November 9th, Hunt was appointed as one of the executors of the will of David Chirbury, a fellow Carmelite and also the Bishop of Dromore in Ireland. Hunt was given 40s. for his labours.

The Carmelite, John Stanbury*, Bishop of Hereford, had probably first met Hunt at Oxford, where Stanbury incepted as a doctor a few years after Hunt. It is likely that he had been one of Hunt's students. So, it is not surprising when, on November 13th, 1461, Stanbury, then Bishop of Bangor, appointed Hunt as the rector of the parish church in Llannynnys (Denbighshire). Then, on June

13th, 1465, Hunt resigned the prebend in Lower Hall, Leominster, and accepted an appointment from Stanbury, to the canonry and prebend of Moreton and Whaddon. Hunt held this appointment for the rest of his life. Hunt was in Oxford on February 25th, when he was named as one of the executors of Bishop Stanbury's will and he received a bequest of £20.

Finally, Hunt himself died in Oxford on November 28th, 1478, and was buried in the Carmelite chapel there. In the subsequent years, his obit was observed by the Oxford Carmelites. The epitaph on his tomb read:

> In the pit below this marble slab, there lie decaying now
> the bones of brother Walter Hunt, the respected doctor;
> I beg you, Flower of Carmel, to help your disciple
> that he may find his home and take his place in heaven.

**References:**

*BRCEW* 450-452: *ODNB* 28, 876-877

Margaret Harvey, "England, the Council of Florence and the End of the Council of Basle", in *Christian Unity and the Council of Ferrara-Florence 1438/39-1989*, ed. G. Alberigo (Leuven, 1991), 203-225.

# 35

# JOHN MILVERTON

**(†1487)**

Castel Sant'Angelo, Rome, where Milverton was imprisoned.

John Milverton can justly be described as the last great prior provincial in the medieval English province. He joined the Order in Bristol, and, after his novitiate, he was sent to do his studies, for the priesthood, in the Carmelite house in Stamford. The diocesan registers show that he was ordained a subdeacon on September 22nd, 1431, and deacon on September 20th, 1432, both occasions in Huntingdon Priory Church. Milverton's intellectual ability was quickly recognised and, after priestly ordination, he was sent to study for a doctorate in theology, at Oxford University c1433-1434.

Milverton was possibly the unnamed prior of Oxford in 1446, one of the delegates from the Oxford distinction (region), who met to discuss the reform of the English province. Certainly he was the prior by January 21st, 1449, when there is a record of him appearing in a court case. Then, in November 1451, he was named as the definitor (delegate) for the province, when he attended the Carmelite General Chapter held in Avignon, France. All these duties clearly distracted Milverton from his academic studies, as he did not complete his doctorate until early in 1452.

By this time, Milverton's leadership qualities were being recognised in the Order. The attempt to introduce a reformed pattern of religious life, in the province in 1446, had not had any noticeable effect so, in May 1456, Milverton was summoned to Paris by Jean Soreth, the great reforming prior general who had been seeking to persuade Carmelite communities throughout Europe to introduce a stricter pattern of religious life, and to follow the Carmelite Rule and Constitutions more faithfully. Soreth was eager to see Milverton introduce the same reformed observance in England and, at the general chapter which met in Paris on 16th May, Milverton was appointed as the provincial for England. The following year, 1457, he was also named as a commissary-general for Scotland and Ireland, which appointed him to act on behalf of the prior general in those two provinces. Soreth clearly hoped that Milverton would introduce the reformed observance throughout the British Isles. As Soreth was over 60 years of age by this time, he was not able to undertake the arduous journeys involved himself.

At the same moment, the mendicant friars were under attack in England, and Milverton was engaged in defending the rights of the four orders, i.e. Dominicans, Franciscans, Carmelites and Augustinians. In 1458, Milverton took part in a debate before Parliament with Reginald Pecock, the bishop of Chichester, who had criticised the friars. Soon after, Pecock was formally censured for his theological views, and he was condemned for heresy by the Archbishop of Canterbury. Milverton continued his criticism of Pecock and, the following year, he wrote to Pope Pius II, supporting the condemnation of Pecock. By now, Milverton's reputation had grown so much, that there was a rumour circulating that he was to be promoted bishop of St. David's diocese in Wales. However, this did not materialise, and then Milverton became involved in a serious dispute which rendered such a promotion impossible.

In 1464, Milverton was caught up in a quarrel with the diocesan clergy, which was to change the whole tenor of his later years. On September 16th that year, a young Carmelite, Henry Parker, preached an inflammatory sermon at St. Paul's Cross in London. St. Paul's Cross was situated in the cemetery, beside

St. Paul's Cathedral, London, and beside it there was an open-air pulpit where sermons could be given to a large crowd of people. In his sermon, Parker argued that Jesus was a beggar, who had had no personal possessions, and that he and the apostles held all things in common. Hence, he declared that those who served the Church should be like Jesus and not have great possessions or receive regular incomes. Parker went on to claim that the mendicant friars, who lived on the offerings from the laity, followed the example set by Jesus most closely, and so lived a more perfect form of the Christian life. These propositions were not new. The Carmelite, Richard Maidstone*, had written a tract on the same subject seventy years earlier, in a dispute with the Lollard John Ashwardby at Oxford. However, in recent years, some Franciscan friars in Italy had adopted this belief with excessive zeal, and, as a result, they were condemned by the papacy. As might be expected, the established clerical hierarchy regarded the resurgence of such notions as extremely dangerous.

Parker's sermon, preached in such a public place, provoked a great uproar and the subsequent events were described in a contemporary chronicle:

> "Also that year began a great schism between friars and priests, but the Friar 'Charmys', that is to say the White Friars, began it first at Paul's Cross. He that began this matter was born in Fleet Street, a skinner's son, and his name is Sir Harry Parker; he blamed men for their great abundance of their goods, and especially he blamed beneficed men, that had great benefices, and priests that had temporal livelihoods. For he said and affirmed that none of the 12 Apostles nor Christ had anything of their own but all in common, and said and affirmed by his reasoning, as strong as he could, that Christ was a beggar and had nought but by way of alms. And that made men to grouse and to mutter bitterly.
>
> "But the Sunday after, there was a doctor of divinity, Master William Ive, the master of Whittingdon College, said against the friar, and proved that Christ was poor and kept no great treasure, but as for begging he utterly denied it, and by holy scripture proved it so that men understood that the friar erred seriously against Holy Church; and then the friars began maliciously against this doctor. Then in Advent they provided a doctor of the White Friars, Master Thomas Haldon, and that he should preach against the Master William Ive aforesaid, and there he talked much of the begging of Christ, and put the people that the same matter should be determined in their school between him and a Grey Friar at the White Friars in Fleet Street the Wednes¬day, 7 nights after. And the Sunday following, a doctor of divinity, Master Edward Story, parson of All Hallows the Great in London, and after, confessor unto the Queen and after that Bishop of Carlisle, preached at Paul's Cross, and as much as he might would have pacified the matter, and said that it [was] blasphemy

so to rehearse and say by our Lord Christ. But that same Sunday the friars set up bills at every church door that the doctor said not truth, but the truth should be showed and said by Doctor Master John Milverton, the prior of the same place, and he was provincial of the same order. And that afternoon in his sermon he railed sore and grievously to fortify his brethren' sayings, that some laymen were wroth with the friar, and withdrew their alms from them; and some men were not pleased with their curates, and said that they had no right to have any offering but live by alms as Christ did; and these men were divided, some well and some ill.

"But the Wednesday, the doctor, Master Halden, kept the school within the Friars and disputed against a Grey Friar as he promised; and at that school were many great doctors and clerks to give him audience. And they thought he went so far that Master Alcock, a doctor of law and commissary unto the Dean of Saint Martin's in the Graunte, asserted the friar that he should appear before the Archbishop of Canterbury at Lambeth. And the friar said he would not obey his citation, for all friars are exempt from all the bishop's power, but it were for heresy; and the doctor of law cited him for heresy.

"Then at the beginning of the term after Easter the friar appeared before Master Doctor Winterbourne, my lord's officer and judge in such causes and others for spirituality. And there were many worthy doctors against the friar, but he leaned ever on his privilege, but he showed none but a bull unsealed. Then the matter was put to my Lord of London, by so much that all this trouble was done in his diocese, and the Chancellor of England, that was my Lord of Warwick's brother, took part against the friars; and the day following the provincial and Doctor Haldon came to Paul's before my Lord of London and brought their privileges with them, but the privileges would not serve that time for no cause of heresy. And my lord lawfully cited them to appear before him that same afternoon, but they came not, for the provincial took his way anon towards Rome. And Doctor Haldon took no leave of the bishop. And then my Lord Chancellor heard that they were gone, and sent for the young friar Harry Parker and commanded him to prison. And he was taken from prison and sent unto my Lord of London. And the Sunday after the same friar, Harry Parker, abjured what he said, and said as we say, that Christ is lord of everything, and he confessed all so that very need caused them to say that Christ begged, so that men should take the order of friars the most perfect of all orders.

"But one friar could not beware by another, for within the vacation time a Black Friar preached almost the same. And he was examined before my Lord of London, and was made to preach again and revoked. Then my Lord of London cursed these 2 doctors, Master John Milverton and Doctor Thomas Halden, at Paul's Cross for their contumacy, and it happened that Doctor Ive did the execution of the curse, and that grieved the friars sore, and said that he was set all in malice; but this Doctor Ive might not choose.

"And before this time the aforesaid Doctor Ive kept the school at Paul's that is under the chapter house, and there he read many full noble lessons to prove that Christ was lord of all and no beggar, and he did it after the form of the schools, for he had his habit and his fur [cape] on, and a verger with a silver rod waiting upon him. And the same friar Minor that answered the White Friar answered him once, and many times he disputed and read in that school; he kept it more then 2 years. Then the friars argued among themselves as to who should answer him. And some friars desired to answer him but at the day of their desire they appeared not. And then men laid great wagers the Provincial would come home and do many things, and caused that a friar of Rome made a treatise of the begging of Christ, that well was him that might have a copy of it, and they were for sale at many places in Rome and some were sent home to the White Friars, but it happened that they came to this Doctor Ive, but he understood the subject well enough and said full little or nought.

"Then the Pope wondering about the complaint of this friar, and inquiring of such men as came late out of England of the matter; and when he understood the matter he wrote down to the Archbishop of Canterbury and to the Bishop of London, and thanked them that they were so true to Christ and Holy Church, and desired to have all the whole matter and process sent unto him by writing. And so it was, everything as near as they could imagine, putting all favour and partiality and malice aside.

"But the very true process this noble Doctor Ive wrote unto the Pope of the manner, saying, and preaching in their sermons, both his doing and saying, as well as the friars, and the acts of both schools. And nine doctors of divinity and bachelors of divinity subscribed their names with their own hands, and testified that all was true that the said Doctor Ive had written, for it was examined and read before all the bishops that time being at London, and by the same doctors and clerks that subscribed. And that large and great letter was sent with the bishops' letters. And if that Doctor Ive's letter had been sealed with some lord's seal spiritual, or a notary's sign thereon, the friar had been burnt in short time; it had no other seal but his own signet.

"And the king took a great part in this matter, for these friars had caused much trouble among his people, and therefore he desired that holy father the Pope to chastise such trespassers and breakers of the peace, and sent forth a letter with the other letters.

"Then the Pope reserved these letters, and understood all the whole process, and made his cardinals to examine the friar, and by his answering they found nine more points that he erred on, and soon after he was put into the castle of Angel in strong prison, and lay therein almost 3 year. And ever his friends and the friars looked after his coming home, but he may not, for he hath bound himself unto the Pope by an iron oblation fast sealed about his 2 heels. And then he lacked money and friendship, submitted him to the Pope; but when he shall come home I know not, but forsooth his articles

> have been damned, whether he be or nought I know not; I trust you shall know after in time coming by God's grace, who have us all in his blessed keeping.

One point which needs to be stressed is that Milverton arrived at Rome at a very inopportune moment. Pope Paul II, who had just been elected, was engaged in suppressing a group of Italian Fraticelli (Franciscan friars), who held these extreme views on poverty. These Fraticelli were imprisoned in the Castel Sant'Angelo in 1466, at the same time as Milverton was held there, and they were interrogated under torture. Many were punished with great severity and a number executed. In view of their treatment, Milverton was probably wise to recant and fortunate to escape so lightly.

The Carmelite prior of London, Thomas Holden, had accompanied Milverton on the first part of his journey but it appears that he stopped in the Carmelite house in Calais and left Milverton to go on alone to Rome.

On his return in 1469, Milverton brought with him a letter from the Pope addressed to the Archbishop of Canterbury. This letter is worth quoting as it demonstrates not only how Milverton had recanted his former opinions but also that he had received the Pope's blessing to retake his former position in the Carmelite Order.

> "To our beloved son and venerable brother, health and our apostolic blessing.
>
> May it be known that we are aware that it was through your devotion that, some time ago, our beloved son John Milverton, of the Carmelite Order and then provincial in England was delated to us for having preached some matters which were not in agreement with the Catholic faith and gave serious offensive to the pious ear of the faithful. We have, in order to prove the sincerity of his faith and in the service of the truth have caused the said John to be detained in chains in prison for two years and more and we have authorised some commissaries who have diligently examined him on these articles which he had preached.
>
> "He continued to deny [his faults] for a long time but, however, true understanding finally returned to his heart and his better senses, so that he retracted his errors publicly before the above mentioned commissaries, and he promised, giving an adequate assurance and also under a sworn caution, that such matters would never again be preached, and also that he would publicly and openly revoke and retract everything which had been contrary to the truth and sense of sacred scripture wherever he or others had preached.
>
> "We have thus extended our mercy to him and we send him to you so that he may freely repeat the aforesaid before you that you will ensure that he revokes [his former opinions] without delay in the places where he has

> preached them, and that he will continue in this better way of life which he has begun. You are to return him to his Order and to all the [former] offices and privileges of the Order, notwithstanding anything to the contrary, as you enjoy, legitimately and freely, our authority.
>
> "Given in Rome at St. Peter's under the seal of the fisherman on the 22nd of December 1468, the fifth year of our pontificate."

On his return journey, as Milverton was passing through France, he arranged to arrive in Orléans just as the Carmelite General Chapter had begun to meet on May 21st, 1469. At the chapter, Milverton was welcomed warmly and he was re-appointed as the provincial for England. When the chapter closed, Milverton continued his way back to England, where he delivered his papal letter to the archbishop. Then, in August, he travelled to Ludlow where the English provincial chapter was held around the Feast of the Assumption (15th August). At the provincial chapter, his appointment as provincial was confirmed, and Milverton presided over the chapter discussions. Later, at the next General Chapter which met in Asti, Italy in May 1472, Milverton was not only confirmed as provincial for England but, once again, he was appointed vicar general for England, Scotland and Ireland.

By this time, Milverton himself was over sixty years of age, and, at some time in the late 1470's, an anonymous letter was sent to the new prior general Christopher Martignoni by an English Carmelite which read:

> "I swear that magister Milverton is a good priest and lives a praiseworthy life but he is incapable of working because of his old age and each day he is easily tired out by his various weaknesses (which is sad), so our religious life is going to ruin. In order that the house of Israel, which has been beaten almost to the ground, should be rebuilt, through proper worship of the liturgy, attention to studies, and the living of the regular life, I do not know of anyone more capable of restoring our province than magister Thomas Gilbert, who lives a praiseworthy life and has a good reputation, etc."

This letter does not seem to have had any significant effect but it does reveal that there was some dissatisfaction with Milverton's long period as provincial. However, it was not until 1482, that Milverton finally resigned his office as provincial. He retired to live in the Carmelite house in London where he died on January 30th, 1487, when he was nearly 70 years of age. He was buried in the chapel there.

John Bale* lists a long series of works which Milverton had written. There was the text of his sermon on *The Poverty of Christ* – which was probably the one which had stirred up so much controversy. This began "By the grace of Our

Lord Jesus Christ …" Another work, probably another sermon, was given the title – *On the Creed* – and begins; "May the Lord open my mouth…" As might be expected, Milverton wrote numerous letters whilst he was provincial, and it is recorded that his letter-book contained the texts of sixty-four of them. Fortunately, John Bale preserved a few notes on their contents at the back of one of his notebooks. One of these letters was Milverton's letter to the Pope on the condemnation of Reginald Pecock, and there was a group of eight letters which were addressed to the cardinals who had interrogated him in Rome. There were also some other more general letters written in Rome and sent to various officials defending his views.

Milverton was clearly a very talented and active leader of the province. It seemed in the 1450's that he had a promising future in front of him with the probability of being consecrated as a bishop and serving the king in some important office. However, it was the rash, ill-considered sermon by the young Henry Parker and Milverton's defence of it which set in train a whole sequence of events, leading to a very unpleasant experience for Milverton in Rome. It was only Milverton's humble confession of his errors that enabled him to escape being formally condemned for heresy and it was thanks to the clemency of the pope that he was permitted to return to England and resume his office as provincial.

**References:**

*BRCEW* 190-192: *ODNB* 38, 350

F. DuBoulay, "The Quarrel between the Carmelite Friars and the Secular Clergy of London", *Journal of Ecclesiastical History*, 6 (1955), 156-174.

# 36

# JOHN HOTHBY

## (†1487)

Music written by John Hothby

It is somewhat strange that, as a religious Order whose daily activities involved singing at the community Mass and the Divine Office, the English Carmelites produced only one notable musician before the Reformation, and he would spend most of his life outside the province. He was John Hothby, born around 1430, the son of William Hothby. He first appears in the records, as being listed as a member of the Oxford community, when he was ordained subdeacon on December 18th, 1451, in All Saints church in Northampton. At this time, Hothby was probably a student in the Carmelite house of studies in Oxford following the advanced course of theology, which led to a Licentiate in Sacred Theology, an internal Carmelite award.

Hothby was evidently a talented musician as, after his ordination, he was given permission to travel widely, pursuing his studies in music. He visited various places in England, and then crossed the Channel and made his way through France, Spain and Germany. There is little information on this period of his life, but it seems likely that he spent some time teaching music in the Carmelite community in Bruges in the late 1450's. Whilst there, he was possibly the compiler, or assisted in the compilation of a collection of church music for use in the Merchant Adventurers' chapel, in the Carmelite church. Although there is no direct evidence, linking Hothby with this choir book, it seems highly likely that he was involved in its preparation. The book, now known as the Lucca Choirbook, arrived in the cathedral in Lucca at around the same time as Hothby took up his appointment as the choirmaster in the cathedral.

After leaving Bruges around 1460, Hothby made his way to Italy, where he spent some time studying music in Pavia university. One of his fellow students there was another noted musician, John Gallicus, a Carthusian from Mantua. Hothby appears to have gained a doctorate in music at Pavia, as a few years later he is described as "John Hothby from England, an expert in the art of music and *magister*". It is worth noting that Hothby had to travel abroad for his music studies as Oxford University did not offer a degree in music until 1507.

After Pavia, Hothby appears to have spent some time in Florence, where he made the acquaintance of Lorenzo de' Medici, the son of Piero il Gottoso, the governor, and other significant figures in the city. Then, in February 1467, Hothby moved to Lucca where he had been offered a position as the chaplain for the altar of St. Regolo, in the cathedral of San Martino in Lucca. His duties included teaching plainchant and polyphony, to the clerics in the cathedral, as well as teaching grammar and arithmetic to the pupils, in the cathedral school. Hothby's appointment was made possible by an endowment from Nicolao da Noceto, who had built a new altar for the chapel, next to his father's tomb. As chaplain, Hothby received an annual salary of 36 ducats.

On November 17$^{th}$, 1469, Hothby wrote a letter to Lorenzo de' Medici in Florence who had just taken over the government of the city following the death of his father. Hothby sought a pardon for one of his friends, and begged Lorenzo to intervene. This letter is the earliest surviving document in Hothby's own hand:

> "Magnificent and generous man and my lord, a lord most esteemed by me, *followed by the due formalities, etc.*

> "Your Magnificence will pardon me if I seem too importunate to You in regard to the acts of that priest, Andrea de Ciampanti, one of my best friends. I should like to hear if Your Magnificence has obtained any pardon for him from the Reverend Father, the Bishop of Lucca, or indeed if You have had to write him for some other reason. I should like, if anyone ought to do me this favor, that it be Your Magnificence, from whom I expect some reply, in spite of my great presumption. But the great humanity that I know has always been shown me, makes me take faith in Your Magnificence, to whom I humbly recommend myself and pray God to maintain always in a happy state, etc.
>
> Lucca, 17 November 1469.
>
> Man of Outstanding Reputation Your son and servant, Hocby the Carmelite"

In Lucca, Hothby proved to be an excellent teacher and so, the same year, the canons of the cathedral wrote to the Consiglio Generale of Lucca, asking for his salary to be increased, otherwise Hothby might be tempted away by more generous offers from other towns. Hothby's fame attracted students to come from the different regions of Italy and, among them was a fellow Carmelite, the Italian, Giovanni Bonadies. It was Bonadies who, in 1473-1474, copied a number of Hothby's treatises on musical theory, and nine of his polyphonic compositions. Bonadies' notebook still survives, and it is the only source for most of Hothby's musical compositions. Another of Hothby's students, Matteo de' Testadraconi, described him as:

> "the first among doctors of music as well as a most talented reader in theology".

As for the Consiglio Generale, they granted Hothby an additional 2 ducats per month. As Hothby's fame grew, there were further increases in his salary, and the granting of various privileges.

Fortunately, a large number of the records for Lucca cathedral survive, and Hothby's name is frequently mentioned in many of the entries related to the payment of his salary. In 1473, Hothby appears to have come into possession of a farm in Brancoli, granted to him by Nicolao da Noceto, which he leased out to Michele di Andrea and Bartolomeo di Giovanni for three years. In 1476, Hothby petitioned the resident chaplains in the cathedral for admission into their community, which would entitle him to receive stipends paid for the celebration of the divine office, and his request was granted on January 30th, 1477 providing that Hothby held no other post than that of a simple priest of San Pietro Somaldi. The latter condition was fulfilled later on September 30th, when, following the death of the previous incumbent, Hothby was nominated by the chaplains as rector of San Pietro Somaldi. In 1479, Hothby was appointed as chaplain of the altar of San Pelegrino in the church of San Pietro Cigoli. Then, in 1484, the community of resident chaplains elected him as their subprior for three months. Soon afterwards, the canons of San Martino nominated Hothby to be the rector of San Vito in Pomorano.

By 1486, Hothby's fame had spread not only throughout Italy, but also further afield and eventually reached as far as his own country of England. In this year, King Henry VII asked him to return and serve in his personal chapel. Evidently Hothby assumed, at first, that this would be a short visit and so, on February 17th, 1486, the *Consiglio Generale* granted his request that he should receive his salary *in absentia* until October 14th, 1486, and that he could choose a substitute to take charge of the school until that date. The *Consiglio* accepted that if Hothby returned within 18 months then he could receive his usual salary and privileges. The decree reads:

> "Then, having read the request of brother John of England, doctor of music performed in public, it was solemnly decreed on it that, in spite of 13 votes against, it shall be ordered and approved that he shall receive not only his salary for his service up to the present day, but also the salary which he would be due to have received up to the day of 14th October next. On which day his contract ends. And he shall have the right to appoint at his discretion whoever he wishes as his substitute while he is away, who shall teach and be in charge of the school until the above date, the 14th October. And also, it shall be given that if it is known after this time that he wishes to return, that he will be re-installed with the same salary and duties that he has had for the years since his beginning from the day of his return providing that he has returned within the next eighteen months."

On his way back towards England, Hothby took advantage of the opportunity to visit Germany and the Low Countries, probably meeting with other musicians and getting acquainted with new developments in music. Then, on October 24th, 1487, the news reached Lucca that Hothby had died "in Britannia". This would imply that Hothby had continued his travels across France to Brittany (not "Britain"), probably visiting some of the French cathedrals on his way. Sadly, Hothby never reached England which is a pity, as his intended post serving in the royal chapel, could have given him the ideal situation to demonstrate his creative talents in composing music for a talented choir.

There is no doubt that Hothby was a well-respected and highly talented musician, with a great reputation among his contemporaries throughout Europe. Unfortunately, few of his musical compositions survive but, as Albert Seay writes:

> "It is clear from these nine compositions that Hothby was well aware of the currents of his own time and was more than just a theorist who also wrote music."

He continues:

> "As a theorist, Hothby represents the 15th-century speculative musician still concerned with the maintenance of Boethian and Guidonian thinking."

Certainly, Hothby was a much admired as a teacher and over twenty of his short treatises on music theory survive. The most important of these is *La Calliopea legale* (The Legal Muse), and Seay commented on this work:

> "It explores in depth the problems of the semitone and its varying sizes. In addition it extends the number of places on which Guidonian hexachords could be built.... The book is obviously an attempt to reconcile the methods and authority of the past with the changing practicalities of the day."

However, Hothby was not only a musician who attracted many students, but he had a wide circle of friends and was held in high regard by the canons of the cathedral and the *Consiglio Generale* of the town. Hothby's eighteen years in Lucca marked a high point for the singing in the cathedral and the town became known as a centre for inspiring music. Hothby's own reputation led to many students coming to Lucca in order to study music under him.

The high regard that the *Consiglio Generale* had for Hothby, can be seen expressed in the letter of commendation which they sent to King Henry VII on his behalf.

> *"Letter from the Elders in Lucca*
>
> To the most serene and invincible King of England, the most illustrious princes, and great lords. We, the Anziani and Gonfaloniere di Giustizia of the Lucchese people and commune, by this our promised and humble recommendation, give assurance that the right venerable priest Brother John Hothby, O.Carm., whose faith, outstanding probity, integrity, and singular erudition in the discipline of music and excellent morals we have experienced for more than eighteen years, to the great praise of himself and consolation to us, has now left our city and is returning to his native land with the favour of [our] entire people, summoned, as he informed us, by the same most serene king. Out of reverence for so great a most serene king, whose regal majesty we revere and observe, we have promised [Hothby] freedom of passage as concerns us. Therefore we recommend him on his departure to everyone and testify to his excellent morals, as noted above, his singular learning, and in particular, which is to be most highly esteemed, his good nature and liberality in teaching students, especially asking from the heart that such a venerable presence shall, both for his own virtues and

> at our intercession, be received with good will by all people in all places and treated with good will as merit demands, and our supplication, because we shall treat as a benefit any kindness and comfort conferred on him. Given the day of March 1486."

Finally, there is a short poem by the Carmelite Giovanni Andrea Ferabos from Verona, which gives another expression of the high regard in which Hothby was held:

> If anyone is here whom music gave a name,
> And who deserved to cover his hair with the leaves of laurel,
> Let him give way to you, Hothby. If you circle the globe
> From the Ganges to Cadiz, none will be equal to you,
> For Nature, the mother of things, poured into you alone.
> Whatever there was of beautiful form, whatever of honour.

**References:**

*BRCEW* 163-168: *ODNB* 28, 266-267

Bonnie Blackburn, "Hothby, John", *New Grove Dictionary of Music and Musicians,* ed. S. Sadie, (London, 2001), xi, 749-751.

Benjamin Brand, "A Medieval *Scholasticus* and Renaissance Choirmaster: A Portrait of John Hothby at Lucca", *Renaissance Quarterly*, 63 (2010) 754-806.

37

# THOMAS SCROPE

**(†1491)**

Thomas Scrope, bishop of Dromore

In the early 1400's, the roads around Norwich would have been very busy, filled with people walking towards to the town, to visit the market or to see the sights there, with the more prosperous travellers riding on horseback and occasionally urgent messengers galloping hard as they carried important messages or reports. Then there were the wagons bringing farm produce for the market, wool for shipping overseas to the weavers in the Low Countries, or going to collect goods, which had been brought by ships from the Continent. Occasionally there might be bands of men-at-arms, or archers marching off on some mission or other; more often, there would be the pedlars, the travelling tradesmen seeking to sell their goods in the local villages and the craftsmen offering to sharpen knives, to repair pots and pans, or to resole shoes.

Around 1425, one might have encountered a strange friar wearing sackcloth and ashes, and with an iron girdle around his waist. He was going about preaching the imminent Second Coming of Christ, proclaiming:

> "… the new Jerusalem, the bride of the Lamb, was shortly to come down from heaven prepared for her spouse."

The friar in question was Thomas Scrope of Bradley, a Carmelite from the priory in Norwich. Little is known about his background, and most of it comes from our regular Carmelite source, John Bale*, who joined the Norwich community himself in 1495, a few years after Scrope's death. Bale would have known elderly friars in the community who remembered Scrope and his curious behaviour.

It has been claimed that Thomas Scrope was born into the family of Richard le Scrope, the first Baron Scrope of Bolton (†1403). However, there is no record of the Carmelite Thomas, in the family history, so it has been suggested that he was an illegitimate child of one of the two sons of Richard le Scrope. The Scrope family owned estates at Medbourne near Leicester. They had the advowson for the parish church there, that is, the right to nominate the parish priests, and they were also prominent benefactors to Bradley Priory, a community of Austin canons in the neighbouring parish of Neville Holt. If Thomas Scrope was born into the Scrope family, then it might explain a curious story preserved by John Bale in his later printed books. This claimed that Thomas joined the Benedictines first, then transferred to the Dominicans before finally entering the Carmelites in Norwich. Such transfers, though, would have been difficult, and there is no record of any dispensations being granted to him in the papal or diocesan registers. What is more likely is that Thomas may have received his early education in Bradley Priory, a Benedictine house (in fact, a child was found to be living in the priory when it was suppressed in 1535). If this is accepted, then it is conceivable that Scrope spent his adolescent years being educated by the Dominicans in Leicester, before formally entering the Carmelite Order as a novice in Norwich, c.1410-1415. In Norwich, after completing his novitiate, Scrope undertook his studies in theology and was ordained a priest.

It seems that shortly after his ordination that Scrope began to develop a conviction that the Second Coming of Christ was imminent, and that he had been chosen to preach and prepare people for this event. How long he spent travelling around Norwich, preaching to all who would listen, is not known but news of his activities soon came to the attention of the prior provincial Thomas Netter* who was not pleased. Netter wrote a letter to Scrope complaining about his behaviour, and giving an order that Scrope was to cease preaching and to remain in his priory. However, this letter had little effect, so Netter wrote again in 1425, to the prior in Norwich, William Thorpe, in which he stated that:

> (This behaviour) "is creating a scandal in the Church, giving rise to divisions and disturbances, and it goes against the intentions of these instructions which he thus disobeys…"

This time, Scrope took Netter's admonition more seriously for, not only did he return to the priory, but he went even further and took up residence in the anchorite's cell, which the priory possessed. There he spent the next twenty years.

In his anchorite cell, Thomas Scrope was not idle. Apart from devoting himself to a life of prayer, he spent time studying the history of the Order. At some time in the 1430s, Scrope was asked by his new prior Cyril Garland to translate a history of the Order which had been written by Felip Ribot, a Catalan Carmelite around 1385. The provincial Thomas Netter* had managed to get a copy of this work some years earlier but, being written in Latin, its readership was limited to the clergy, and other scholars. Scrope did as he was asked and the text of his translation was carefully preserved by John Bale. The text is in Middle English, as spoken in the fifteenth century, and has just been edited with great care and skill by Dr Valerie Edden.

Scrope, however, was not satisfied with just translating works by other writers and so he commenced writing some compositions of his own. He was fortunate in that there was an excellent library in Norwich as the house was the centre for higher studies in theology for the communities in the Norwich distinction. Three of the works written by Scrope while he was an anchorite still survive. One work, entitled *A Book on the Foundation of the Order of Carmelite Brothers*, bears the dedication:

> "Brother Thomas Bradley, monk and anchorite, to his beloved brother John Blakeney, a black monk, greetings in Him who rules over the whole world…."

John Blakeney was a Benedictine monk in Norwich Abbey, who was professed in 1427, and had been ordained by 1446. A second similar work, *A Tract on the Foundation, Title, Antiquity, Rule and Confirmation of the Order of the blessed Mary of Mount Carmel*, divided into seven chapters, was written around the same time.

However, it was the third of his books which led to a remarkable change in Thomas Scrope's life. This composition was entitled, *A Description and Supplication to the Supreme Pontiff Eugene IV,* which concludes with the words:

> "Written in the anchorite's cell in Norwich, on 3rd September, in the year of Our Lord 1441."

Earlier, that same year, on May 5th, Scrope had received papal permission to choose his own confessor, who would have the power to grant him a plenary absolution of his sins, when he was on his deathbed. It is possible that Scrope wrote this work, addressed to the pope as a thanksgiving for this indult. The book was said to have greatly pleased the Carmelite prior general, Jean Facy, who had probably met Scrope when he conducted a visitation of the province in 1442.

Around this time, there are records of small legacies being left to Scrope in the wills of local citizens. One will in 1442, is addressed to "the anker of the Carmels", and another in 1443, to "friar Thomas, the recluse of the Order of friars Carmelites". Then in 1445, Thomas Bumsted leaves a bequest, to "the anchorite dwelling in the convent of the Carmelites, in Norwich".

However, Thomas Scrope's name was becoming known in Rome, partly due to his book which had been addressed to the pope, but probably helped by influential members of his family. As a result, in 1449, Scrope received a summons from the pope, and he left his quiet cell in Norwich, and made his way to Rome. Once there, on January 12th, 1450, in a papal bull where he was addressed as "our beloved son Thomas Scropbolton alius Bradley", he was appointed bishop of Dromore in Ireland. He was consecrated bishop in the church of Santa Maria in Aquiro, in Rome by bishop Angelo Capranica, bishop of Ascoli Piceno, assisted by the bishop of Chiusi and the bishop of Bojano on February 1st, 1450. Two notaries for the diocese of Lincoln were present – John Wardale and William Stanley – which indicates that some powerful voices in England were supporting Scrope's promotion. However, there was a problem with Scrope's consecration to Dromore as the diocese was not vacant. Another Carmelite, David Chirbury had been appointed bishop of Dromore in 1431, and was still alive, acting as suffragan bishop in the diocese of St. David's in Wales. Even Chirbury, though, had not been the only bishop of Dromore as a Franciscan friar, Nicholas Warter, had also been consecrated bishop of Dromore in 1419, and was serving as suffragan in the diocese of York, until his death in early 1448. It was the death of this latter occupant of the diocese, which had led the papal authorities to think that the diocese was vacant, and so approving of the consecration of Thomas Scrope.

After his consecration, Scrope made his way back to England, and evidently was intending to travel onwards to visit his diocese. The text of a letter survives, written by the Carmelite provincial, Nicholas Kenton, which was addressed to the bishops and prelates of Ireland, commending Scrope as a worthy and devout man. It begins:

> "To the venerable in Christ fathers and lord bishops and prelates, and also to all the Christian faithful in all the land of Ireland, the humble brother Nicholas, in office as the prior provincial, and servant of the brothers of the Order of the most blessed Mother of God, Mary of Mount Carmel in England, every form of reverence, also the spirit of wisdom and intelligence to understand the truth.
>
> Moral conduct and life, fame and reputation are each acquired in the home of this earthly dwelling by a way of living praiseworthy or evilly, for this reason it is that I am led by a sincere, faithful conscience, to write of the venerable man, our brother Thomas Bradley, who was recently by chance raised to the episcopal dignity. He was formerly a priest and professed member of our Order, living praiseworthily for a long time in our aforesaid province, and now, aware of his episcopal ministry, is coming to the lands of your province. I will give you a true testimony of his life and way of living,"

In the event, Scrope did not travel to Ireland and, instead, he accepted a request to serve as a suffragan bishop in the Norwich diocese. On September 12th, 1450, Scrope was given authority to officiate in the diocese, and he served there for most of the remainder of his life. His presence can be traced through the episcopal registers, where he is recorded as performing ordinations and other duties. As he had little hope of receiving any income from his own diocese, he was appointed rector of the parish of St Mary's, Sparham, near Norwich, on November 24th, 1454. Then in 1461, he was admitted as rector of All Saints, Belton, near Great Yarmouth, and finally he was admitted as rector of St Andrew's, Trowse Newton, just outside Norwich on June 3rd, 1466. In all these parishes, Scrope would have appointed a curate to look after the daily pastoral duties whilst he was engaged in diocesan affairs.

After June 1466, Scrope vanishes from the episcopal records for nearly three years. His absence would seem to be explained by a number of references in John Bale's* notes, which claim that Scrope had served as a papal legate to the island of Rhodes, which was then under the control of the Knights Hospitallers. The Hospitallers had held a general chapter of their Order in Rome, in 1466, where pope Paul II introduced a number of reforms into the Order. It is conceivable that the appointment of Scrope as a legate to Rhodes, was part of the Pope's plan for having some impartial oversight of the Order's activities there. John Bale dates Scrope's period as legate to c1450, but this is impossible as Scrope was active in the Norwich diocese during this period. No trace of Scrope's appointment or his presence in Rhodes has been found in the records of the Knights Hospitaller, but there are a few stories about his activities in Rhodes which have been preserved in the notebooks of John Bale and the antiquarian John Leland. It is claimed that, whilst in Rhodes, Scrope had frequent conversations with a Franciscan friar from Jerusalem, a converted Jew, and that Scrope learned much from him about the Jewish faith, and the situation in the Holy Land, under the Muslims. John Leland writes that Scrope was popular among the soldiers in Rhodes, but other sources state that he was not liked by the local population because he never learned to speak Greek.

Scrope appears to have returned from Rhodes early in 1469 as, on February 25th, 1469, he is recorded as performing ordinations for the archbishop of Canterbury in Maidstone parish church. It is likely that Scrope was staying at this time with his Carmelite brethren in Aylesford, three miles away. In one of his later works, Scrope records seeing a copy of *The History of Jerusalem* in the Cistercian Abbey in Boxley, near Aylesford. It is possible that Scrope saw this work on his outward journey to Rhodes in 1466 but it is more likely that it was on his return in 1469, as Scrope is recorded as staying for some time in Kent. He is listed as consecrating the holy oils at the high altar in Christ Church Monastery, on Holy Thursday during Easter Week, March 30th, 1469, and on the following Saturday, he carried out ordinations in the prior's chapel there.

Then, Scrope continued his way back to Norwich, probably spending a few days in London, where he could have met John Milverton, the ex-provincial, who had just returned after spending nearly three years imprisoned in the Castel Sant'Angelo, in Rome. Scrope reached the Norwich diocese sometime later in 1469, the year when he was admitted as rector of St. Peter's, Freston. Then, he is recorded as administering ordinations on March 17th, 1470 and, once again, his name appears regularly in the diocesan registers until 1478.

In the Hilary Term, 1477, Scrope features in the court records, being listed as "Thomas Scrope of Hevingham, clerk, bishop of Dromore" when he was sued by Simon Randys, clerk, for a debt of 40s. From his address, it would appear that Scrope was acting as rector or administrator of the parish of Hevingham, 10 miles north of Norwich, where the previous rector had died in May 1471. Later, in 1477, Scrope was invited to consecrate the new church in the Carmelite priory in Ipswich.

On the 7th and 21st March 1478, Scrope performed his last ordinations in Norwich diocese, in the parish of Hevingham, where it seems that he was still living and acting as rector. Then, evidently, Scrope decided to retire, and he was admitted as the rector of St Margaret's Church, Lowestoft, where he passed the rest of his life.

During all these years as a bishop, Scrope had continued to study and to write. He acquired a number of books, three of which have survived. The most notable one is preserved in the British Library (Ms. Harley 211). This is a "common-place" book which contains a collection of inspiring or useful texts which Scrope acquired. Some of these may have been copied by Scrope himself. One significant text which the book contains is a copy of the Carmelite Richard Lavenham's* – *A Little Treatise on the Seven Deadly Sins.* This work was intended to help priests and lay persons preparing for confession. Many of the entries are in English but some of the prayers are in Latin. One notable entry contains a hymn, and prayers to a list of saints, all of whom were named Thomas, which was probably assembled by Scrope himself. There is also a liturgy for the enclosing of a person as an anchorite, which could have been used by Scrope whilst he was a bishop. Scrope's own name occurs on a couple of pages as "pray for the soul of Thomas Scrope", also there are numerous prayers to various saints, especially Carmelite ones. Two other significant texts are a copy of Nicholas de Lyre's *Postill on the Gospels,* and a psalter of the blessed Virgin Mary.

Scrope wrote another history of the Carmelites during this period with the title: *A Chronicle of the Foundation, Succession, Title and Diffusion of the Order of the Brothers of the blessed Virgin Mary of Mount Carmel,* which bears the dedication:

> "Thomas, by the grace of God and the Holy See, bishop of Dromore and Legate of the Holy Roman Church, sends his greetings, grace and blessings to his beloved son Cyril, archdeacon of our church in Dromore".

This work would appear to have been written early in the 1470's, after Scrope had returned from Rome, as it includes Scrope's title as a papal legate, and it contains the reference to the book, which he saw in Boxley Abbey. It is also claimed that Scrope wrote a short work on the Ten Commandments in English. This might be a text copied in in Ms. Harley 211, but scholars are doubtful that this version was written by Scrope. Alternatively, it may be that John Bale and other early writers, knew of this work and assumed that it was by Scrope. Bale does not record an *incipit* for this composition, which is usually an indication that he has not personally seen the work. Another piece, *A Life of Saint Brocard, Second Prior General,* was attributed to Scrope when it was printed in the 17th century. Unfortunately no manuscript copy of this work survives and the work was unknown to Bale.

In his later years in Lowestoft, it is recorded that Scrope walked barefoot around the surrounding villages and fields every Friday, teaching the Ten Commandments, to those who could not read, and giving away all his possessions to those in need. Finally, he died on January 15th, 1492, aged over 90 years of age, and was buried in the chancel of the parish church. A local historian, Edmund Gillingwater, writing in the 18th century, records:

> "There was formerly on the stone the effigy of the bishop in his episcopal habit; his crozier in one hand and his pastoral staff in the other, with several escutcheons of the arms of his family, etc. and ornamented with a border, all in brass; but scarce any remains of them are now to be seen and the matrices wherein they were placed are almost empty. Here this venerable and pious bishop was buried …"

Following the restoration of the church in the 19th century, Scrope's tombstone was moved into the War Memorial chapel, in the north aisle, and can now be seen on the floor in front of the altar.

Thomas Scrope was one of those inspiring characters, who spent his life in prayer, and the service of others. He was someone whom it would have been a joy to meet, and from whom one could have learned much. Our Carmelite John Bale*, whose knowledge of Scrope, came from the members of his community in Norwich who had known him, held Scrope in high esteem. Bale was sufficiently impressed to compose the following epitaph in his memory:

> Here lies the venerable body of an outstanding bishop,
> A sorrow for Carmel, a joy to those in heaven.
> Of noble birth from the line of Scrope, Thomas
> Bradley took his descent, which endowed him with great talents.
> Life in Carmel attracted Thomas, and also its cloak,
> In Norwich, he lived a life as in a tomb when,
> Enrolled as a religious in Carmel, he became a recluse.
> He wrote many works for his brethren (which still survive)
> Especially he wrote on the founders of his religious life,

Of the Order of Elijah and the holy Virgin.
Then, summoned by Eugene for Dromore in Ireland
He was, at last, found worthy of episcopal honours.
Thus was his worthy life raised up on high,
As was his purity of thought, devoid of all ambition.
He was appointed legate to care for the people of Rhodes,
And with great honour, he carried out this high office.
Here, with grace and a virtuous life, he inspired all;
A learned man, with his soul free from all pride,
He preached eloquently on the glorious commandments of Christ,
Opening the true way to ascend to heaven above.
Then came the moment, struck with an awful illness,
His spirit ascended on high, only his body remained on earth.
Already that light (which converted the pious Paul)
Has prepared the soul of this father for the heavenly kingdom. 1491.

Scrope was listed as "venerable" in some old Carmelite calendars with a feast day on 15th January. At the general chapter of the Order in 1908, his name was put forward for beatification but, sadly, the cause did not proceed any further.

**References:**

*BRCEW* 431-435: *ODNB* 49, 566

English translations of some of Scrope's writings will be published in a later volume of *Early Carmelite Documents*.

# 38

# JOHN PECOCK

**(†1537)**

Ruins of Walsingham Abbey where the conspiracy met.

It was in 1534 that King Henry VIII's quarrel with Rome, came to a head and the Act of Supremacy was published declaring the king to be head of the Church in England. Led by Thomas Cromwell, the king's chief minister, a series of reforms were introduced to ensure that the English Church recognised the king as its head. As for the religious orders, there was to be an inspection of all religious houses, and their communities were to be "persuaded" to sign a public assent to the Act of Supremacy. This was followed a few years later, by the suppression of all religious houses. Inevitably, there were protests against these actions and, after a short-lived uprising, in Lincolnshire early in 1536, the major resistance came from the Pilgrimage of Grace, an armed uprising which was launched in Louth in October 1536. Two Carmelites figured in this rebellion. One was the prior of Doncaster, Lawrence Cooke*, who was involved in the negotiations between the rebels and the king's army in Doncaster (see

Chapter 39), and another unnamed Carmelite, probably from Appleby, who was exempted from the pardon given to the participants in the Pilgrimage.

It would be gratifying to be able to state that the English Carmelites put up a united front against all these changes. However, sadly, this did not happen. The steadily increasing attacks, introduced by the all-powerful royal authority, coupled with the savage punishments meted out to those who resisted, deterred most Carmelites from making any open show of resistance. Also, as will be described in Chapter 41, the prior provincial John Bird*, not only did not oppose these changes but, in fact, he became an eager supporter of the king's pursuit of a divorce from his first marriage, and he added his signature to the declaration of the king's title as Head of the Church in England. So, those Carmelites who were opposed the changes, could not expect any support from the provincial if they chose to resist the royal decrees. As a result, only a few heroic Carmelites gave any open witness, in defending the traditional Catholic faith.

One example of Carmelites being involved in resistance to the suppression of the religious houses happened in Norfolk. There, two Carmelites were members of a plot, known as the Walsingham conspiracy, which was led by two of the lay choristers from Walsingham Priory, who planned an armed insurrection to resist the suppression of the priory, and the other religious houses. A group of around 30 sympathisers met together near Walsingham in April 1537 to prepare their plans. Among the group were John Pecock and Walter Gibson, members of the Carmelite community in Burnham Norton. Unfortunately, the plot was quickly betrayed by one of those present, and all involved were arrested. They were held in Norwich Castle for some weeks before being indicted for treason at the Norwich Assizes on May 25th. Fortunately, a glimpse of how the two Carmelites behaved in prison, was described by two of their fellow conspirators when they were interrogated on 10th June. These two, James Hindley and Harry Capon, described how they had been imprisoned in a house in Norwich Castle, together with the two Carmelites and five others, who were involved in the plot. Occasionally, the group were allowed to go to the chapel in the castle and, once there, the Carmelites would sing the "anthem of Our Lady". Afterwards, the two friars would spend some time kneeling in prayer before the altar.

Most of the conspirators were found guilty, and Pecock together with eleven others, were condemned to suffer a traitor's death. On June 1st, 1537, he was taken to King's Lynn where, after making a good end, that is expressing his remorse and exhorting the onlookers to obey the king in all things, he was hung, drawn and quartered. Peacock's companion, Walter Gibson, was more fortunate. He was condemned to life imprisonment for his part in the Walsingham conspiracy. Then it emerged that he had also been involved in a second conspiracy, which had met in the village of Fincham, 30 miles south of Burnham Norton. This second plot had started in April before the Walsingham group, but details of it only reached the authorities in June. Gibson was indicted again, and once more sentenced to life imprisonment. However, a few months later, on November 27th, 1537, he was granted a pardon and released early in 1538.

A sad aspect of the Walsingham conspiracy is that Pecock may have been betrayed to the authorities by his own prior John, who was possibly the brother of Walter Gibson. On the same day as Walter Gibson received his pardon, November 27th, prior John also received a pardon:

> "…Pardon of all treasons, rebellions, etc. committed by [him] before 1st August last."

However, in a letter sent to the king's chief minister, Thomas Cromwell, by Sir Thomas Townsend, there occurs the passage:

> "Sends, by the prior of the White Friars of Burnham, Norfolk, a book of 'conjurations' and a paper of prophecies rehearsed by one Ric. Laund, pinner of Norwich. The prior can show him the good service done by Austen Styward, alderman of Norwich. Asks him to thank the prior, who was the taker of one of the most rank traitors that were privy to the conspiracy at Walsingham. …"

Whatever the actions of the prior, one can only admire the bravery shown by John Pecock. He must have known what would be the punishment for any resistance to the king, and yet he risked his life, not only to stop the suppression of the religious orders, but even more to preserve the Faith, which he had served throughout his life. His courage was recognised much later when the Carmelite general chapter meeting in 1908, put forward his cause for beatification.

**References:**

*BRCEW* 200:

C. Moreton, "The Walsingham Conspiracy of 1537", *Historical Research*, 63:150 (1990), 29-43.

# 39

# ROBERT AUSTEN

## (†1538+)

St Bride's Church, London (before the fire of London)

As mentioned in the previous chapter, there were a few brave Carmelites who resented the religious changes introduced by King Henry VIII, especially his assumption of the title of Supreme Head of the Church in England, and the suppression of all the religious houses. However, most of the friars kept a prudent silence and behaved as they were commanded, even if unwillingly. Just occasionally, there is the record of an individual Carmelite speaking out and revealing what he feels, and one such protest was made by Robert Austen.

Very little is known about Robert Austen's life, or where he joined the Order. It is most likely that he joined the Order at the Carmelite house in London, or possibly in Winchester. Austen's name first appears in the records, whilst he was studying in Oxford. He is listed as being ordained subdeacon on May 25th, 1510, deacon on September 21st, and then priest on September 20th, 1511. There is no evidence that Austen studied for a degree in the university, and it is more likely that, as a talented student, he was sent to take advantage of the

Carmelite study house there, and the opportunity to hear other lecturers in the university town.

Once Austen was ordained, his name disappears from the surviving records, and it is not until over twenty years later that it re-appears. In 1534, by an Act of Parliament, king Henry VIII assumed the title of Supreme Head of the Church in England, and in April of that year, all religious communities were ordered to give assent to the king's actions as follows:

> "All friars of every monastery must be assembled in their chapter house, and examined separately concerning their faith and obedience to Henry VIII, and bound by an oath of allegiance to him, Queen Anne and her present and future issue. They must be bound by oath to preach and persuade the people of the above at every opportunity. They must acknowledge the king as the supreme head of the Church, as Convocation and Parliament have decreed. They must confess that the bishop of Rome has no more authority than other bishops. They shall not call the bishop of Rome pope either privately or publicly, or pray for him as such. They shall not presume to wrest the Scriptures, but preach the words and deeds of Christ sincerely and simply, according to the meaning of the Holy Scripture and Catholic doctors. The sermons of each preacher must be carefully examined and burnt if not Catholic, orthodox and worthy of a Christian preacher.
> Preachers must be warned to commend to God and the prayers of the people, first the King as head of the Church of England, then Queen Anne with her child, and lastly the archbishop of Canterbury, with the other orders of the clergy. Each house must be obliged to show their gold, silver and other moveable goods, and deliver an inventory of them. Each house must take an oath under their convent seal to observe the above orders."

In April of the following year, Austen's name occurs in a complaint made by three witnesses, Guydo Lilley, John Eglyston and Rychard Curll, who protested about:

> "Certain articles of treason spoken by friar Robert Austen white friar."

They listed the following statements made by him about the pope, the newly elected Paul III:

> "... That whoever wrote otherwise than charity would require against the bishop of Rome, he would regard him no otherwise than as a schismatic, paynim (pagan) or Jew.
>
> When I alleged the mischievous and proud usurping of the bishop of Rome, that so used king John, he said the chronicles were false, and he was accused maliciously of malice and of false heretics; that we should see a new turn of the bishop of Rome if we lived; that we were a many wretches of this realm, without any charity thus to blaspheme him, seeing

> that he does not write against us, but we malicious wretches write and rail upon him without any charity; that though some of his predecessors were evil, he is a good man."

This complaint seemed to have had no effect on Austen, and he preached another sermon on June 10th, in St Bride's Church in Fleet Street, near to the Carmelite house, London. Once again, there was a complaint against his words as follows:

> "The information of Francys Turpin of the words and preaching of Robert Austyn, White Friar, in the church of St. Bride's in Fleet Street, 'the 10th day of June of this present month'.
>
> 1st. That he did not pray for grace.
>
> 2. That he omitted the reverence due to his Prince and Supreme Head under God.
>
> 3. That he did not preach against the usurped power of the bishop of Rome, according to the commission lately proclaimed by the bishop of London.
>
> 4. that he had abused a preacher who had preached at St. Bride's on the gospel of the Rich Man and Lazarus for applying it to women.
>
> 5. Item, he said, although the rich man in that parable had no name, 'yet right well he might have named his steward called Nemo.'
>
> 6. That the preacher aforenamed called Our Lady a maintainer of bawdery.
>
> As he left the pulpit, informant asked him by whose authority he preached, and he replied by the bishop of London's. [Added] with the good will of the curate, then being present."

The year that this sermon was preached is not given, but it was probably on June 10th, 1535. After the sermon, Austen was arrested but he seems to have been released fairly quickly. This time, after being freed and probably thinking that discretion was the better course to follow, Austen left London and retreated to the small Carmelite house in Winchester. There he remained until the house was suppressed in 1538. On October 20th, 1538, he was granted a dispensation by the archbishop of Canterbury, to hold a benefice and to change his habit. As Austen was the only Carmelite to be granted a dispensation when the house was suppressed, it would seem that he was the only priest left in the small community.

There is no further clear information on Austen, which is sad and, as a man in his mid-fifties, it is to be hoped that he found some useful employment in a parish. It is possible that he can be identified with the Robert Austeyn, whose name occurs in 1548, as the curate in St Peter's church, Lodworth, Sussex (30 miles east of Winchester). This Robert Austeyn is mentioned, in a submission to the bishop, for defaults in the administration of communion on the Sunday before the last Rogation (6th May).

References:

*BRCEW* 329-330:

# 40

# LAWRENCE COOKE

## (†1540)

Rebus of Lawrence Cooke carved in the Tower of London

Our next Carmelite, Lawrence Cooke, came from an illustrious family in Doncaster. He was the eldest son of Edward Cooke of Arksey, mayor of the town from 1504-1508, and the brother of William Cooke, one of the ancestors of the Baronets of Wheatley. Sometime around 1505, Lawrence joined the Carmelite community in Doncaster, and was sent to pursue his studies for the priesthood in York, the senior house in the northern distinction. On Saturday March 12th, 1513, he was ordained acolyte in the Carmelite chapel there. After completing his studies in York, Cooke was sent to pursue higher studies in theology, but which university he attended is not known. However, he was awarded a B.Th.

After his return, Cooke was appointed as prior for a few years in Scarborough, where his signature occurs on a lease in 1527. Sometime before 1531,

Cooke was transferred to become prior in the Carmelite house in Doncaster, his home town. As has been mentioned earlier, this was the moment when King Henry VIII decided to seek for a divorce from his first wife, Catherine of Aragon. Guided by Thomas Cromwell, the king made preparations to break the link with Rome, and all monks and friars were to be required to sign an oath accepting the king's supremacy over the Church in England. As prior of Doncaster, Cooke made known that he refused to sign the oath and so, in 1532, he was imprisoned in the Tower of London. Presumably, Cooke was persuaded to change his mind as he was released at Christmas. In the meantime, John Bale* was appointed as prior in his place.

On July 24th, 1534, Cooke was given a licence to preach in the diocese of York, which confirmed that he was now back in good standing with the authorities. Then in 1536, Bale departed and Cooke was re-appointed as prior. However, later that year, events occurred which completely destroyed Cooke's peaceful life in Doncaster. There was widespread anger in the north of England against the suppression of the monasteries, and the result was an open revolt against the king, which became known as The Pilgrimage of Grace. Late in 1536, the armed forces of the Pilgrimage of Grace, passed through Pontefract and started making their way south to Doncaster. The nearest royal troops under the command of the Earl of Shrewsbury were at Rossington Bridge, five miles south of Doncaster so Gostwick, the Earl's treasurer, sent for Cooke and ordered him to cross the river Don to view the rebel army, and to bring back details of their numbers and equipment. Evidently, Cooke secretly sympathised with the rebellion but he was fearful of disobeying a royal command. So, he went to meet the rebel army, where he was allowed to move freely, and he had an interview with their leader Robert Aske. Cooke gathered information on the rebel numbers and their plans, but, in exchange, he told them of the numbers and disposition of the royal troops. Aske asked if the Earl of Shrewsbury's troops had reached Doncaster, and learning from Cooke that they were some distance away, Aske stated that he would be in Doncaster before them and spend the night there. However, the plague had broken out in the town, so the rebels remained on the north side of the river. Back in his priory, Cooke informed Aske that Gostwick was expecting a large sum of money from the king. This arrived in Tickhill the next day but Cooke lied to the messenger sent by Aske and said it had not come. Then Cooke went out again to inspect the rebel army and, on his return, he informed the Earl of Shrewsbury of all that he had seen.

In the meantime, the Duke of Norfolk had arrived and a meeting was arranged in the Carmelite house between the Duke and his Council and Robert Aske who brought 10 knights, 10 esquires and 20 commoners with him. After a long discussion, it was agreed that the rebels would all be pardoned, if they returned home quietly and their complaints would be considered by the king. Unfortunately, once the rebels had dispersed, the king reneged on the promises which had been made on his behalf and the leaders of the rebel army were declared exempt from the promised pardon and orders given for their arrest. A list of those exempted from the pardon was drawn up by the Duke of Norfolk and sent to Thomas Cromwell. Among those exempted from the pardon was:

> "… the late prior of the White Friars of Doncaster…"

Cooke was arrested and sent to the Tower of London where, in 1537, his name occurs among a list of prisoners and the cost of their maintenance:

> "… the prior of Doncaster, for three months at 10s. a week. Total: £6".

Evidence of which was Cooke's prison cell can be found in a room in the Beauchamp Tower, where there is a rebus composed of the words: "Doctor Cook 1537". Exactly when and where Cooke obtained this doctorate is unknown and he was still being described as B.Th. in July 1534.

A letter written by Cooke survives where he explains to the royal authorities what he did when the Pilgrimage of Grace came to Doncaster. This letter, written in 1537, was evidently composed to defend his actions and deny that he was guilty of any act of treason.

> "Acts of me, friar Lawrence Cooke, prior of Duncaster, at the first insurrection in Yorkshire.
>
> By command of the earl of Northumberland I went to the captain of the commons, Robert Aske, for a passport for my lord to go to Northumberland to his office. The captain was abroad, but a priest named Mansfield said I should have none. I was sent for to Tickhill by Mr. Gostwick, who sent me to ascertain the number of the commons; which I did, and returned to my lord Steward; Captain Aske said he feared them not, if they were 40,000. As for the King's treasure, it was for fear of life that I informed them of it. They sent next morning to know if it were come, and I answered No, though it was come to Tickhill. Concerning my communication with Mr. Aske at the meeting at Doncaster; I came to the vicarage where he lay, and he asked what the lords said. I answered, "they were sore therefore of that business." He said, if they had crossed the water most of them would have turned to them, "and that he knew right well. And I to see what he would say by that death that I shall suffer if false," told him I had spoken with lord Darcy and bade

> him "stick fast," and that 15 lords were confederated to suppress heresies; "and I never did know one [pure] in my life." Begs pardon of the King and "your good Lordship."
>
> When I went to the commons from Mr. Gostwick, the captain asked if the town were taken by the King's army, and I answered No. He then said he would have it that night."

In 1538, Cooke was moved from the Tower to Newgate Prison and his presence there is mentioned in a letter from Hugh Latimer to Thomas Cromwell, dated 18 May:

> "… Hears that Forest is not duly accompanied in Newgate for his amendment, with the White Friar of Doncaster and monks of the Charterhouse, in a fair chamber more like to indurate than to mollify, whether through the fault of the sheriff or the gaoler or both, no man could sooner discern than Cromwell. …"

Cooke was condemned by an Act of Attainder in June 1540, a few days before Cromwell himself was arrested. There are two contemporary accounts of Cooke's execution on August 4th, 1540, where he suffered with William Home, a lay brother from the Charterhouse, Giles Home, gentleman, Clement Philip, gentleman, Edward Bromholme, priest, Darby Gening and Robert Bird. An eye-witness account can be found in a letter sent by the French ambassador, Charles de Marillac to King Francis I of France, in which he recounted recent events in England, and dated August 6th, 1540:

> "Wrote before of the execution of Mr. Thomas Cromwell and lord Hungerford, which was followed two days after by that of six doctors, three of whom, named Pol, Abel, and "le prieur Dancaster," were hanged as traitors, for speaking in favour of the Pope, and three named Bernes, Guyard and Hierosme burnt as heretics. It was wonderful to see adherents to the two opposing parties dying at the same time, and it gave offence to both."

The second account is found in an early London chronicle, collected by John Stow:

> "The iiij. day of August were drawn from the Tower to Tyborne 6 persons, & one led between 2. sergeants, & there hanged & quartered: one of them was the prior of Doncaster, a monk of the Charterhouse of London, Gyles Herne, a monk of Westminister, one Fylpot, & one Carrow, & a friar: all were put to death for treason."

Some have doubted whether Cooke was executed, as a pardon was issued in his name on October 2nd, 1540 to cover all faults committed before August 8th, that year. However, this pardon seems to have arrived too late to save Cooke, and the two contemporary accounts above confirm that he was executed on August 4th. It was a sad end for a brave Carmelite, who had tried to do his best, and finally gave his life holding on to the unity of the Church.

**References:**

*BRCEW* 246-247:

# 41

# SIMON CLERKSON

All Saints Church, Rotherham, where Simon Clerkson was Rector from 1539-1554

Most of the portraits in this book have focussed on the contributions made by individual Carmelites, during their time in the Order. However, although Simon Clerkson, did spend over twenty years in the Order and was the prior of the community in York at the time of its dissolution, more is known of his later life, and it is that period which is of interest here. Many of the friars who were expelled when the Order was suppressed, must have found life difficult and we know little about what happened to them.

Those who were ordained, would have sought positions as curates or chaplains, in local parishes or other institutions, but these were not easy to obtain, with so many ex-religious seeking employment. Clerkson, though, was more fortunate, and the surviving records give us a glimpse of what happened to one friar after he left the Order, and embraced the new church order. As a graduate of Oxford University, and prior of the house in York, Clerkson must have had some influential relatives or friends as, following the suppression of the Order, he was able to secure an appointment to a prosperous parish, where his talents quickly came to the attention of the king. Clerkson, therefore, gives us an example of how to survive and do well, amidst all the upheavals and changing situations, during the reign of King Henry VIII.

Clerkson appears to have been born in York around 1500-1502, probably to wealthy and influential parents. He joined the Carmelite community in the city, and his name first appears in contemporary records when he was ordained acolyte on September 20th, 1522, in the Dominican church in York. He was evidently a talented student and so was sent to continue his studies at Oxford, where he was ordained priest on September 23rd, 1525. Whilst in Oxford, Clerkson was mentioned in the will of Edmund Pilkington, on December 12th, 1528:

> "Also I will, that one Friar, Simon Clerkson, or else some other honest priest, do sing for me, and for the souls of my father and mother, and for all Christian souls, the space of one whole year, in what place my wife will assign him to sing; and to have to his wages 40s. and meat and drink with lodging."

One would imagine that Clerkson was a friend of Edmund Pilkington and his family, and that the generous bequest helped to pay for Clerkson's expenses whilst he was in Oxford. At that time, it was common for the parents of a friar or a rich patron to help to pay for the expensive university studies. Clerkson made good progress and, on January 2nd, 1533, after nine years of study in logic, philosophy and theology, he supplicated for his B.D. (bachelor in divinity).

Shortly after this, Clerkson appears to have returned to York, as he was probably the prior who gave the sermon before the Corporation of York, on the morrow of the Feast of Corpus Christi in 1535. He was still in office in 1537 when, in July, accompanied by John Gybbes, the prior of London, he assisted Bishop John Longland of Lincoln in the examination of William Cowbridge for heresy at Aylesbury. Clerkson was still prior of York at the dissolution of the house on November 27th, 1538, when his name comes at the head of the thirteen members of the community, who signed the surrender document. He was given £1 from the sale of the property.

It was at this point that Clerkson's family, or the influence of his friends, served him in good stead. On July 17th, 1539, he was presented to the vicarage of All Saints church, Rotherham, by Francis, the Earl of Shrewsbury. The Earl had just acquired the advowson (the right to propose the parish priest), for the parish together with a number of other properties, which had belonged to the suppressed religious orders. The appointment was quite lucrative and came with an annual salary of 25 marks (£16 13s, 4d). This compares to the annual salary for one of the choristers who received 5 marks (£3 6s 8d.). Clerkson was to hold this position for the next fifteen years.

Following the execution of Thomas Cromwell in 1540, the religious approach of King Henry VIII, became more traditionally Catholic (which caused the more Protestant ex-Carmelite John Bale* to flee to the Continent and remain in exile until the king died in 1547). During his early years in Rotherham, Clerkson achieved a reputation as a good preacher, and his moderate views appear to have appealed to the king and his advisers. So, when King Henry VIII visited Hull on October 3rd, 1541, Clerkson was given a special licence to operate as a travelling preacher throughout the country, on behalf of the king for the next ten years. This licence, as issued formally under the Privy Seal, still survives:

> "The king to all, &c., greetings. In order that our beloved Simon Clerkson, perpetual vicar of the parochial Church of Rotherham, clerk of the diocese of York, who, as we understand, is bachelor in theology and excels in sacred learning, may make use of and enjoy the liberty of preaching the word of God throughout our kingdom of England. Know that we of our special grace, and from our certain knowledge & own motion, have granted & given licence, and by these presents do grant and give licence to the aforesaid Simon Clerkson that he, for the sake of preaching the Word of God can and may be away and absent himself from the said parochial church and its perpetual vicarage for the term of ten years, to be reckoned from the time of the date of these presents, and may preach and set forth the Word and the Gospel of God through our said kingdom in Latin sermon or the vulgar tongue as may be thought suitable for the hearers, in times and places convenient thereto; also during the term of the ten years he may receive the fruits, rents and profits of his said vicarage in the time of his absence from the same, as if he resided there personally and continually, and may freely and lawfully convert and apply them to the use and service of himself and his vicarage; so that he, Simon, be by no means bound to reside in his vicarage in the meanwhile, nor shall he be able unwillingly to be forced thither by any authority whatever;

> And this, though there is no express mention of the annual value or of the certainty of the premises here made, any Act or Statute hitherto in Parliament or otherwise to the contrary published or to be published, or any other matter, thing, or cause whatever, notwithstanding. Provided also that the said church of Rotherham and its perpetual vicarage shall not on that account be deprived of its due funeral services, and the cure of souls in the same shall no wise be neglected, but the usual charges shall be fitly supported; and that the said Simon Clerkson four times in every year of the said ten years, that is once a quarter, shall serve in his said church of Rotherham aforesaid, shall publicly preach and set forth the Word and Gospel of God to his parishioners and others coming to it for the time, otherwise our grant and license will be void and without force, and he shall be censured. Witness the King, at Westminster, 27th October. By Writ of Privy Seal."

Clerkson would have needed to employ a curate to look after the parish, whilst he was away but the salary for a curate was only around £5-£10 per year and Clerkson would have received payment for the sermons he preached whilst away from the parish. In fact, later the same year, on November 4th, Clerkson was also appointed to a second living as the vicar of St Oswald's church, Crowle in Lincolnshire. Presumably, this was due to the fact that Clerkson had just been granted his licence to be away preaching for the next ten years, and was in need of more funds. However, on March 10th, 1548, Clerkson was presented to be the rector of St Peter's Church, Stainby in Lincolnshire, with permission to hold this position in plurality with his other living in Rotherham. Presumably, this appointment replaced his previous one as the vicar of St Oswald's. Three years later, Clerkson had to exhibit his "plurality licence", when there was an episcopal visitation of his parish. Clerkson also held a third position, for a while, as the perpetual vicar of the parish church in Hatfield, Yorkshire, but he had resigned from this position by June 1549. Finally, Clerkson was presented to the living of St George's church, Doncaster but he was never instituted.

Holding more than one appointment was not uncommon at that time although in each case, Clerkson would have had to find a curate to look after the pastoral duties. However, he was able to retain a significant proportion of the annual income. At some time before 1553, Clerkson took the opportunity to be married and it was this act which caused him serious problems when Queen Mary came to the throne. He was summoned to appear before the Chancery Court in York on April 16th, and then again on October 29th, 1554. However, Clerkson remained completely unrepentant. After his first appearance before the Chancery Court, Clerkson was deprived of his position in Stainby, and another priest was installed as the rector of on October 5th. At its second meeting in October, the Chancery Court deprived Clerkson of his position in Rotherham as well.

What happened to Clerkson after this is unknown. It is possible that he and his wife emigrated to the continent, during the reign of Queen Mary, but, more likely, the two of them retired from public view and lived as a married couple in some small village in the Yorkshire countryside.

**References:**

*BRCEW* 366-367.

# 42

# JOHN BIRD

**(†1558)**

John Bird, bishop of Chester (attributed)

John Bird was born in Coventry in the 1470's, probably into a family who had moved south from Chester, and joined the Carmelite community in the city. A very able student, he was sent to study at Oxford University around 1495, and was awarded his doctorate in February 1514, "after 18 years of study in logic, philosophy and theology". Later in the same year, he was the preacher in St. Mary's, the Oxford University church, on Ascension Day, 28th May.

At the provincial chapter held in King's Lynn in August that year, Bird was elected provincial. The prior general, Battista Spagnolo (Baptist of Mantua), was unwell and unable to visit the province, so he appointed Bird together with the prior of London, William Brevie, as his vicars-general to make a canonical visitation of the province in his place. For use during their visitation, Bird and Brevie had a blank letter of confraternity printed which they could present to prominent donors and patrons of the Order. This is the first instance among the Carmelites of a mass produced letter of confraternity which could be widely distributed – in return, of course, for a significant contribution. The letter of confraternity declared that the recipient was a *confrater* or brother/sister of the Carmelite Order, and shared in the graces gained from all the good works, prayers, penances, etc. which were done by the members of the Order and also that, when the recipient died, the Province would have masses said for them, and they would be remembered in the prayers of the Order in the same way as would be done for any friar who died.

The following year, Bird attended the general chapter held in Siena, where his appointment as provincial was confirmed. Then, as a new statute was passed limiting the provincials in England to a three year term of office, Bird stepped down in 1519.

It seems likely that Bird spent the next three years as prior of Coventry, before being elected provincial again at the chapter held in York in 1522. Soon after his election, Bird had the statute limiting provincials to a three year term removed, and he held office from then on until 1537. Bird was also appointed vicar general from 1522 to 1534, conducting visitations on behalf of the prior general, and representing him at provincial chapters and other official functions. In a report on the situation in the various provinces of the Order, the new prior general, Nicholas Audet, wrote of the English province;

> "The provincial is a worthy man and outstandingly learned".

In 1523, Bird was in the Carmelite house in Calais, which was then under English control, where he preached the sermon at the funeral of the Carmelite Edmund Bury. In August 1526, after a discussion at the provincial chapter held in Hitchin, Bird wrote a letter to the Chancellor of Oxford University in which he gave a licence for the Carmelite Thomas Giles, to proceed to a doctorate in theology. This letter still survives.

Bird was possibly serving as the confessor or similar office for the Duke of Northumberland as, in 1527, there is a record in the Duke's accounts:

> "To Dr Bird, provincial of the White Friars, for his annuity, £6 13s. 4d. (10 marks)"

Then in 1531, Bird was sent to argue with Thomas Bilney, a Lollard, who was in prison in Norwich for heresy. Bird attended the trial of Bilney, where he was condemned to be burnt and the sentence was carried out on August 19th, 1531. Bird's presence was remarked upon by John Foxe in his book on the Protestant martyrs:

> "Another great doer against him was one friar Bird with one-eye, provincial of the White Friars".

However, Bird was a faithful supporter of King Henry VIII, and he wrote a treatise supporting the king's petition for a divorce. This treatise was purchased a few years ago, by an unknown buyer, but a photocopy is preserved in the British Library. In April/May 1534, Bird was a signatory to the royal declaration against papal supremacy and, the following year, he was chosen to accompany the Bishop of Hereford, Edward Fox and the lawyer Thomas Bedyll, to try to persuade Queen Catherine of Aragon from using the title of queen but she refused. After the act of royal supremacy was passed in Parliament in 1535, Bird was given the title of "general" of the Carmelites in England, Ireland and Wales by king Henry VIII. On the Wednesday in Easter Week (4 April) 1537, Bird was chosen by John Hilsey, the Bishop of Rochester to preach before the king. Interestingly, on May 18th, 1537, Lord Thomas Darcy, who was in the Tower of London awaiting execution, asked for a confessor and Bird was one of the two names he put forward. He described Bird as:

> "the Doctor of Our Lady Friars in Fleet Street, a big, gross, old man…"

Then, on June 11th, 1537, John Bird's name was proposed to be the bishop of Pentreith in the diocese of St. David', where he would act as suffragan bishop to the bishop of Llandaff. Bird was consecrated in the chapel at Lambeth Palace on June 24th, 1537 by Thomas Cranmer, Archbishop of Canterbury. After two years, Bird was translated to the diocese of Bangor on July 24th, 1539. However, Bird did not wish to spend too much time in his diocese, and he leased a house in Holborn in London. On July 9th, 1540, he was present in the chapter house at Westminster when the marriage between Henry VIII and Anne of Cleves was declared null and void, and he attended the synod of the Canterbury Province in St Paul's cathedral on July 28th, 1540.

Finally on August 4th, 1541, Bird was translated to the newly erected diocese of Chester. It was probably early in the 1540's that Bird married and he remained as bishop of Chester, until dispossessed on the accession of Queen Mary. Bird's name occurs on many official documents during his time in office, and as a bishop he attended Parliament and undertook various duties for the king. The major problem that he faced during these years was financial. The new diocese of Chester was not well-endowed and Bird had to work hard to establish an adequate income. He was forced to appeal to the king and to negotiate a number of land exchanges with the king, which were not always beneficial to the diocese.

The arrival of Queen Mary on the throne finally ended Bird's problems in Chester as, due to his marriage, he was deprived of the diocese. Bird seems to have had no hesitation in choosing what to do. Quickly he repudiated his wife, whom he had married, so he alleged, against his will "for bearing with the time". His repentance was accepted by Queen Mary, and Bird was appointed as a suffragan to the bishop of London. On November 6th, 1554, Bird was appointed vicar of the parish of Great Dunmow in Essex, which provided him with a regular income. However, at his age, conforming to the new situation under Queen Mary which had re-introduced Catholic practices, was not easy.

John Strype, writing about the Protestant Reformation in England, has some less than complimentary remarks to make about Bird:

> "This Doctor Byrd was well stricken in years, having but one eye; and though he, to flatter with the time, had renounced his wife, being made of a young Protestant an old Catholic; yet as Catholic as he was, such devotion he bare to his man's wife that he had them both dwelling with him in his own vicarage, she being both young, fair, and newly married, that either the voice of the parish lied or else he loved her more than enough."

There is another critical account, written by the Protestant John Foxe, describing an episode when Bird was called upon to preach at Great Dunmow, in front of Bishop Edmund Bonner of London.

> "Thus the suffragan, at the bishop's assignment, went up to the pulpit, with no small expectation of some great account of learning to be looked for at his hands. The theme which he took was, "You are Peter and upon this stone I will build my Church, etc. Upon which ground, his intent being to advance and extol the high pre-eminence of St. Peter's excellency, he waded so far, as himself knew not where he was, nor any man else understood whither he would. So deep was he drowned in the profoundness of that divinity, that the more he strove to get out of the labyrinth, the further he wound himself in that subtle maze: so far had he overreached his key, that he was gone clean beyond *Ela*, and almost beyond himself. So that where the drift of his sermon was, if he could have brought him out, to prove the stability of St. Peter, and so successively of the Pope's seat, suddenly he slipped into the weakness of St. Peter, and of all mankind, reciting this text, "Before the cock crows, thou shalt deny me thrice, &c." Meaning belike, by the fall of

Peter, to excuse his own weakness, and of all Adam's children, if he could well have discharged the matter.

These two contraries standing so disjointly, were more than a wonder to the audience, and no less trouble also to the preacher himself; who still dwelling in this fruitless babble, and, as you would say, hanging still upon a note, might not well tell how to wind himself out. All this while the bishop was disquieted not a little, and stood upon thorns; for he made faces, his elbow itched, and so hard was his cushion whereon he sat, that many times during the sermon he stood up, looking towards the suffragan, giving signs, and such signs as almost had speaking, to proceed to the full event of his cause in hand; which was, as he looked for, either to establish the usurped seat of Rome, or else to maintain the altar-god. For in these two consisted the chief scope of all that visitation. But my lord's suffragan either could not or would not take up his meaning."

Foxe, also, records an episode, later in 1555, when Bird visited Bishop Bonner's house in Fulham. Bonner, was interrogating Thomas Haukes, who was being detained for refusing to have his child christened.

"The next day came thither an old bishop who had a pearl in his eye; and he brought with him to my lord a dish of apples, and a bottle of wine. For he had lost his living, because he had a wife. Then the bishop called me again into the orchard, and said to the old bishop: "this young man hath a child, and will not have it christened."

Haukes: "I deny not baptism."

Bonner: "Thou art a fool; thou can't not tell what thou wouldest have;" – and that he spoke with much anger.

Haukes: "A bishop must be blameless or faultless, sober, discreet, no chider, nor given to anger."

Bonner: "Thou judgest me to be angry: no, by my faith, am I not:" – and stroke himself upon the breast.

Then said the old bishop, "Alas, good young man! you must be taught by the church, and by your ancients; and do as your forefathers have done before you."

After Bird had left, Bonner continued his argument with Haukes and, as Haukes refused to change his attitude, he was condemned and burned.

Bird did not live much longer after this episode and the parish register records:

"John Birde, Doctor of Divinity, late Bishop of Chester, but now Vicar of this Parish of Great Dunmowe, was buried on the 15th of October 1558."

The Carmelite John Bale*, who knew Bird well, wrote a more sympathetic description of him in his history of the Province composed in 1536:

"A man of modest abilities, with a honeyed tongue, he was a keen disputant and a not ineffective preacher."

And later in the same book, Bale states that he was:

> "… a particularly handsome man … but (to be deplored in such a man) he was rather remiss in correcting the faults of others, being swayed by his own good nature."

In his efforts to serve the king and his country, Bird conformed to the changing beliefs and religious practices around him. In that time, many followed his example, fearful of the savage consequences if they did not conform. It is easy to condemn their weakness but how many of us would have the courage to do otherwise?

**References:**

*BRCEW* 116-120: *ODNB* 5, 816-817

F. Sanders, "John Bird D.D., Bishop of Chester 1541-1554", *Journal of Chester Archaeological Society*, 3 (1907), 110-126.

# 43

# JOHN DOVE

**(†1560)**

Notre-Dame Church, Calais, rebuilt in the English Perpendicular style whilst the town was under English control.

As has been stated before, for the large majority of Carmelites in the English Province, at its suppression in 1538-1539 little is known about their subsequent careers. A few protested against the suppression and were severely punished for their temerity, others welcomed the new Protestant ideas and were suitably rewarded. There were some, however, who became unwittingly involved in the ferment of new ideas, and had to struggle hard to survive unharmed. One of these was John Dove, who was prior of the Carmelite house in Calais, in the 1530's. Calais had come under English control, following its capture by king Edward III in 1347, and the king had immediately ordered all the French inhabitants of the city to be expelled and replaced by English merchants, and other settlers. Among these new inhabitants were a community of English Carmelites, who were asked to take over the Carmelite priory in the town. This priory had been founded by their French brethren sometime before 1314. The Carmelites were the only mendicant order of friars to have a community in the town, and they remained there, until the suppression of all the religious orders under King Henry VIII.

In 1538, the prior of the Carmelites in Calais, John Dove, became involved in a dispute over the doctrine of transubstantiation, that is the nature of the changes to the bread and wine, which take place during the celebration of mass. A young man had recently arrived in Calais named Adam Damlip [*alias* George Bucker], who claimed to have been a chaplain to St John Fisher, bishop of Rochester, until his execution in 1535. Following Fisher's death, Damlip left England, and made his way through France and Germany down to Rome, where he was befriended by Cardinal Pole. However, after a brief stay there, Damlip became disgusted with the state of the Church in Rome, and he adopted Protestant beliefs. Thanks to a gift of some money from Cardinal Pole, he made his way back, reaching Calais early in 1538. Once there, he impressed the Lord Deputy of Calais, De Lisle, and John Butler, the Archbishop of Canterbury's Commissary, who gave him permission to preach and give talks on theology. Damlip started to preach in the chapter house in the Carmelite priory, where he attracted big crowds. As the numbers grew, Damlip transferred his preaching to the pulpit in the larger parish church of St Nicholas, where he warned the congregation against Roman errors and abuses, especially on the Eucharist. He preached against transubstantiation, the doctrine of propitiatory sacrifice, idolatry and false miracles, especially those which were linked with image of the Virgin Mary in the parish church. Dove made his objections to Damlip's preaching clear, and he himself began to argue in defence of the Mass and other traditional Catholic beliefs. Dove attempted to convince the more Catholic members of the Council in Calais to stop Damlip and, on June 19th, the Council ordered the Commissary, John Butler, to ensure that Damlip did not preach "against the king's pleasure". Then Dove sent secret letters to the authorities in England and this resulted in Damlip being summoned to appear before the Archbishop of Canterbury, Thomas Cranmer.

At this time, Thomas Cromwell, the Lord Privy Seal, was in a delicate situation as King Henry VIII was beginning to retreat from his more extreme Protestant ideas and to adopt a traditional Catholic approach. Hence Thomas Cromwell had to tread a delicate line between his eagerness to support the introduction of the new Reformed ideas, and the king's more Catholic approach. Faced with this dilemma, Cromwell was eager to see the controversy over Damlip's preaching settled quickly, and so, on June 16th, he ordered that Dove and Damlip should be examined in Calais; however, his letter arrived too late as Damlip had already been sent to England. Dove, though, was questioned in Calais before he too was sent to England, to be examined by Thomas Cranmer, the Archbishop of Canterbury. On his arrival, Cranmer had Dove placed in detention and recommended that he should be suspended from office, and the Carmelite priory in Calais suppressed.

In August 1538, Dove was summoned before the members of the royal council and a series of questions were put to him. The list of questions survives, though sadly, only Dove's answer to the first question had been copied. The questions were as follows:

"a. Where he was made friar? "He answereth in Ichchen [Hitchin] in Hertfordshire where he tarried from 10 to 14 or 15 years of age."
b. Where he has studied?
c. Where he has been master and in how many places?
d. By whose means he has been promoted to any office and who has chiefly helped him?
e. By whose means he was made prior of Calais?
f. By what means and by whose help he became acquainted with the lord Deputy there?
g. How many of the Council of the town he took to be his friends?
h. And how many his enemies or unfavourable to his opinions?
i. How many of the retinue he took to be of his faction?
j. And how many of the contrary opinion?
k. Who encouraged him to hear the sermons of one Adam, who came lately out of Germany?
l. Who encouraged him to come to England to depose against the said Adam?
m. Who directed him to the bishops of London, Chichester, and Durham?
n. What letters he had to them, and whether he were privy to their contents?
o. What intercourse he has had with the said bishops, or any of them [whether] before his going over or not?
p. What conferences he has had with them since his coming over; how often and in whose presence?
q. What letters he has written to those or other bishops any time these four years, and what letters he has received from them or any other person within this realm, and what they contained?
r. What intelligence he has with my lord Chamberlain, to whom he lately wrote, how many letters he has written to him, how long have they been acquainted, and what letters he has received from my lord Chamberlain, or any of his household?
s. Who directed any letters from Calais to John Gostyk in his favour, and what communications have been between them?

t. Who directed him to my lord of Durham, why he went to him, what communication he had with him, how often, and how he departed from him?
u. Who directed him to the bishop of London, how often he was with him, whereupon they conferred, and what conclusions passed between them?
v. Who addressed him to my lord of Chichester, &c.?
w. Whether he were privy to the bishop of London's letters to the lord Deputy of Calais, what the bishop meant by the ending, "wherein he prayed that all should not perish there as it is lost here," and what words were between the bishop and him at the delivery of the letters?"

Following Dove's interrogation, Thomas Cranmer sent a written account of his questioning of Adam Damlip and John Dove, together with his recommendations, to Cromwell. He wrote:

> "Adam Damlip, of Calais, denies that he taught or said that the body and blood of Christ was not presently in the Sacrament of the Altar. He says the controversy between him and the prior was because he confuted the opinion of transubstantiation, and therein I think he taught but the truth. Two friars, however, came to testify against him that he had denied the presence of the body and blood in the Sacrament, and he straightway fled. Thinks it rather from suspecting the rigour of the law than the defence of his own cause. Has appointed two of his chaplains to go to Calais and preach, but it is thought they will do little good if the prior returns home. No one has hindered the Word of God so much as he, or maintained superstition more. Sends two letters about his subtlety and craft. Prays that he may not come to Calais any more to tarry, but either that the house be suppressed, or an honest and learned man appointed in his room. As he is here now, asks for Cromwell's authority to forbid him to return.... Lambeth 15th August."

Cromwell was out of London at this time, but he acted swiftly. He sent letters to Cranmer, one of which was to be forwarded to Lord de Lisle, the Lord Deputy of Calais instructing him what to do, and the other had advice for Cranmer about what to do with Dove. Cranmer replied on August 18th, saying:

> "...Will keep the prior in safe custody till Cromwell's return to these parts. Doubts not there will be matter enough for his deprivation."

Dove remained in prison for several weeks more, until a decision was taken about his future. What this was to be is contained in a letter from John Husee, the servant of Lord de Lisle, who informed his master on 3 October:

> "... The prior goes to Calais, there to recant the things by him ill-spoken, and so doing, my Lord of Canterbury and [my Lord] of the Privy Seal promise him favour."

Dove arrived back in Calais later in October, and evidently he did what he was asked to do. He was released and orders were given for the suppression of the Carmelite house. Dove himself, was eager to keep on good terms with the authorities and so, sometime between the 8-15th November, 1538, he wrote a letter to Lord de Lisle who was eager to obtain the Carmelite property for himself.

> "Jesus. Whereas my especial good lady (to whom I pray God send prosperous fortune in all her affairs and suits) hath promised your lordship to do her diligence for a commission for the Friars, I beseech God shortly to send it to your good lordship with all your other suits, for I would as gladly be delivered of it as a horse would be of his heavy burden, considering the trouble and misery that I live in. And if it please your lordship to have a writing under our convent seal, with the whole assent and consent of all the brethren to render up to your lordship all our title and interest that we have in the house (which I think would be no hindrance to the expedition of your suit in it) keeping it close to yourself for because the people shall not wonder at me in surrendering it to your lordship, I shall desire you to devise a writing by counsel secretly, and it shall be sealed with all our names underneath. As whereas your lordship has perused the counterpane of Mr. Porter's indenture, if it be your pleasure to send it to my good lady to know whether the re-entry may take effect or no, your lordship shall have it again at your pleasure. If your lordship will not do it, I think I shall be compelled to seek some friend in England which shall weigh against him and put the matter in execution; which I would be loath to do but he deals so unkindly with me that I shall be forced to do it. The sooner your lordship doth follow your suit in these premises I think it the better and specially before the return of Mr. Wrysley, for his great trust is in him. I would I could devise anything to do your lordship pleasure with: you shall have my faithful service, with heart and mind, as God knows, whoever preserve your good lordship with long life and much honour.
>
> Amen. Your Lordship's daily orator, John Dove, inceptor in divinity and prior as yet.
>
> I beseech your lordship to have me most humbly and heartily commended to my especial good lady in your letters next (if it your pleasure). I am her assured bedeman and servant to the uttermost of my poor power."

The following year, Dove was once again in London when, sometime between November 8-15th, 1539, he wrote another letter to Lord De Lisle:

> "After due form of humble salutation premised, your daily orator doth most heartily and lowly salute your good Lordship, certifying you that my Lord Chamberlain hath him most heartily commended unto your lordship, and gives you hearty thanks in my behalf. And, where it hath pleased your lordship of your goodness to grant me my chamber with the containings

thereof, I have sent my servant to Calais to take up all such things as doth appertain unto me with your lordship's licence; wherefore I most humbly beseech your good lordship to aid him in the way of right.

Moreover, whereas your lordship of your goodness hath granted me £5 pension, if it were your lordship's pleasure to give it me in writing under your seal of arms, I should be much more bound to you. I wholly put it to your goodness. I beseech your lordship to give me the hangings of green and red silk about the high altar for my chamber. And as for such rents as Mr. Porter doth owe unto me I put them wholly to your lordship. My lady hath a bill of all. Also, Mr. Ryngeley hath a vestment and a chalice I left with him. If it please your lordship to give me the vestment it shall be a memory as long as I live. They be in Mr. Porter's inventory as yet.

My servant shall deliver to your lordship the keys of all such things as be in the house. As for the feather beds, I left four in the vestry when I went into England the last year, and when I came home I found not one there; and also one Edmund Gates stole 2 feather beds and sold them to the parson of Offchurch [Offekerque?], and Mr. Porter's servants hath the rest. And if Mr. Porter be grieved with me for because I let him have no quittance, I shall desire your lordship to make the matter whole, if it may be.

Finally I most humbly beseech your good lordship to take me as your faithful servant and daily beadsman [i.e. pensioner who prays for his benefactor], and so shall I be during my poor life, as I am most specially bounden by duty, as knoweth Almighty God, whoever preserve your good lordship with much honour, and long life, to his high pleasure and your heart's request: Amen; and good lady also.

Your Lordship's daily orator & dutiful beadsman, John Dove inceptor in divinity."

After this, what happened to Dove is unknown. His experiences in Calais, though, illustrate the problems which faced many Carmelites at the Reformation. Dove, as prior of the Carmelite house there, sought to restrain the disturbance caused by the arrival in the town of an enthusiastic follower of the Reformed views of Luther and Calvin. However, as Dove sought to counter the new views being preached, he found himself unwittingly involved in the political tensions between the king and his senior advisors. Dove's attempt to hold on to the traditional Catholic beliefs led him to risk his freedom and even life itself. Of the key figures in this affair, Thomas Cromwell was soon to lose the king's favour and was executed in 1540. The original cause of all this affair, Adam Damlip, was released, and is said to have spent a year or so teaching in the West country, before he was re-arrested, taken back to Calais and executed as a traitor. Damlip lost his life not because of his Protestant views, but because he had accepted money from a known traitor, Cardinal Pole!

**References:**

*BRCEW* 140-142.

Philip Ward, "The Politics of Religion: Thomas Cromwell and the Reformation in Calais, 1534-40", *Journal of Religious History*, 17:2 (Dec 1992), 152-171.

# Illustrations

All photos are by the author unless otherwise noted.

1. John Bale (†1563)
   Engraving from Thomas Fuller's *Abel redivivus or The Dead Yet Speaking: the Lives and Deaths of the Modern Divines*, (1651).
2. Simon Stock (†1265)
   Painting by Seán Keating in the chapel of the Carmelite house, Gort Muire, Dublin.
3. Ralph Fryston (†1276+)
   Painting by unknown artist preserved in the Carmelite house, Krakow, Poland.
4. Gilbert of Norwich (†1287)
   Painting by unknown artist preserved in the Carmelite house, Krakow, Poland.
5. Henry de Anna (†1300)
   T.N.A. SC 1/15/194 Letter to King Edward I, c1283
6. John Baconthorpe (†1349+)
   Fresco on the wall of the old library in the Carmelite house, Krakow, Poland.
7. John of Welwyk (c1347)
   Coloured woodcut of Monte Cassino from the Nuremberg Chronicle by Hartman Shedel (1493): [from *Wikipedia*, by Michel Wolgemut & Wilhelm Pleydenwurff].
8. William of Coventry (1360+)
   Remains of cloister garth of the Carmelite Priory, Coventry.
9. John Paschal (†1361)
   Llandaff Cathedral, nave looking eastwards. Paschal was buried in the Lady Chapel at east end. [Michael D Beckwith, CC0, via *Wikipedia Commons*]
10. Osbert Beaufeu of Pickenham (c1360-1370)
    Illumination from manuscript copy of Osbert's *Determinaciones*, Paris, Bibl. Mazarine, MS 3519. [image provided by the library]

11. John Reppes (†1373+)
    The Papal Palace in Avignon where John Reppes travelled on missions for the Early of Derby and King Edward III. [Jean-Marc Rosier from http://www.rosier.pro, CC BY-SA 3.0 <https://creativecommons.org/licenses/by-sa/3.0>, via Wikimedia Commons].
12. Walter Kellaw (†1367)
    Excavations in 2007 on the site of the Carmelite Priory, Northallerton, founded by Walter Kellaw in 1356 and where he was buried.
13. Thomas Brome (†1379+)
    Letter from Thomas Brome to the Chancellor of England, John Kyyvet
14. John Mepsale (†1390+)
    Tomb of Constance, Queen of Castile, (by Borjaanimal – Own work, CC BY-SA 4.0.)
15. Nicholas of Lynn (†1390+)
    The first page of Nicholas' *Kalendarium* for January [Oxford, Bodl. Libr., Ms. Laud Misc. 662, fo. 1v.
16. Richard of Maidstone (†1396)
    Cloister garth at Aylesford Priory where Richard of Maidstone is buried.
17. Richard Northalis (†1397)
    Painting by unknown artist preserved in the Carmelite house, Krakow, Poland.
18. John Swafham (†1398)
    Bangor Cathedral in 1831, an engraving by William Wallis, National Library of Wales.
19. John Kynyngham (†1399)
    Unknown Carmelite doctor in a roundel from Carmelite house, Cambridge. [Photo by Dr Brian Callingham]
20. Richard of Lavenham (†1401)
    Beginning of Richard Lavenham's *Tractatus de decem generibus*. [Oxford, Bodl. Libr., Ms. Digby 77, fo. 191v]
21. Walter Disse (1404)
    View of the Carmelite house in Lisbon by Guilherme Francisco Lourenço Debrie, *Crónica dos Carmelitas* (1745), from a copy in the *Biblioteca Nacional de Portugal.*
22. William Southfield (†1414)
    Remains of the anchorite cell in the Carmelite Priory, Norwich.

23. Robert Mascall (†1416)
Plaque commemorating the site of the Carmelite Friary, Ludlow erected by Ludlow Civic Society: Historical Marker Database (HMdb.org: photo by Stephen Palmer).
24. Stephen of Patryngton (†1417)
portrait from Mackenzie E. C. Walcott, "Bishops of Chichester from Stigand to Sherbourne", *Sussex Archaeological Collections*, 29 (1889), 1.
25. Thomas Peverel (1419)
View of Worcester Cathedral where Thomas Peverel was bishop from 1407-1419. [https://www.visitworcestershire.org/business-directory/worcester-cathedral]
26. Emma Stapleton (1422)
The enclosing of an anchorite [Cambridge, Corpus Christi College, Ms 079, fo. 96r]
27. Thomas Netter (†1430)
Painting by Adam Kossowski in the Carmelite house, The Friars, Aylesford.
28. Aleyn Warnekyn of Lynn (†1432)
Surviving gatehouse of Carmelite Priory, King's Lynn
29. John Keninghale (†1451)
Illustration of the delegates at the Council of Florence, in the Nuremberg Chronicle (1493), taken from a Latin copy in Sao Paolo [Accessed Wikipedia, 29/10/2023]
30. Roger Alban (†1453+)
Roger Alban's scroll, *Progenies regum Brytanniae*. [University of Pennsylvania (Philadelphia), Ms. Lehigh Roll 8 (1461-1465)]
31. Richard Misyn (†1462)
Colophon at the end of Richard Misyn's translation of Richard Rolle's *The Mendynge of Lyfe* (1434) [B.L. Ms Additional 37790, fo. 18]
32. John Hauteyn (Scharyngton) (†1466+)
Picture of Oxnead Manor as it appeared in Stuart Times. [courtesy of "This is the Paston Portal": https://www.thisispaston.co.uk/oxnead01.html]
33. John Stanbury (†1474)
Chantry chapel of John Stanbury, bishop of Hereford, in Hereford cathedral. (photo by Gerry Lynch)

34. Walter Hunt (1478)
    "Carmelite" at his study. [B.L. Royal MS 14 E 1, fo. 3] The friar is actually a Dominican, Vincent de Beauvais, and dates from 1478-1480. It occurs in a manuscript copied for the English King Edward IV who was in Bruges at the time. The illuminator was evidently not familiar with the habits of the friars and portrayed Vincent as a Carmelite in a white cloak!
35. John Milverton (†1487)
    Rudolf Wiegmann, "View of Rome with the Castel San Angelo on right" (1834). Milverton was imprisoned there during his trial in Rome. [Wikipedia Commons: accessed 24 March 2023].
36. John Hothby (†1487)
    Modern transcription of John Hothby's composition *Amor ch'ay visto* [https://musescore.com/user/35121661/scores/6702274]
37. Thomas Scrope (†1491)
    Painting by unknown artist preserved in the Carmelite house, Krakow, Poland.
38. John Pecock (†1537)
    Photo from Walsingham Architecture, (walsinghamvillage.org)
39. Robert Austen (†1538+)
    Drawing of St Bride's Church (before the fire of London) [accessed Wikipedia 27/10/2023}
40. Lawrence Cook (†1540)
    Rebus of Lawrence Cooke carved in the Tower of London. [Photo – courtesy of the Tower of London].
41. Simon Clerkson (†1554)
    View of All Saints' Church, Rotherham where Simon Clerkson was Rector from 1539-1554. [Photo courtesy of Neal Theasby (2014): accessed via Wikipedia, 26/10/2023]
42. John Bird (†1558)
    Alleged portrait of John Bird from F. Sanders, "John Bird, D.D., Bishop of Chester, 1541-1554", *Journal of Archaeological Society of Cheshire*, n.s. 13 (1907) 125.
43. John Dove (†1540+)
    Photo of Notre-Dame Church in Calais. [Photo courtesy of Nilfanion: Wikipedia Commons, accessed 24 March 2023].

# Saint Albert's Press

Saint Albert's Press is the publishing title for the British Carmelite Province and prints books on Carmelite spirituality and history. The present book is the first of a new series.

**Exploring Carmelite History**

1. *The English Followers of Elijah*, Richard Copsey, O.Carm. (2024)
2. *Carmelite Fioretti, Carmelite miracle stories and legends*, Richard Copsey, O.Carm. (in preparation)
3. *In the Footsteps of John Bale through France and Italy* 1526-1527, Richard Copsey, O.Carm. (in preparation)

Other more academic series contain:

**Carmel in Britain: Studies on the Medieval English Carmelite Province**

1. *People and Places*, ed. Patrick Fitzgerald-Lombard, O.Carm. (1992)
2. *Theology and Writing*, ed. Patrick Fitzgerald-Lombard, O.Carm. (1992)
3. *The Hermits from Mount Carmel*, Richard Copsey, O.Carm. (2004)
4. *Thomas Netter of Walden: Carmelite, Diplomat and Theologian*, ed. Johan Bergström-Allen & Richard Copsey, O.Carm. (2009)

**Early Carmelite Spirituality**

1. Felip Ribot, *The Ten Books on the Way of Life and Great Deeds of the Carmelites*, ed. & trans. Richard Copsey, O.Carm. (2005)

**Other titles include:**

*Climbing the Mountain: The Carmelite Journey*, ed. Johan Bergström-Allen (2010).

*Friar beyond the Pale: A Biography of Carmelite Friar Fr. Elias Lynch* (1897-1967), Wilfrid McGreal (2007).

Copies of these books can be ordered from the address below or through the Carmelite website at https://www.stjudeshrine.org.uk/ Our books are also sold on Amazon and by the Carmelite Book Service at https://carmelite.org.uk/

**Saint Albert's Press**

Carmelite Friars
P.O. Box 289
Faversham
Kent ME13 3BZ
Tel: 01795 539214